D1460151

UNEARTHED

Unearthed

On Race and Roots, and How the Soil Taught Me I Belong

Claire Ratinon

Chatto & Windus

LONDON

1 3 5 7 9 10 8 6 4 2

Chatto & Windus, an imprint of Vintage

Chatto & Windus is part of the Penguin Random House group of companies
whose addresses can be found at global.penguinrandomhouse.com

Copyright © Claire Ratinon 2022

Claire Ratinon has asserted her right to be identified as the author of this
Work in accordance with the Copyright, Designs and Patents Act 1988

First published in the United Kingdom by Chatto & Windus in 2022

penguin.co.uk/vintage

A CIP catalogue record for this book is available from the British Library

HB ISBN 9781784744472

Typeset in 10/16.85pt MillerText by Jouve (UK), Milton Keynes
Printed and bound in Great Britain by Clays Ltd, Elcograf S.p.A.

The authorised representative in the EEA is Penguin Random House
Ireland, Morrison Chambers, 32 Nassau Street, Dublin D02 YH68

Penguin Random House is committed to a sustainable future
for our business, our readers and our planet. This book is made
from Forest Stewardship Council® certified paper.

To my parents, my grandparents and to all
who came before us.

Dad, aged five, with his siblings in their house in Trou d'Eau Douce

Introduction

I let the chickens out at the same time every morning. 7 a.m. Even though they wake with the sun somewhat earlier on July days like today. They hear me coming and I can hear their chatter grow more urgent as I open the back door and crunch across the gravel towards their coop. I see one prehistoric eye peering at me through the small window on the side of their henhouse as I go to slide back their door, then all four squat, feathered bodies tumble through the gap, skidding down the ramp and past my feet towards where their food is waiting. I pause for a minute to admire their impressive bustles that point in the air while their hungry little beaks tap-tap-tap at the dull grey pellets they eat for breakfast.

Most mornings I rush back to bed for another hour's sleep, but the still air of this balmy morning is worth lingering in. The sun glints through the morning dew that covers the ground at my feet, and the tall grass in the field beyond the vegetable patch bows its soft pink seedheads gently to greet the day. House martins dance wordlessly overhead, their black bodies, white bellies, forked tails flitting through the sky. All is quiet, but for the soft buzz of bumblebees searching the persicarias' spiked flowers for their nectar, and the sound of the chickens, whose attention has shifted from their feeder to scratching at the ground in search of tiny bugs. I open the greenhouse door to allow the moisture trapped inside to escape. The tendrils of cucumber plants and a lone bitter melon, planted too late but with optimism, reach towards me and curl in the hope of finding something steady to hold on to. Their jagged-edged leaves and yellow flowers press themselves against the steamed-up windows like sweaty palms. Turning around, I smell the sugary scent of jasmine spiralling towards me from the vines that clamber up and over the wooden fence. As I devour its fragrance and the sight of its star-shaped flowers, I spot something familiar entangled amongst the chaotic midsummer growth spilling out from the nearby bed.

Bright-green, heart-shaped leaves, coming off a stem wound tightly around whatever it can grab hold of, cling on to and strangle as it scrambles upwards in search of the sun. This particular specimen has been left to grow for long enough that there are buds appearing and the topmost has broken into a white, trumpet-shaped bloom. On seeing it, I start to panic. There is no doubt. Whether through negligence or distraction or incompetence, bindweed has been rampaging through the garden on my watch. So much so that it has had time to settle in and flower.

I first met bindweed as a child when it was climbing its way up the chain-link fences around my school playground. I'd slowly press the plump flower buds until they relented with a satisfying pop. I didn't know then that those blousy blooms would one day be the mark of my nemesis, and that just the sight of them would fill me with panic. I think every grower and gardener has one plant that torments them. One with a rampant growth habit or that sows its seed a touch too prolifically or monopolises the water, earth or sun so that the plants they are trying to grow have to compete for what they need to thrive. A plant that follows them from garden to garden, reminding them that no matter how they try, there is much in the garden beyond their control. Bindweed – with her anticlockwise twirling, suffocating ways and her roots that burrow as deep as three metres below the ground but snap easily under a too-heavy hand – is my ever-present enemy.

I once spent a spring trying to excavate those brittle white roots from the first piece of land I'd been given permission to steward – a small plot at the bottom of a vicarage garden in Hackney. One side of the site was neat and organised, with five vegetable beds where salad leaves had been grown in rotation for a number of seasons already. The other side, though, had been left to grow with abandon and was shoulder-high with nettles and brambles. I devoted those winter months to hacking back the thorny, stinging tangle and finding the raspberry canes, gooseberry bushes and a pond hiding beneath. Yet it wouldn't be until the days started to warm that the bindweed made itself known – crawling under and across the path that kept the rowdy side separate from the tidy side, before emerging above ground to smother the perennial herbs and bother the overwintered chard. It was a futile task, but I was driven by the determination of a new grower who foolishly believed she could be more tenacious than this pernicious wanderer.

Tenacity and idealism marked my first few seasons of growing food. Career-changers, like me, can be like that. Evangelical – and occasionally unrealistic – about their new direction, because they've committed themselves to a path that rescued them from a work life that made them miserable. That's how I felt when I found my way to the work of growing plants. I wasn't looking for it, but it found me. I'd like to believe that it would have found me some other way if I hadn't walked down that New York street on that one sunny Saturday in June. I was working as a documentary producer when I stumbled upon Brooklyn Grange and fell for what was happening there. I found myself on a rooftop farm at a time when I was falling out of love with the work I was doing. The urge to grow food coaxed me back to London where, one foot in my old career for steadiness, I volunteered and trained, learned and worked my way into any job that called for me to be outside and in the presence of plants and their allies. I sowed seeds, planted seedlings, watered and weeded wherever I was allowed. I learned how to keep bees and tended hives in Central London before turning away from the conventional bee-keeping that I was taught and adopting a natural approach that does a far better job of honouring how honeybees would behave without our interference. I taught children how to garden in primary schools and community centres, explaining that soil is not dirt and just because you think a fresh vegetable tastes yucky does not mean it's okay to spit it out into my hand. I grew feisty mustard leaves and zesty sorrel, hefty beefsteak tomatoes, crates-worth of climbing beans and implausibly shaped courgettes for restaurants, cafés and a veg-box scheme. I did anything and everything I could to find my way to the plants that dared to grow in the city – and it changed me.

I came to understand and appreciate the life in the ground beneath my feet and the preciousness of what grows from it. I unlearned the instinctive panic I had once felt when surrounded by the sound of buzzing insects flying by. As I came to know what it takes for a seed to germinate and a plant to grow, all the systems and organisms that it relies upon and all the systems and organisms that rely upon it once it has appeared, I began to weave together an understanding that nothing exists in isolation of other things. We are all – humans, animals, plants, elements – deeply and profoundly connected. Even the bindweed, which I will likely do battle with until my last gardening day, is part of this divine and infinite web and is as entitled to its place in the ecosystem as I am to mine. Although I'll untwist its stems before it chokes my redcurrants and keep it far away from my compost heap, I do so with the belief that its determined root system is part of what figuratively and literally knits the earth together. And that it is as miraculous as it is ordinary.

The act of growing food is decidedly ordinary. It is one of a handful of things that we have in common with one another – and with our forebears. We all rely on it and we all come from a lineage of land workers. And yet it was extraordinary to see it in action for the first time, to participate in it for myself, to learn its intricacies and to choose to make it my life's work. The fact that it felt so remarkable to (re)discover it in my late twenties shows how distanced from this vital process so many of us have become. When our parents and teachers encourage us towards academic accomplishment, and governments and the societies they shape urge us towards work that forgoes meaning in favour of productivity and financial gain, it's no great wonder that the humble work of feeding each other is not presented as a respectable and worthy path.

Yet, for me, it has come to be the only path of meaning I've ever known. Growing food has helped me to come back to myself, to know who I am beyond the grasping and unbelonging. It has shown me the many ways in which I am woven into a tapestry of being, of which we are all a part. It has allowed me to tune my ear to the call of the Earth and tread on its surface with an ever-loving step. And it has shown me how to walk in the footsteps of my ancestors when I couldn't find their stories in the history books. It has taught me how to tend my wounds by holding the soothing leaves of healing plants against them, and to know that I am part of something profound and divine, after living for many years believing that I belonged to nothing.

It is not an untroubled journey. While I don't and will never know the names of my ancestors, I know they suffered. I know that some were stolen and sold while others migrated and left behind their motherlands, and that labouring on the land was the work that held too many of them captive. The field was the site of their oppression, and many of their descendants resolved never to return to that wretched place. I know this because I am one of those descendants, who once thought it unfathomable that I'd do the same work that enslaved them. But so much is forsaken when we turn away from the earth and sneer at it, deeming those who cultivate it and nurture it as lowly. If we keep ourselves removed from the green places beyond our brick walls, I believe we can never be whole. Had I not found my way to this work, I'm quite certain I would still be lost.

I found my love for growing food in the city. It was a defiant and determined love that I tried to cultivate on any patch of soil that would have me. And it was the love that I had for the plants that grew in those implausibly small and sunny spaces that had me craving more. I wanted more space, more green, more plants. I wanted a garden where I could grow whatever I chose because it was my right to tend the land. For all my adult years I had lived in cities, because feeling different is easier when you don't feel conspicuous; and yet, in hungry pursuit of more room to grow, I find myself now in the countryside. With a garden and a vegetable patch, four chickens and a greenhouse, standing outside in the early-morning light with my pyjama bottoms tucked into wellies, pulling at a tangle of bindweed stems.

I saw those heart-shaped leaves when we viewed the house for the first time. I knew that if we ended up living here, this old friend would be waiting to greet me. I spent the early days of that first spring trying to extract its roots from under the gravel and quietly (and unreasonably) cursing my new neighbours when the roots led me to the fence we share, then snapped. Even the tiniest piece of bindweed root left in the ground will happily regrow and so, as with every season that I've grown through thus far, I expect to see the bindweed again next year.

It is oddly reassuring to see a plant that I recognise growing here when so much of the garden remains a mystery to me. At least there's one thing about moving to the countryside that I know how to deal with.

CHAPTER 1

The house sits halfway up a hill. From the front there is a view of a woodland that stands between our village and the nearest town. The back garden looks over a field with ancient trees scattered throughout it. The nearest are two pine trees growing side-by-side: the older is large and poker-straight and the younger curves north-east in a gentle bow. I step out of the house, leaving the unpacking behind, to take myself on a circuit around the garden. Autumn has blown through already here, it seems. The leaves have been yellowing and falling to the ground for a while and they turn to squelch under each footstep. I'm trying to remember what flowers I saw blooming so joyfully and convincingly in the spring when we first saw the place, and then in the summer when we returned to make doubly sure it was somewhere we wanted to make our home. I can't recall what plants I saw growing – and can't tell now, as their annual retreat into the ground is well under way – but I do remember feeling excited by the prospect of getting to know them and learning how to meet their needs.

But it is the wrong time to ask the garden to tell me who it is. It was wrong of me to think I could arrive and, in my excitement, come to know its secrets so quickly. This garden has had many lives. Many cycles of growth and senescence. This is my first garden, but it has belonged to many before me and all the plants that grow here were brought in by someone else. Plants grown from seeds scattered, or carried on the breeze, or caught on passers-by, alongside those that retreat down into their deep, established root systems through winter to gather strength and wait for the first suggestion of spring to rouse them. It is a place of many layers, of decisions and labours and chance encounters. I can sense the energy that's gone into creating it, the graft and craft of training and pruning, cultivating and planting done by those who have sculpted this place. The cumulative energy of a hundred years or more of beings who touched this soil and sought to nurture it. A nourishing energy that radiates out, even as the plants are dying back.

I imagine all of this garden's gardeners, wilful and unintentional, shaping it while they were resident. Some choices (the slippery death-trap decking) I dislike, while others (the cascading marjoram) make me feel hopeful. I imagine how each gardener surveyed this space and envisioned the plants that they'd tuck into the bed that gets the most sun or, if they thought it would survive, nestled into the shady part overshadowed by the neighbours' fragrant thorny olive. I imagine how they welcomed the wildflowers in and willed them to behave, watching, just as I will, as they stray beyond the edging and take up residence elsewhere, but find that they are just too pretty to remove. I imagine how they made tough decisions to bid farewell to ailing roses, lopsided shrubs and unpruned bushes that flower every summer but are growing too far into the path to be left there for another year. I imagine how they lovingly or begrudgingly or tentatively tended this space on sunny days and drizzly days, frosty days and hazy ones; and how they made their mark, whether they meant to or not, and left the garden for me to inherit and now steward into the seasons to come.

I look for clues. I study what remains, examining the leaf shapes and headless stems, inspecting the detritus for a hint – something characteristic, a sign of who or what was growing here in the midst of the season. I find the dark skeletons of something that bloomed not long ago, poker-straight but now devoid of leaves, chlorophyll and colour. Two clusters of a kind of sedum have started to yellow from the bottom of their stems; their once-bright flowers, which would have vibrated joyfully with winged insects in the late summer, are closer to blood-red and of no use to the bees now. Dandelions and docks have made themselves at home in the cracks in the path where the cement has worn away, their taproots pushing deep into the earth. The last owners were just passing through and the plants they had added to the flower beds have been dug up and moved along with them to their new home. From here, I can see the holes they have left behind, which are now filled with twigs and wet leaves. What bushes and shrubs remain in the ground have been left to grow straggly and unwieldy, bushy on the outside and bare underneath. Where the garden dips down and the coldest air gathers, the once-tall, primeval leaves of the ferns shrivel and curl, collapsing in on themselves, darkening. I push my thumb through the seedhead of an anonymous plant and watch the little flecks of fluffy seeds as they separate and drift to the ground. I wonder who they were, and who their young will grow up to be. An impressive clump of ornamental grass with striped leaves, and drooping seedheads like soft pink feathers sways in the almost-winter wind as what little is left of the day's sun starts to disappear. It's a garden of remnants and detritus. Of decaying abundance, negligence and glory.

Coming to know a garden is like making a new friend. It is a process that asks for patience, to be allowed to unfold on its own timeline. It is a process that is forcing my hand, for winter at least, to accept inaction as the most useful approach and this year, especially, I'm thankful for the invitation. I know, beneath the soil and fallen leaves, the stories that the garden has gathered await me. Of bulbs dropped into dibbed holes, bare roots firmed in with muddy heels and burred seeds caught on cotton or wool or fur. Of plants grown by friends or neighbours, passed over fences or picked up by the roadside in exchange for a few coins dropped into an old tin can. Of rootballs divided, cuttings rooted and seeds collected on dry days in paper bags and passed on – passed down – to hands wearing gloves so encrusted with soil that they can stand up straight, on their own. Of fat balls and feeders made of pine cones and coconut shells filled with suet and seeds. Of holly and ivy and hawthorn berries hanging heavy for the birds, who dart between branches. There's a lot for me to learn about this garden, but with each day that passes, there will be even less to see. Another stem snapped, another leaf blown into the path to tumble down towards the pile that's gathering over the storm drain.

I head back inside the house and there's a pile of Tupperware on the kitchen table. Lanti rouz, cari pwason, some kind of sautéed greens, and the rice cooker is on, filling the air with that warm, familiar smell. I breathe its starchy sweetness in and then slowly out. My body knows it well. My mum, in rubber gloves, is scrubbing the oven and my dad is pulling nails out of the wall that a week ago had another family's photos hanging from them. He fixes and she cleans, and that's their routine. If nothing is broken and everything is spotless, then all is right with the two of them. I used to be the same way. But now my life is messy and muddy – not broken, but cobbled together and haphazard. I know it's not what they imagined for me but, then, it's not what I'd imagined for myself, either.

I grew up in the suburbs with my nose buried in books. I didn't grow up playing in grassy meadows, wearing wellies or climbing trees. The outdoors unnerved me. I'd read Enid Blyton's stories of children romping through the English countryside and knew those adventures weren't meant for a child like me. I liked the nature that lived between pages and in the magical corners of my imagination, but I was reluctant to experience it, with all the itching, sneezing, snagging, grazing and filthiness that I thought were the sum total of venturing outdoors. Nature was all the things that I believed had no value, all the things I thought best to avoid.

I spent my teenage years with my eyes trained on the city. Young and intoxicated by what I imagined life there could be. Wild, free and joyful. I wanted to live in a place where I could hide amongst a mass of people, in the relief of being inconspicuous. I wanted to experience the possibility of a quiet acceptance, and to feel not unwelcome. And I couldn't see that happening anywhere other than in the city. And it was the only place that I could imagine myself building the kind of successful life that achieved the sole thing that really mattered – making my family, both here and in Mauritius, proud. So I did just that for nearly a decade. Tucking myself onto buses between other squashed-together commuters, behind desks in open-plan offices and in little rented rooms, a brick wall between my life and that of the neighbours I'd never meet.

But in the last few years, with every growing season that passed, a quietening was happening inside me that made the city seem too loud. The more I fell in love with the nature that I found there, the more I fell out of love with the city itself. I had a burgeoning hunger for proximity to the natural world, and it made the roads seem more congested and the city air taste more polluted. The peace that I craved felt unreachable when the lorries that drove by our London flat shook the walls and early-morning techno had me standing on the street, pyjamaed and pleading with our young, drunk neighbours. It may have been the trickery of a mind that was craving more green and less concrete-grey, but living in London came to feel stifling, and the countryside life that I once thought unfathomable became the focus of my daydreams with every turn of the seasons.

We wound up leaving in a hurry, even though our minds had been changing for some time. We'd been bumping up against the edges of our flat since we moved in together three years earlier. Two in a space meant for one. Me, a food grower coming home in muddy boots, and him, an artist renting a studio next to a cement factory, returning with paint splattered all over his jeans and shoes. I'd bought that flat in a past life when I had a job with a contract and a salary, and after three years of very close proximity, a bathroom without a window and sharing almost everything, we've swapped our little flat for a house in the East Sussex countryside. Three bedrooms, a garage and a garden.

On the day we left, the sky was grey and as we ran down the stairs from our flat, raindrops dampened the boxes we had filled with jars of home-made jam and books and the sturdy boots we hadn't worn since spring. Our whole life was packed in cardboard boxes and thrown into the back of a removal van heading south. I watched the van speed off with the big, heavy things while we loaded what we feared might break, and the plants we hoped would survive the journey, into the back of the car and said goodbye to London. The rain began to fall more heavily as we journeyed through the city, but when we crossed into Kent, the sun broke through the clouds and I turned the music up loud and, through the excitement and uneasiness, smiled at Sam as he gave my hand a reassuring squeeze. Out of the window, trees and fields and sheep flew past. I looked out for thatched roofs and oast houses and tried not to notice how often I saw St George's flags flying by the roadside.

I was eighteen when I moved away from home for the first time, leaving for university like most of my friends. I wanted to live in a city and, determined to be brave, I headed to Nottingham instead of London, which felt a bit too close to where I grew up. Around six months into my time there, the war in Iraq was declared and I, filled with youthful outrage, went to the city centre to protest alongside hundreds of others. I was fearless about adding my voice to the cry of all the citizens who stamped their feet alongside me to tell the government that their actions didn't represent us. After the marching and chanting and speeches, I was leaving with a friend when a man stopped me.

'What was going on over there?'

'It's a demonstration against the war in Iraq.'

'Right. And where are you from?'

'Oh, we go to the university...'

'No, where are you *from*?' he asked, turning towards me and sidelining my friend. I'd been asked this question before and, from the quivering, rising fury in his voice as he got worryingly close to my face, I knew it was not a benign enquiry. I told him I was born here, that our passports looked the same and, with blood pounding loudly at my temples, that the English he spoke was the language I knew best. And he told me that I had no right to an opinion, that this wasn't my country and that I should leave if I didn't like it here and had the cheek to go to a protest.

'Why don't you just go back to where you came from? Why don't you fuck off back home?' he hissed at me as he backed away from us. My friend, who'd been holding fast to my side, took me by the arm and dragged me into a nearby restaurant where I collapsed into her, hot tears burning painfully down my cheeks.

I grew up knowing I was different. Feeling uneasy and sad about that fact was normal for me. I knew from a young age that I was seen by many as a foreigner – an outsider, an other from an elsewhere. In that man's words, in the poison that spat from his lips, I understood the fullness of his disdain. Not for something I'd done, not really, but for who I am. And who I am, he made quite clear, was not welcome here in England. And my opinion was unwelcome, too. To him, I had a home elsewhere and he wanted me to leave, to go and live there and not here, in this country, which was his and could never be mine.

When I was a child I willed my face, my hair, my skin to be other than they were. I wasted years wishing I were someone else, but until that moment at the protest I hadn't wished myself to be *somewhere* else because I'd never called anywhere else my home. With those swift and venomous words, that stranger robbed me of the capacity to believe that where I was born was where I belonged. He drew a line of whiteness around this island and ordered me to stand outside it. Ever since then

I've seen that sentiment over and over again: that to be Black or Brown here in England means that this place couldn't possibly be your home. To not be white here means that you're the property of another land and your right to be here will always be up for debate.

I didn't last much longer in Nottingham. The whole city became toxic to me after that day. He'd poisoned it with his words and his rage, and everywhere I looked I saw disdain and hopelessness. I fell ill and fell out with my flatmates, so by Easter, a month later, I'd quit and was on my way back to live with my parents again. Back to my barely cold childhood bedroom.

*

Port Louis, 1964

Apples were a rare and expensive treat in Mauritius when she was a child. Her father would go to the first Mass on Sunday morning at 6 a.m. or so, and afterwards head to the market to buy the meat that the family would eat on his one day off, the day reserved for God. And if there was a little money to spare that week, he'd buy a few apples to bring home to his children. She liked apples well enough, but she really loved the longan that was in season from New Year, at the height of summer, or the fat mangue dauphiné that arrived each November. Her mother spent most of her day in the kitchen, cooking for her family, as most housewives were expected to – although she took more pride in it than others. She would stir simmering pots of dal, knead dough to make rotis, massage spices and mustard oil into thinly sliced cabbage, carrots and green beans, and preside over perfectly steamed rice while the children were at school and her husband was fixing shoes and reminiscing about those few adventurous years that he spent working for the British Army over in Egypt after the Second World War.

Her mother would ask her to listen out for the call of the roaming vegetable seller, pushing his bicycle along the road that ran alongside their home. The wheels would squeak gently, complaining under the weight of woven vacoas baskets full of ziromon, bred malbar and pomme d'amour. All grown from the fertile red earth on his small plot of land and brought to sell to the women who'd step out onto their doorsteps upon hearing his voice. Whenever she heard a merchant approaching, she'd secretly hope it was the one with the glass box attached to his tricycle filled with gato pima or gato patat or dal pouri. And when he came, she would ask her father hopefully for a few cents to buy herself and her sisters a greasy treat wrapped in paper.

When she was old enough and strong enough to carry the groceries without dropping them, her mother would send her to la boutique chinois to buy rice or lentils or little packets of curry powder en roulement. The shopkeeper would write down a list of what she'd purchased in a little notebook next to their family name, so that her father could settle up when pay day came around. She often wondered when the shopkeeper slept, because even when the store was closed for the night, you could sneak around the side, knock on the window and they'd push whatever you needed through a little hatch in the wall.

Trou d'Eau Douce, 1964

His mother was slightly less enthusiastic in the kitchen but benefited from a husband who, unlike most, was a very good cook. He and his five siblings loved to see their father hunched over a bubbling pot on the fire, because it meant that something special – cari poul or la daube maybe – would be for dinner and their mother would be happier for spending the day chatting to neighbours instead of stuck inside. They would push and shove each other, trying to be first in the queue in the hope that they'd get the best of what Pa had cooked. Then he'd take himself to his little bench and, plate balanced on skinny knees, eat his small piece of meat or fish before anything else, to save it from being stolen by one of his brothers. Meal times were the best part of the day and there wasn't much that he wouldn't eat, but whenever he was served patol, he would scrunch his little nose at the unpleasant texture. His mother, sharp as she was, would tell him that this special vegetable had come from Curepipe – the part of the island where the weather is cool, the chou chou grows wild and the rich people live – and he'd gulp it down, believing it to be precious. His father loved to watch his children eat, basking in how eagerly they gobbled up what he'd prepared. His father was too able a cook for his own good and couldn't resist interfering when others were in the kitchen, suggesting that maybe, 'sa mank inpe di sel'. And he, his son, who had learned to cook under his parents' feet, would one day turn out to be the same way.

She grew up on the west side of the island and he grew up on the east, yet they both had their sights set on England. The Mother Country. They arrived at different times, but ended up in the same place and found their way to each other after one too many insipid, cornflour-thickened 'curries' stirred through with tinned pineapple and raisins and poured over cold boiled eggs. The food in the cafeteria in the hospital where they were training wasn't quite what they had imagined when they left Mauritius. She missed banane zinzli, fresh coconut water and her mother's cari pwason with kutcha made from green mangoes. He missed frying ourit on an open fire with his pa, pineapple flavoured with chilli and tamarind, light-skinned cucumbers, and celebrating special occasions by eating vindaye and playing dominoes until it got dark. So although she didn't really know how, she decided to learn how to cook to save herself from living mostly on biscuits. And even though he could cook – and could cook very well – he didn't let on, so that he had an excuse to spend time with her and their new friends as, together, they made the food that reminded them of home.

*

Our new kitchen is far bigger than the one in the flat and was what I felt most excited about, after the garden. I've never had a lot of space to cook and, since we arrived, I've been filling the cupboards with all the things that I'd not had room for before. Big pots of turmeric, jeera, mustard seeds and different kinds of dried chilli, bottles of rice vinegar, sriracha and good olive oil, and jars of lemon pickle, tamarind paste and all our jam – gooseberry, apricot and blackberry flavoured with gin – dating back to 2017. We bought a palette of tinned tomatoes, a ten-kilo sack of basmati rice and a butternut squash, so I'm making rougaille and toufe ziromon for dinner tonight. I don't know how to cook many Mauritian dishes, but I know how to make the food that helps me feel settled. I chop onions and then, through watering eyes, crush garlic and ginger in a pestle and mortar. I peel the squash, cut it into cubes and pop open a can of plum tomatoes. The base ingredients for both recipes are the same, so I put two pans on the cooker to heat up side-by-side. The onions hit the hot oil with a sputter and, after a few minutes, start to soften and colour at the edges, then in go the garlic and ginger to complete the holy trinity.

By the back door, next to a variegated sage, there's a scraggly thyme plant with just enough leaves to flavour this one meal. This herb is one of the few edible plants that grew in our garden when I was young and its smell, in moments of longing, can move me to tears. I pick a few sprigs and make a mental note to get a new plant next year. The warm, savoury smell of the thyme meeting the heat fills the kitchen as Sam calls down the stairs to ask what's cooking. Tomatoes go in one pan, lid off to sauté and reduce. Squash goes in the other pan, lid on to sauté and steam. The rice cooker burbles quietly, and the jar of pickle Dad made waits on the side, ready to be served.

Sam has a fire going in the log burner and we settle in to eat our dinner off our laps, rewatching *Withnail & I*. While we're laughing at its depiction of a countryside made of rolling fields, bad-tempered cattle and hostile locals, I remember why I'd never thought to live anywhere but the city in my twenties.

The following weekend is the first I spend here alone. I don't change out of my pyjamas, because it's Saturday morning, Sam's up in London and I've got nothing planned. From the sofa where I've curled myself, I watch as a head of red hair bobs up the path towards the house. Probably a new neighbour. We've met a few already and most have been pleasant so far. On one side, through a wilderness of a front garden and past a rusty old camper van, there's a sweet elderly woman who welcomed us with stories about homing pigeons and swimming in the sea, and a jar of home-made pickled onions. The neighbours we share a wall with have made it quite clear that they're not interested in being friendly. But Linda, who lives down the lane, does want to be friends, and the door's barely open before she pulls me in for a bear hug, clutching a welcome card in her hand.

'Welcome to the village! How are you settling in?' she asks as I jostle her into the house and close the door against the cold. News of our arrival has clearly made it around the neighbourhood. She politely declines my offer of tea and instead tells me about the church on the other side of the village where she goes, compliments the colour of the kitchen cupboards and tells me about nearby planning applications. As expected, she asks me what I do, and I try my best to explain. 'Well, I used to grow food in London and sometimes I write and talk about it, but I'm not quite sure what I'm going to do now I'm here. I probably should have made more of a plan before we moved. Oh no, I'm not a gardener exactly, as I don't really know about ornamental plants or how to take care of a lawn, which I don't really believe in doing anyway.' I explain myself more than is probably necessary, but Linda's too warm and kind to notice my embarrassment at not having a 'real job' and not really knowing what I'm doing here. She talks over my discomfort with suggestions to join the village gardening club; stories about her husband, the ex-pilot, and her son, the landscape gardener; and that time when she lived in Singapore.

'You're going to get along great with Graeme and Rachel, who live up the hill. I think she works for a charity and they've got a flock of chickens, if you ever want some eggs or advice on keeping hens,' she tells me as we swap numbers and another hug. Linda doesn't stop chatting even when she's halfway out of the front door, encouraging me to come to the Sunday service as she heads back down the path. By the time she's out of sight, I'm back under a blanket and using my phone to find the planning application website for the county. The rest of the day is lost to stress-reading a hundred or so angry letters from the people who live in the village who are objecting to a proposal that they say would ruin this Area of Outstanding Natural Beauty for ever. I've got nothing better to do than submerge myself in their outrage and worry that we made a mistake moving to this house.

*

The day that follows is clear and crisp. I turn my watch back by an hour and open the curtains to see the first frost. This day is an important one in any gardener or farmer's calendar. The first of many mornings when the temperature will drop close to or below zero and will turn the water in the air to ice on all that is outside, from the ground up. It is a beautiful and dangerous time. Each blade of grass, each protruding vein on every low leaf is outlined with a delicate etching of crystal. Sharp edges in blue-white until the morning sun rises high enough to dull them and melt the frost into the soil.

This year is the first since I started growing that I haven't had plants that I am duty-bound to protect. It's the first winter that I haven't checked the weather forecast and the sky for clouds, before rushing off on my bike to pre-empt the possible damage of the year's first freezing night. The urge remains, though. The instinct has become hard-wired in the last handful of seasons, where laziness or absent-mindedness or tardiness might have dented my harvest, come the following spring. Instead, this year I peer at this first frost through the back bedroom window, thighs pressed against the radiator, jumper over pyjamas. Nothing to run outside for just yet – not as far as I know. The frost runs from our scruffy patch of lawn, over fallen leaves and into the field beyond the back gate, carving out the low tussocks and growing heavier and harder where the ground curves away down the hill.

Some plants can withstand this onslaught. Leaf cells so robust that the frost remains merely ornamental. Other plants are ill prepared for the extremity. The expansion of the water in their cells, as it turns from liquid to solid, bursts their walls and heralds imminent, if not immediate, death. It's a time of the year when those of us who have devoted ourselves to stewarding plants through their lifecycles pay close attention to the weather. At this juncture between autumn and winter, we watch with vigilance. This work asks us to move with the seasons and, while we respect them, we relish the challenge of meeting a season's margins and nudging at what is possible. When a profound and chilling shift in the weather threatens our less hardy plants, we rush outside, arms filled with bolts of fleece to throw over the leaves and pin the fabric down, as though we were tucking a child in at night. We try to eke out autumn's grace by trapping a little warmth under a blanket to prevent the demise of our charges before the Persephone period begins. When the days have only ten hours of sunshine, then steadily less and less, that year's growth comes to an end.

Sam returns just after lunchtime and we spend the rest of the day shuffling the last of our boxes from one room to another, slowly unpacking bits and pieces and tucking them away into the corners of the house. Our voices echo around the empty rooms, stripped of all the things that had us believe, six months ago, that we could make a home of this place. The weather changes quickly. The wind is gathering momentum and blows through the tiny gaps in the walls and under the doors, whistling like breath pushing past a blade of grass caught between thumbs and, every so often, it plays a discordant tune. Rain falls, steadily and heavily, and whenever the wind changes direction to blow eastwards, it pushes raindrops through a barely visible gap where the roof meets the wall above our bedroom window, so that when we try to sleep, it is to the sound of the drip-drip-drip of water seeping in.

CHAPTER 2

The November days here are grey and short and slow, but the birds in the garden don't seem to mind. It's possibly an illusion caused by the trees becoming steadily naked, but it seems like there's more of them appearing each day. Starlings and great tits, dunnocks and wrens fly through the tree branches, knocking dead leaves to the ground and chatting and chirping from early morning until the sun sets in the mid-afternoon. I used to think that people who watched birds were dull, but watching them dart around the feeder I've hung on the knotted branches of the wisteria that curls around the living-room window has convinced me otherwise.

The blue tits are adept at negotiating the feeder, with their slender outlines, which are ideal for dangling upside-down so that their beaks can tap indentations into the fatty balls of seed. Their thick necks are surprisingly mobile and the way their heads tilt is terribly cute. They can swivel at awkward angles, doing whatever's necessary to fly off with a full belly. The robins, though, can just about manage to land on the feeder when they're smaller and younger, but those that have shed their juvenile feathers develop puffed-up red breasts that prove obstructive, leaving them to flap furiously as they thrust their hungry beaks towards the food, before getting exhausted and retreating to catch their breath. The sparrows swoop into the hedge nearby and poke their heads out to calculate their approach. Some dart out with precision, claws out and ready to grasp the cage; others take more time to survey the landscape, edging gradually closer to be sure that all is safe before they approach. The sparrows are birds that I thought I knew well enough. Along with pigeons, there were plenty that landed in the garden of my childhood. Yet, up close, they are far more special than I realised – the males with their dark masks and finch-like beaks, chestnut-and-black striped wings, soft taupe almost everywhere else and tails that flute at the tip. The females are altogether more demure, wearing the less striking of the males' colours, with a lighter beak and a less heavy-handed approach to their eye make-up in a gentle streak of tan, brushed from their eyes to the backs of their heads. The sparrows are teaching me to look anew at what I once thought familiar.

I'm still hesitating in the garden, though, despite having little else to do. I didn't make time to think about what I'd do once we got to the countryside. I let myself be distracted by the last of the beans and courgettes and summer salad leaves in London. Harvesting them, and then planting out mustard greens and kale seedlings in their place. I kept growing until we left. We didn't even have enough time to throw a leaving party, and I didn't mind that. I didn't want to tell my friends that I wasn't sure what I'd do with myself once we'd moved. Part of me didn't believe we would go through with it and thought I'd just stick with growing plants in London – and that part of me still can't believe I'm here.

I have taken to doing one thing outside – sweeping up the never-ending supply of fallen leaves that cover the slippery decking. It is a somewhat futile task but it feels reassuringly simple. Every other day I put on my thickest gardening gloves, pull a woolly hat over my uncooperative hair and step out into the early-winter chill for an hour. Our neighbour's spectre of a willow tree is oddly shaped and looms overhead, pruned out of necessity and with little discernment. Its torso and its many branches lean over the fence and its thinnest, weepiest branches reach low so that, with every gentle puff of wind, it scatters pointy, yellowing leaves all over the garden. A new blanket every forty-eight hours. I use the little broom that I found amongst old paint cans and spiders' webs in the rickety shed to push the leaves into small piles, leaning into the repetition and unsteadiness. Sweeping and slipping, sweeping and slipping. It's good to have something to do.

Weeping-willow trees can often be found growing on the banks of rivers and streams, their love for moisture making them ideal for holding in place soil that's boggy and heavy with water. It offers me some insights into what I might expect from the soil of this garden. Before we moved, I investigated the soil constitution using a soilscapes map and was hoping that I'd be working with a loamy soil that would be ideal for growing vegetables. Somewhere between clay and sand and silt, able to hold as well as dispense with water with an exactitude that a root system would rejoice in. It is clear now that my map-reading skills have failed me, because what I am standing on is categorically clay. Sticky and weighty and resistant in Britain's cold, wet winters, then unrelenting and dusty when it dries out in the summer. A challenge to work with, but full of nutrients if you can get to them.

In the bed that edges around what could loosely be described as a lawn, the bushes and shrubs look like they have had a good season of growth, but the soil they're rooted into looks grey and as solid as concrete. It's a little too late in the year to offer the soil the mulch of compost that it needs, since the mornings are liable to freeze from now on. So I keep sweeping and stuffing handfuls of rain-soaked willow leaves into the recycled bin bags that I rescued from the move as a gesture of commitment and hope that, in two or so years' time, I'll still be here and will harvest the dark crumbles of leaf mould to lay over this earth as a thick and generous mulch, to improve the soil's structure for the sake of the roots of these plants that I'm trying to take responsibility for.

Sam had two main criteria for where we would move to: a good pub that he could walk home from, and space to dry our clothes outside. He would get so frustrated when even our clean clothes smelt fusty from being dried inside the flat. While it will be a few months before it is warm enough for this aspiration to come to pass, we head towards the village green for a first drink at our new local. We met in a pub, five years ago, on a snowy evening in South London. He was playing saxophone in the band that was playing that night and, after the set, we shouted over the music to each other about yoga and veggie-burgers, and then danced around until the boots he was wearing started to fall apart.

We struggled to find time for each other at first. He was working in a gallery during the day, and my evenings were taken up by production meetings with colleagues and clients based in San Francisco; but it was only a year before he'd moved into my flat and we'd both given up those jobs and were trying to spend our days doing the work we actually cared about. He helped me get over my fear of cycling on the roads in London and taught me how to choose a proper water-proof jacket. He bought me the same Flexothane trousers – the ones made for dairy farmers – that he grew up wearing, and they have kept my legs dry on all the winter days that I've spent shifting compost, and through all the springs when I've harvested kale and chard and cauliflowers. He helped me learn how to be comfortable in the outdoors, so that I could go after my love for plants without discomfort getting in my way. And he has worked with me on almost every patch of earth I've grown in, shovelling woodchip, teaching children about earthworms and digging out brambles all over East London. The salad leaves we harvested together paid our council-tax bill and I don't think it would have occurred to me to move out of London if it weren't for Sam. He was the one who planted that seed. Seeing the ease with which he moves through rural places and open spaces made it easier for me to do the same, following his lead. In the proximity of his reassuring presence, the move seemed more possible because we'd be doing it together.

As we walk down the road, we spot two of our new neighbours who are in their front garden, tidying up and sweeping leaves, and we stop for a minute to chat. She tell us about their plans to redecorate their house and he proudly points to their new garage door. Sam tells them about the work that takes him into London once a week, and I mutter something quietly about how I've not been up to much. I'm awkward when I chit-chat, but it's part of village etiquette and I want to get better at it, so I nod and laugh along as much as I can. She comments on my hair and, without warning – as many have done before – she reaches for it and pushes her fingers into my curls. I can't stand the feeling of my hair being touched, or the uninvited overstep of someone I barely know doing so. I take some small steps backwards and slowly drag my hair through her fingers and out of her reach, wince a smile and try to keep chatting as I tie my hair into a bun on top of my head.

We say our goodbyes and head down the hill and over the bridge towards the village green and, while I'd rather go back to the house, I resist the urge to turn around. The path to the pub veers upwards and as we walk past the flock of geese that roam around freely, one lifts its head and delivers a few warning honks as the rest waddle alongside us for a minute. The geese, the green, the cottages, the pub whose building dates back to the fourteenth century. The history of this place, with its stories about the sixteenth-century gang who frequented the pub, bringing smuggled tea, brandy and rum with them; and how the village powder mill made some of the best gunpowder in Europe in the seventeenth century; and how, during the Second World War, a doodlebug was dropped in a field nearby, blowing out all the windows of the workers' cottages. It all feels characteristically English, as does the village itself and the landscape around it. It's the domain of an Englishness that I don't quite know how to describe.

On a busy Sunday afternoon like this one there are no seats in the pub left empty. The floor is littered with dogs and the air is filled with the smell of meat, roasted potatoes and gravy. A man in his seventies is perched on a stool by the bar, with a pint in his hand, chatting to his friend who's sitting opposite. He pauses to watch us as we walk up to the bar and his eyes narrow slightly, inspecting me as I take off my coat. I feel a familiar heat creeping up my neck towards my face and turn away, wanting to escape the burn of his stare. 'I'll just have a half of whatever you're having,' I tell Sam, as I slip around the corner and look for somewhere out of the way to put myself. He's probably stopped staring now and it was probably because he doesn't recognise us, but I don't dare look behind me as Sam hands me my drink. I try to hide behind him, lining my body up with his silhouette, but he's waving and grabbing at my hand. 'Hey, it's Graeme from up the road. I met him the other day. Let's go over and I'll introduce you.'

*

I grew up not far from the Hogsmill River. More of a stream at its source, it bubbles up through a chalk spring next to Bourne Hall library, where I spent many Friday evenings choosing books to borrow and read over the weekend. Legend has it that William the Conqueror (also known as William the Bastard) once stopped to let his horse drink the water there. Along the banks of this tributary the Pre-Raphaelite painter Sir John Everett Millais painted the landscape in which he would place a wistful depiction of Shakespeare's Ophelia, floating amongst pond weed and strewn with wildflowers. He spent five months by the riverside, painting and perfecting the fauna that surrounds her. The thick horizontal trunk and straggly branches of the willow from which she fell is where a robin sits and watches; a dog rose tumbles white-pink flowers towards the water; the falling seedheads of teasels, the soft blue of water forget-me-nots and what look to be the pink spires of veronica surround her. Millais painted her into the moment before her gown is overwhelmed with water and she is pulled beneath the surface.

I remember seeing this painting for the first time when I was exploring London as a teenager. She hangs in Tate Britain, gifted by the sugar merchant Henry Tate at the gallery's inception. I was captivated by this painting not because I saw something of my childhood in her surrounds, but because of how beautiful she looked to me: fair-skinned with blushed cheeks, at ease despite the imminence of her demise. The parts of the river that looked like this painting, where Millais once sat, were off the paths and in the patches of wildness that I'd avoided as a child.

When the century turned, just over a hundred years ago, Ewell was still distinctly rural. There were farms and farmland where now there is row after row of modestly sized houses on roads laid out at neat angles. While much of the area remained green through the Second World War – allotments full of vegetables, and gardens being dug for victory – it was close enough to the city to have suffered from the bombing. British fighter planes flew over where my family's house would later be built, heading towards Epsom Downs to intercept the German bombers on their way to drop their payload on the docks and factories of London's East End. The holes left by a devastating war were filled with new houses, and about thirty or so years later my parents and brother moved into one of them and made it our home while they waited for me to be born.

By the time I arrived, where the Hogsmill River started comprised the suburbs, and where it met the River Thames in Kingston would be considered the edge of London. Where I grew up was an in-between space, not close but not far from the nearest town. Road after road of semi-detached houses, each with a modest garden, somewhere to park a car and enough room to raise a family. The occasional bungalow, a suddenly grand property here and there, but mostly the same two-bedrooms-and-a-boxroom houses, side-by-side with gardens laid cheek-to-cheek. Not a rolling meadow or agricultural field for miles. It was all suburbia.

My parents were invited to emigrate to England as subjects of the former British Empire from a newly independent Mauritius, as part of a mass recruitment drive aimed at filling empty NHS nursing positions. To be able to move to Britain, to the Land of Hope and Glory, and train to be a nurse was the opportunity – a dream – they had always hoped for. It was the height of achievement to study hard and earn enough to send money home to support your family. My parents both thought they'd be training in general nursing and didn't realise that instead they'd been enrolled into the area with the most severe staffing shortage – psychiatric nursing. And so they didn't get to choose where they would be living when they arrived and they ended up in Epsom, a suburban town in Surrey.

They were stationed within a group of five psychiatric hospitals in an area of about a square mile – the 'Epsom Cluster' – which was the largest concentration of psychiatric institutions of its kind in the world, and it became the point where people from all over the former British Empire would congregate and start their new lives. This assembly of people, many leaving their homelands for the very first time, was a unique meeting of cultures and ethnicities, of nationalities and languages and religions. People from India, Sri Lanka, the Philippines, Ghana, Nigeria, the Caribbean and Mauritius – including my parents (who arrived independent of each other) – all lived and worked together. The hospitals were multicultural – like the Mauritius that my parents had just left – and it was this diversity that gave their community its protective quality. It shielded most of the new nurses from the more caustic racism that was commonplace for those assigned to the general hospitals. It was a place of solidarity and sup-port, where being assigned shitty jobs and being passed over

for promotion was everyone's burden to carry. And the prejudice that they did experience was tempered by the deference
they were taught, at home and in this new place, to show their
English bosses. My parents found their way to each other
through a group of Mauritian friends who would meet and
cook together in the student-nurse accommodation where
they both lived.

By the time my brother, Daniel, and I were born, my parents were qualified nurses and had moved into a house of their
own and were busy building the good life they'd long hoped to
create for themselves, for their family back home and to pass
on to their children. They took opposite shifts, so there was
always someone at home, apart from on Sundays, when we'd
spend one crossover hour on the ward where Mum worked,
writing stories in old notebooks or filling bags full of conkers
from the chestnut trees that grew outside her office window.

Every summer we would pack ourselves into the car – me
with a bag of books, Daniel with a Walkman, my dad with jars
of spices and my mum with everything else – and drive south to
France. Apart from that one summer when I was four, when
we went to the Lake District instead. We drove up in our red
Ford Escort to Cumbria, before passing through Blackpool
and ending up in Edinburgh. We set out to explore the lakes in
the cool, wet Cumbrian summer, but we didn't have the right
gear to protect us from the weather. We were the only ones
wearing optimistically summery clothes and thin jackets that
weren't waterproof. There's a picture of me, my brother and
my dad standing on a stony path, against a backdrop of rocky

grey and green, a narrow waterfall cutting through the rockface behind us. I'm holding my dad's hand in both of mine and pressing it against my face, squeezing out a smile for the camera. The three of us, standing there in the wind, wearing terribly-short shorts, our knees unprotected from the cold. The best part of the trip, my dad told me, was coming back to the warm apartment, where he'd cook and we'd sit down for dinner together. We spent that week doing our best to resist the cold before driving the eight hours or so back to Surrey. And after that, we never travelled north for a family holiday again.

It didn't occur to my parents that my emotional experience as a child would be quite so different from their own. They couldn't have foreseen how my feelings of otherness and ugliness, and desperation to assimilate, would shape me. I suppose no parent can anticipate how their child will feel when faced with their world, but back then I badly wanted them to understand what I was going through, although it was beyond their comprehension and I couldn't find the right words to explain it.

I can conjure up the moments when I still believed my mum when she'd tell me that I was the beautiful daughter she'd hoped for. I remember trying on a flouncy white dress for my first Holy Communion and us both agreeing that I looked like a princess. But I don't know when that started to change. I only know that I started to see more of what made me unlike my friends than what made us similar. I don't remember the first time I was called a name, or was told I wasn't invited to play, or was winded by the blunt force of a slur. Monkey. Mowgli.

Shitskin. The words that sent me weeping into my mother's arms, confused and hurt by their inaccuracy, of all things. She'd hold me close and tell me sincerely that what they said didn't matter, because they were wrong. 'We're from Mauritius, not from Pakistan,' she'd tell me.

'You felt different and were always trying to find an explanation for it. I never knew what to say or do, so I just felt guilty,' my mum tells me now. It's as painful for me to hear this as it is to remember how much heartache I carried through my childhood, and what I did with it. I wanted to be the same as my friends, and the only way I could see how was to copy them – to beg my parents for the things they had, the food they ate and the clothes they wore. I contorted myself to appear 'normal' and did all that I could to hide the signs that betrayed how, when I got home, my life was different from theirs. Language became my inner battleground. I wanted to excel in English especially, to write impressively and make the words mine. I talked and read and kept talking, because words were the way I took up space and hid my pain. By the time that man abused me on that Nottingham side street, I was all As in English Literature and Language. I was studying English at an English university when he assured me that England was not a place I could call my own.

My childhood was not one without joy though. I was – and I am – deeply loved by my parents, who made sure I went without nothing that I needed. We celebrated birthdays at Pizza Hut, and always ended our evening by stealing a tomato each from the salad bar and rolling it under the wheels of passing cars outside. Whoever's tomato went splat first won the game. Christmases were spent either at our house or at my uncle and auntie's – who weren't my auntie or uncle by blood, but because of love – and always ended in raucous games of Pictionary and poking fun at how my uncle insisted on pronouncing salmon with a hard 'L', and laughing at my cousin (who I called my brother) when he cried because we told him that our Christmas gift was to put him in the bin. Although we were Catholic and they were Hindu, we celebrated Raksha Bandhan every August, tying dark-maroon thread around each others' wrists to honour the sibling-like bond between us. On sunny days my brother and cousin would be outside kicking a football around, and I'd be inside in the company of books, trying to disappear into imagined worlds or watching telly to find comfort in seeing other girls who looked a bit like me – on *Sister, Sister*, *Moesha* or *Desmond's* – who didn't waste their time, as I did, wishing they were someone else instead.

I grew up inside the embrace of a Mauritian community that felt like family and created home where it found itself. Constructing islands like floating lily pads upon which our family and familiars could climb for safety and a sense of collective identity. And then we, their children, the next generation, were tasked with venturing into the water and trying to swim, trying to fit in, doing our best in choppy water. Then we returned for dinners cooked in big pots by loving aunties so that, with bellies full, we might bolster ourselves for the next time we find ourselves trying not to sink. When in the midst of our Mauritian family and its raucous, ground-shaking laughter and sunny music and generous portions, I basked in feeling part of something special and loving and delicious. At other times, though, I winced and cringed and complained, and tried to hide how we sound and taste and smell different from our friends and neighbours. And with every objection, I inched myself away from belonging. My mum tells me how stubborn I was when I refused to speak Kreol as a child, choosing to fall into ill-mannered silence rather than respond in our mother tongue. I can't imagine getting away with being so rude, but I take her at her word because it explains why I can barely speak the language of my family now.

I crave a sense of home because I've had it before and, when I did, it felt good and steady. I have felt it when our house was filled with the smell of frying garlic and ginger and the warmth of steamed white rice. I've felt it in the balmy heat of nights sat outside my auntie's home in Belle Mare, after the crescendo of music and laughter has settled and we sit, whisky on the table, watching tiny lizards gather near the light and casting shadows while the curling smoke of burning citronella wards off biting insects. I have felt it in unexpected moments, too. In times of beauty and peace it feels more present and possible. When the sun is setting over hazy days in the park with old friends, or when a spring breeze nudges me along while my fingers are intertwined with my beloved. It rarely lingers, though, this feeling of knowing home. It pains me that I can't keep hold of it for long enough to fill the hole in my heart. Home is more than a place, a building or a land. It is a feeling, an action and, like all feelings and actions, it is not static. It is made of tastes and smells, of individuals and community. It is colours and textures, sounds and songs, and the comforting feeling of your heart-space filled to the brim. Belonging is a human need. One we only know the importance of in its absence. To know it is to not have to name it. Home and belonging are intertwined and they both evade my capture.

I wanted to make England my home, to belong to it and, for me, that meant denial of all that kept me from it. I couldn't fathom, through the fog of idolising whiteness and Englishness, how it could be possible without dissolving all that made me different. I'd curse my hair and hiss at my dad for making me this way, because it was his curls that had met my mother's texture and made my hair impossible to brush. I'd have fairy-tale dreams of being white with blue eyes, feeling blessed and chosen at last, then wake in tears to find myself still in my pink bedroom and crimson bed sheets and brown body. I'd use a wooden ruler to trace the distance between England and Mauritius and Pakistan on an atlas, as though knowing the geographical distance could protect me from that weapon of a word, and cushion me from the feeling of being punched in the stomach every time it was thrown in my direction. I'd make mental lists of all the ways in which I was closer to being English than I was to being Mauritian, and would try to ignore anything I couldn't argue away. I didn't understand the difference between determining yourself English and British back then but I hoped that English was something I could become, and then I'd belong and finally be able to call this place my home. I don't feel that way any more, though. I don't crave Englishness like I once did because I don't really know what it is. I ask Sam what it means to him and he just shrugs and doesn't answer. Even so, we've managed to move to a place of great significance in the historical timeline of England.

When you cross the county line leaving Kent, heading towards the coast at Hastings, the sign does not welcome you to East Sussex but, instead, to '1066 country'. It's already become the marker that tells us that we're nearing our village. The Battle of Hastings took place three miles from our front door and this is one of the few history lessons from school that I can remember quite well. I remember learning about how the Duke of Normandy, William the Conqueror, came ashore near Pevensey to challenge the army of the recently crowned King Harold for the throne. A few miles away from where we now live is where an English army descended from a hilltop to fight the French and watch as their new king, after a full day of sustained and cunning attack, died, either having been hacked to pieces or finished by an arrow piercing him through the eye (depending on whether you believe the story of a Norman soldier or the Bayeux Tapestry). For the next twenty-one years England was ruled by a French monarch. So if you identify as English, there's a decent chance that some of your ancestors were French.

Despite having grown up and gone to school in Mauritius, more than 6,000 miles away, my parents also know the story of William the Conqueror. They learned about Henry VIII and his six wives as well. Under the eye of the British Empire, following a curriculum determined by Englishmen in England, the history they were taught as children was the history I was taught as a child. They were not taught the history of Mauritius, not in any kind of meaningful way. They were taught that first came the Portuguese, followed by the Dutch who killed the dodo, then the French took control but they lost it to the British. Then, 150 or so years later, came independence. Scant mention of how Mauritians came to be there, in all their remarkable diversity; and certainly no mention of the colonial rule that they were born into and under.

*

Dina Arobi. Ilha do Cirne. Mauritius. Île de France. L'Île Maurice.

A volcanic island rising out of the Indian Ocean, 500 miles to the east of Madagascar, 790 square miles in area. Believed uninhabited, but certainly not unknown. Frequented by passing Arab and Swahili sailors and traders who called it Dina Arobi (meaning Abandoned Island) from the tenth century. The Portuguese were the first Europeans to land there in the early sixteenth century and they found wax tablets bearing inscriptions believed to be Arabic (or Greek, depending on which account you believe) on the beaches, by those who had reached the island's shores before them. Diogo Fernandes Pereira, a Portuguese captain, named it Ilha do Cirne in 1507 in honour of the ship that had carried him there. The Portuguese introduced goats, monkeys and rats over the following decades but, finding it had no resources they wanted, decided against settling on and colonising the island.

The Dutch then claimed the island as a Dutch possession in 1598 and named it after Maurice of Nassau, the Stadtholder of the Dutch Republic and Prince of Orange. For the forty years that followed they were preoccupied with the island's strategic position in the Indian Ocean for facilitating trade, but during that time no Dutch inhabitants committed to living there permanently. Eager to prevent the English or French from taking possession of the island, they began their attempts to establish Mauritius as a colony in 1638. Over the next seventy years they tried repeatedly to turn the island into a prosperous entity, bringing hens, deer and sugarcane with them, and sowing seeds that had never before grown in the island's soil. They brought the first enslaved people to the island, too: 105 men and women from Madagascar, tasked with cutting down the island's precious ebony trees to feed a trade hungry for tropical hardwood. Within weeks, half of those stolen people had escaped into the densely wooded interior of the island – the first Maroons.

The Dutch struggled. They blamed the droughts, storms, locusts, rats and monkeys for sabotaging their attempts to cultivate potentially lucrative commodity crops like rice, indigo and tobacco, and for chasing away the colonists they hoped would settle there. There were never more than 400 people on the island under the Dutch – with far more men than women – and they never quite managed to grow enough food to sustain themselves or supply the Dutch ships that stopped off at Rade des Tortues (now Port Louis, the capital city). After they had denuded the land of its valuable ebony trees, there was little left of value worth staying for. In 1710 the Dutch abandoned the island, destroying all that they had built as they left.

For a handful of years after their departure, the island was left unoccupied – other than as a base for passing pirates – until 1715, when Captain Guillaume Dufresne d'Arsel called in to Mauritius on his way to Île Bourbon (now Réunion), coffee plants in hand, and claimed it in the name of France. In the near-century that the French possessed the island, which they renamed Île de France, there were nineteen governors, yet there is one who remains held in hagiographic regard to this day: Mahé de La Bourdonnais, the so-called 'founding father' of the island. Under his rule the cultivation of sugarcane expanded, the population – both free and enslaved – grew, infrastructure was developed and the stage was set for the plantation economy that the island would eventually become.

The French Revolution saw slavery abolished in 1794, but while the law changed in France, it was ignored in Île de France, as the 50,000 enslaved people were integral to the economy of the island, where they made up more than 80 per cent of the population. Despite repeated efforts to establish Île de France as a productive as well as strategic colony, the island was still unable to sustain itself and remained most coveted for its optimal geographical position – for both trade and warfare. During the Napoleonic Wars, Britain fought France for possession of it and won. The French capitulated to the British on generous terms, such that their customs, laws, language, religion and property remained intact on the island. Under the British the island reverted back to being called Mauritius, sugar production and trade boomed and slavery was abolished – although Mauritius was the last of the British colonies to grant their enslaved population their freedom. After abolition, indentured labourers, mostly from India, were imported and, although technically free, were subject to the same brutalities of the formerly-enslaved people they were brought over to replace. In 1839 the British and Foreign Anti-Slavery Society described the indenture system as 'slavery under a different name'.

After years of struggling against the colonial authorities, universal adult suffrage was instituted in 1959, which paved the way for 12 March 1968 when, after a week of heavy rain, the sun broke through the clouds to shine over a newly independent Mauritius. Today nearly 1.3 million Mauritians live on the island, making it the most densely populated African country. English remains the official language (and is the principal language spoken in parliament), while education and the media mostly use French; 90 per cent of the island's population speak in Mauritian Creole – Kreol Morisyen – day-to-day, alongside a number of other languages, including Hindi, Tamil and Bhojpuri which are spoken by those of Indian descent (who make up more than two-thirds of the Mauritian population), as well as Chinese dialects spoken by the Sino-Mauritian community.

The story of Mauritius is the story of a nation brought into being by the forces of colonial plunder and imperial ambition.

A story of European empires wrestling for the power to trade and exploit, for financial gain. A story of occupation, trade and warfare. This is the story that the history books tell. Yet what they fail to adequately describe is how the island's plentiful and unique ecosystem of dense tropical forests with palm trees and grand ebonies, where giant tortoises and flightless birds roamed while doves flew and parrots squawked overhead, was deforested and devastated, ravaged and razed by those who arrived and saw an abundance that they sought to exploit. A natural landscape was wrecked and its pieces exported for sale, and the fertile plains that remained were transformed into a patchwork of plantations and monocultures that decimated the island's biodiversity. The history books fail to describe how, over a handful of centuries, a nation of people was created from generations of stolen and oppressed humans, with their wisdom and ancient spiritualities demonised and suppressed, and their names and stories erased. Or how an entire people created themselves from their intertwined lives – one hand clinging to memories of their motherlands and the other stitching together new identities, new languages and new songs to sing together. Imperfectly and urgently inventing new ways of being so that they might survive their unspeakable subjugation.

*

On a Tuesday evening two years before we moved I was sitting on the sofa in our London flat, trying to take a deep breath. I felt as though there was a brick in each lung and I couldn't gasp even half as much air as usual. My breathing had been laboured since the weekend, when I'd come into contact with a shaggy black cat that left a trail of fur wherever it sauntered. I pulled hard on my inhaler, desperate for the relief it usually brings, but nothing was changing; fearing that I'd only get worse, Sam ordered a taxi and we went to A&E.

I've had asthma for as long as I can remember – ever since I caught pneumonia as a two-year-old in Mauritius – but I hadn't had an asthma attack before. And while I sat with my head between my legs with all the other sickly people in the waiting room, I was still in denial about was what was happening. But by the time I got to see a doctor, my oxygen levels were too low for me to leave and, panicked, I had started to think that I might be closer to death than I'd realised. For the five nights that I was in hospital I was gripped with fear and barely slept. I lay awake, listening to the other people groaning and crying and throwing up, and I was consumed with one thought, in the face of my mortality: why did I spend so much of my life depressed?

In moments of clear-mindedness it can seem as though depression is a rational thing, and that it's amenable to logic. My mind during that hospital stay, sharpened by breathlessness, certainly thought so. The way my depressive states could shift and fluctuate has, at times, caused me to believe that I could be convinced out of feeling unhappy. But depression isn't a rational thing. At least mine isn't. And no rational argument has ever soothed me in the midst of a downswing.

I would read voraciously through the depression of my

childhood. Always looking for new words. But I haven't ever found the right ones to describe the experience of never feeling part of something rich and rooted, of never feeling known or understood. I was in a perpetual state of mourning, caught in the chasm between two cultures and identities. Disconnected from both my family, whom I was rejecting, and my friends, with whom I could never truly connect. I never felt whole.

As I got older, those feelings transformed somewhat. They outlasted my childhood and became more vulnerable and conflicted. I believed it was impossible that anyone would love such a fractured being as I was. I'd lose whole nights of sleep, believing that I was destined to see out my days bewildered and alone. So I trained myself to perform joyfulness, to keep those wretched parts of myself obscured. I hid behind rambling chatter and forced laughter. And even when I was performing honesty with friends, I would hide the bedrock of my anguish. I got so good at pretending that, in the moment, my performance could feel almost genuine. Almost.

At its most disturbing, the depression robbed me of clarity. Plunging me into a fugue state where time became endlessly slippery, causing me to feel as though I was half-trapped in a dream during the day, and at night I'd half-wake to the presence of a malevolent shadow by my bed, unable to scream or move. But day-to-day I lived with the low rumble of anticipating misfortune, my body braced for the worst to happen. It made the feeling of ease in the present moment nearly impossible. And it only lightened when something awful finally did happen, as if to say, 'Ah, there you are, catastrophe, I've been waiting for you. Now you're here, I can finally breathe.'

In those moments under the hospital strip-lighting I was in awe of what it was to be alive. I couldn't stop thinking about all the time I'd spent engulfed by anxiety and swinging in and out of depressive states, and how much of a waste it had been. I was foggy and oxygen-deprived and desperate to be discharged, and then consumed with the thought that I should have been able to coax myself out of a depressive period with a little logic. If only my depression was amenable to logic, maybe then I wouldn't have let it devour so many years of my life.

I chase the splinters of sunlight that find their way across the garden and into the house. It illuminates the cobwebs that hang from the corners of each room it passes through. The spiders have woven so much webbing throughout the house that I wonder if it would remain standing if I got rid of them. I've got to know when to expect a sunbeam to find the top two stairs, and every day I take myself to sit there. Face warm, toes cold. In the early afternoon the light finds the bedroom and I lean out of the window for a time, watching the last leaves on the wisteria fall while I absorb what of the early-winter sun I can catch hold of. The warmth I accumulated over the year's longer days is fading steadily, and I try to trap it and hold it against my body with woollen blankets and mugs of hot tea. Although we can't turn sunlight into food, like our plant friends, I'm certain I absorb it and turn it into something akin to energy. I am phototrophic and I pine for the sun on my face, no matter the temperature or the sludge of grey clouds surrounding it.

'Why don't you go on a walk?' Sam asks.

It's a gentle and reasonable suggestion. We haven't done much walking since we got here, and there are fields and woodland and streams to hop over nearby. But I don't much like to go for walks alone, so I find an excuse – something to tidy or an unpacked box to deal with. I know getting out and exploring would do me good, and might go some way towards helping me feel settled here, but I'm too uneasy. I've worried myself to a standstill.

I've walked in the countryside alone a few times before, on meditation retreats held in sacred silence. For a week at a time I'd head south-west down to Devon, onto Dartmoor, and disappear into days split into hours of sitting practice, meals eaten in silence and solitary walks in the woods, on the moors, over the tors. Every day a walk would be part of my practice. I absorbed the seclusion and the foliage as a tonic from city life. Being alone is the point when you withdraw from your everyday life, and the silence that I committed to for those days felt protective. Even when I got lost and couldn't find my way back to the centre, pacing back and forth, hoping for a flicker of remembering to guide me to the right path. Even when I was scrambling through a forest, feeling like a wild thing, thinking I was far from civilisation, only to skid down a bank onto a riverside path full of dog walkers. Even when I was quietly feeding fistfuls of long grass to a pony and the serenity was broken by a farmer driving by, brandishing a rifle. In all of these moments I felt that the silence was my shield. I was able to embark on explorations, climbing heather-covered hills, with the meditative tradition of withdrawing into nature to guide me, holding on to the permission that I'd given myself to dispense with politeness and eye contact and greeting passers-by – and allowing myself to pretend that I could blend in to the landscape, at least for those few days. On retreat, I could feel invisible and, by hiding behind the silence, was able to walk by myself.

But here I don't know how to walk alone. I can't use a protective veil of silence because I'm not just passing through. I can't hide in anonymity when I'm trying to make this place my home. Sam knows that I want to be outdoors, but I'm uncertain in a way that I can't fully explain. I feel less visible with him to hide behind and less nervous about getting lost, so he suggests coming with me and tentatively I say, 'Okay.'

We decide to walk by moonlight. The stormy rain and wind that have been whipping the bare trees against each other have moved on at last and have left behind a still and cloudless night. As we cross the field, the full moon starts to appear over the skeletal treeline, crisp and cool against the nearly-night sky. The moon here is fearsomely bright, like nothing I've seen before. It shines with such intensity that our bodies cast dark-blue shadows across the ground as we walk. Some of the fields are still flooded from the recent storms, so Sam walks ahead of me, using a stick to find a path. He moves through the land with more certainty than I know how to, and I feel safer when he leads the way. I find myself following his stride carefully, placing my feet where his footsteps tell me is safe. As the light fades into deeper darkness, my eyes start to adjust. The outlines of trees and branches crystallise into moonlit blues. The chill in the air catches around my lips. I follow Sam over a barbed-wire fence that's been bent low by other walkers shortcutting across this corner of private land, through a boggy field and over a stile towards the woodland. Each one of his steps is followed by each one of mine. He seems to know where he's going and if he doesn't, I can't tell.

The path through the woods is clear and well trodden, even though all the recent boot-marks have been washed away by the rain. In the darkness I try to commit this route to memory as we snake through the silent woods and to a clearing on the other side. I am drawing a map in my mind's eye of the track carved out by the steps of others. Along the path I see a gargantuan tree shining silver-grey under the light of the full moon. The trunk is made up of weighty undulations, like hefty swatches of draped fabric, marked with the fissures and fractures of a few hundred years of growing and widening. Between the folds and creases are lodged brackets of thick shelf fungi, the size of dinner plates, their many ridges betraying their old age. The tree is remarkable. Elegant and sturdy, shimmery and statuesque. I place my hands against the cool, smooth bark and sense that I am one of many who have pressed palm to trunk.

The moon is climbing higher, growing smaller, and the temperature is steadily dropping. The chill finding my toes tells me it's time to go home. We turn on our heels and retrace our steps, back through the woods and across the swampy fields, leaping over the puddles that look deeper than our boots. We pass a stream that appears swollen from all the rain and in it see a reflection of the round moon, rippling into shards as it flows slowly south towards the sea. Tawny owls hoot gently into the night as we pass by. We trudge, semi-frozen, towards the village, following the smell of wood-smoke and the faint twinkle of lights from the houses to guide us back.

CHAPTER 3

I've always found winter challenging. As the nights get longer and the days chillier and gloomier, my tendency towards depression gains ground. Before plants, I had little sense of winter's utility, the cycle that makes the onset of cold times both inevitable and renewing. I met cold weather as though it were an inescapable suffering, a yearly punishment. I'd look up the weather in Mauritius – winter here is summer there – and daydream of a life close the equator.

This year is no different. The wind howls and the sky hangs low. The leafless trees cower as one windy day after another rattles through the house. It blows our neighbours' stagnant water-butt into our fence, sending it crashing into the garden. The drains overflow and we make a panicked trip to the DIY shop for the rods to unblock them. I arrange and rearrange the bookcase. We paint the hallway and the kitchen walls white, and Sam drills holes to hang pictures I've not seen before. On the days that we're not scrubbing off or painting over the marks left by the last occupants, I'm worrying that we shouldn't have moved here. I worry that I'll remain too afraid to explore, or that I'll be too nervous to make friends with the neighbours and always feel too uneasy to settle in. The frost arrives most mornings. The cold is consistent and tiring. Although nothing compared to the chill of the four winters I spent in New York.

Despite my resistance to the cold, the first snowy days in that city could coax me outside. The first romantic flutters of snowflakes drifted down as I, and the other transplants to New York, excitedly pressed our noses against freezing window-panes and hoped for frosty walks and days off work to skid around the snow-covered streets. The initial flurries of snow-fall are dreamy there. Crisp blue-whiteness would crunch and click underfoot. The intensity of the cold, after the searing forty-degree heat of the summer, was startling but invigorating. But after a few short days of wonder, the snow would start absorbing the city's filth, turning from pristine white to a dirty grey-brown. It would be ugliest by the kerb where the cars turned, cutting tyre marks through the blackened slush that would turn to invisible ice, poised to whip a hurrying commuter down onto their tailbone. When it snowed really heavily, even the lumbering city buses and garbage trucks couldn't make it down the streets. Trash would pile up along the sidewalks ungathered. When the inevitable next blizzard came, the black bags would get buried underneath. They would melt and refreeze until they formed glass-like sculptures that would take weeks and weeks to fully defrost.

When I first left for New York it was early October, almost

a decade ago, and I'd barely got my bearings before my friend Ben first asked when I was going to come home. Ben and I had been friends for four years, having met on a Channel 4 training programme for television researchers from 'diverse' backgrounds. We didn't like each other much at first, but ended up forging a friendship built on supporting one another other to withstand the demands of a tough industry and the emotional burden of being the 'token ethnic' person. Working in the TV industry was both a gift and a curse. It was exciting and draining, and filled with as many smart, joyful people as there were egomaniacs and bullies. Ben was one of the smart and joyful ones, and we spent much of our time together plotting how to escape the management styles of the egomaniacs and bullies.

It was about three years after we'd first met when Ben fell ill. She had been feeling unwell for a few weeks but putting on a brave face because she, like everyone who worked in TV, was too busy working to find time to see a doctor. One Saturday her skin had started to turn yellow, so she took herself to A&E and, suspecting jaundice, the weekend staff gave her a blood transfusion and admitted her. By the time I visited her on the Monday, she was back to her usual hue and was waiting to be discharged, eager to make way for someone else to use the bed. But the next day they told her it was leukaemia and that treatment needed to start as soon as possible. I remember the swift blow of anguish that I felt when she called to tell me that night, although I can't remember a word of what she said. I was crying so hard that Ben was the one comforting me as I wailed into the darkness of my bedroom.

A week after her diagnosis I was perched on the edge of her hospital bed. She promised that she'd fight it, and I promised to love her while she did, so that we could be friends until we were good and old. Even though she was about to start her first rounds of chemotherapy, she refused to succumb to hopelessness and wallowing and she wouldn't allow me to, either. She insisted that we maintain our dynamic of complaining about work and then figuring it out together, so as we sat in the not-knowing of what the next weeks and months would hold, she helped me to write an overdue resignation letter to my boss at the BBC. Using herself as a cautionary tale, Ben hit 'send' on the email that untethered me from a job I'd stayed in so that I could apply for a mortgage. But it took me another year to drum up the courage to quit London and get on a flight to New York.

The decision to leave was a knee-jerk one. On the surface, I wanted to untangle myself from yet another crappy TV job working for someone who couldn't stand me, but beneath that, I wanted to get away from London and the life I'd wandered into. Tending the wounds of a break-up, a personal trauma and one too many conflicts at work had me planning my escape. So when I was presented with an offer to extend my contract, I told my boss that I was leaving the country and had no plans to return before Christmas. I flew out of Heathrow and then, eight hours of sleep later, landed at JFK Airport, despite never having visited America before and not knowing anyone who lived there. I hadn't planned to stay more than a couple of months, so with every postponed flight, Ben became more suspicious that I wouldn't return. I was falling into a life there and as my temporary escape looked to turn into a migration, she'd ask more insistently when I was going to come back.

The first twelve months or so were haphazard and blurry. I moved three times, shared rooms with near-strangers, had meltdowns and spent hours and hours trying to figure out how to apply for a visa that would buy me a little more time in New York. I was naive and romantic. I made friends and I lost them. I worked for tips and sometimes came home with not even a dollar more to my name. I was desperate for a chance to start from scratch, to move across an ocean and feel brand new. I wanted to see if somewhere else would have me. I wanted to feel like I didn't belong to where I lived because I'd chosen that state of being, instead of having it forced upon me. And for a while it worked. I made friends with people who liked the sound of my voice and didn't mind that I might not be staying long. I made friends over cans of warm beer, shots of cheap whiskey and dollar slices of pizza. I made friends with people who showed me what it looked like to be themselves, fearlessly and carelessly. An elderly woman selling costume jewellery at an East Village flea market said to me, 'I didn't know they had Black people in England,' and her passing comment left me bemused but glowing. I felt more unique and interesting because, to some of the people I met, my existence was unexpected. Implausible even. I began to feel like a mythical creature and, as odd as it was a reason for it, I loved feeling special.

I chose adventure over facing myself. I danced with my

hair down and sang karaoke until the sun came up; rode
around Manhattan on the back of my new friend's Vespa; and
drank the dirtiest of dirty Martinis whenever I had the chance.
I dated carelessly, ate greedily and fell asleep on subway trains
as they transported me across the bridges that joined borough
to borough in the middle of the night. And it was all to keep
myself moving, so that the sadness that had been gathering
since my teenage years wouldn't catch up with me; and I
wouldn't have to keep remembering the abusive workplace
that still gave me nightmares; and so that I could pretend I
wasn't still heartsick over the love that had left me. New York
City's a good place to disappear, and to convince yourself that
you're happy when you're not. It's electric and enlivening and
sleepless and delicious – and it's ideal for keeping you from
dealing with your stuff.

It was a hot mid-June day in my third New York summer when
a friend and I found ourselves following a treasure hunt of
notes pinned to doors, scrawled arrows and 'THIS WAY's
through a coffee shop to a lobby and then in a lift up to the
eighth floor of an industrial building on a busy street. The
doors slid back and, shielding my eyes from a suddenly brighter
sun, I stepped off metal and out onto soil and gravel. The warm
air smelt sweet and earthy, and before me lay row after row of
kale and carrots, spring onions and chard, basil growing in
bouquets, alongside aubergines and tomatoes and lettuce. All
manner of plants emerging from a few feet of chocolate-
coloured soil beneath me. I watched as sun-kissed, sweaty

workers and volunteers hustled past, carrying full-to-the-brim watering cans and crates filled with pak choi and the first of the season's peppers. The Manhattan skyline glinted in the background and all I could see was basking in the bright sunlight, coming to life under the endless blue of the New York summer sky. A bucolic wonderland framed by a cityscape.

The thrill of this unexpected place stayed with me when I got back down to street level and buzzed through me for days and so, eagerly, I returned the following week to spend a day among plants and soil for the first time. I arrived wearing denim shorts and canvas slip-on shoes – the wrong clothes for manual work. I'd never willingly touched the ground before. I'd never felt compelled to dirty my hands intentionally. I moved between squatting and kneeling, brushing away the gravel that had pushed itself into my knees and intermittently emptying out the soil that had gathered in my shoes. Fragments of earth and tiny stones wedged themselves under my nails as I learned how to weed and wondered how these little opportunistic plants had found their own way up to this piece of land so high above the ground. The dirtier I got, the keener my eye became as I removed the unwelcome competition from around these young plants who were still finding their feet, to encourage them to grow strong and fruitful. I was hooked.

Sneaking out onto the rooftops of apartment buildings was one of my favourite ways to spend summer evenings with my New York friends. It wasn't something I'd ever done in London, with all of its pitched roofs and rain showers. We'd wiggle up clanking fire escapes or squeeze awkwardly through hatches propped open with a brick and, clutching beer and snacks, climb up and out to escape the sweat, smell and noise of the city streets below. When the evening started to cool, we'd slither back down, leaving no evidence for a landlord or super to discover. So while a farm in the city would have been novel enough, I couldn't stop thinking about this farm on a city rooftop.

They called it Brooklyn Grange because their first farm was supposed to be in Brooklyn, but they found themselves setting it up on top of the Standard Motors Building in Queens – the borough I'd adopted – instead. It came into being in 2010, when a group of farmers and the contractors they'd hired laid down a green roof system, before hoisting ton after ton of soil up by crane and planting seedlings straight into the newly-laid earth. It is unfathomable that on a roof in the middle of a city, crops could be grown, in actual soil, and produce enough to really feed people, but in this implausible place a leafy sanctum rose out of higher ground. A feat of big dreams and tenacity.

By the time I found myself at the farm, I'd managed to secure myself a visa and was working in documentary production. I'd fought hard to get through the immigration process, so when I'd made it out the other side, with permission to work for three years, I was determined to convince myself that I was happier than I had been working in London. But my situation felt precarious and I was barely making enough money for the rent. I worked long hours on projects I wanted to care about, but I was searching for a feeling that making films didn't give me. I felt drawn to the plants on that rooftop as well as to the people there who were growing them. I'd plough through the working week just so that, come Saturday, I could leap up those flights of stairs and out onto that roof. Some days I manned the market stall, telling the customers what was at its best that week, and how considerately the vegetables had been grown – with no chemicals at all – before weighing what they had chosen and chatting about how they were planning to cook it. Other days I'd plant out seedlings or weed with the other farm workers. I liked to work near the chicken coop, picking beans or ground-cherries or leafy greens, then stopping once or twice to push some damaged chard or kale leaves through the wire for them to peer at and then peck to shreds.

On busier days I'd take a moment to catch my breath next to the beehives, sitting close enough to hear their steady thrum while they zipped back and forth, laden with fuzzy bags of yellow-orange pollen. Next to the compost bays, the cut-flower bed was filled with rose-pink and purple-blue cornflowers alongside amaranth, with its blood-red tasselled flower heads cascading towards the ground. The nectar of the flowers called out to monarch butterflies who – with their wings patterned in black and white lace against burnt orange, and their exquisitely spotted bodies atop slender legs – would come to feed there. As I watched one butterfly place its feet daintily on the open petals of a dark-orange zinnia and unfurl its proboscis, I realised I'd never seen a butterfly like it in New York City before.

Spending time on the farm felt like an antidote to the creeping dissatisfaction I was feeling towards the work I was doing during the week. It was work too, but it felt different. Engaging, yet somewhat monotonous, repetitious in a way that felt satisfying and worthwhile. Hiding amongst the rows of plants up there, I started to find a little respite from the city. For a few hours, once a week, I'd walk home with leaves in my hair and soil under my fingernails, carrying a hefty bag of vegetables and somehow feeling less overwrought. The relief I found in this otherworldly green space was like nothing I'd felt before. It was somewhere safe and kind to be, when life felt like too much of the opposite. I'd got used to diluting whatever was bothering me in Happy Hour cocktails or brunch with a Bloody Mary. But I was growing sick of doing that: sick of commuting on deafening subway trains, sick of breathing in smog-heavy air, and sick and tired of feeling unfulfilled.

I found out on Facebook, of all places to hear the news. The last message I'd sent was on her birthday. There were a couple of messages before that one, a few texts and a call or two that went straight to voicemail. With the five-hour time difference, I'd grown used to how lopsided my communication with old friends could be. While it was weird not to have heard from Ben, there had been times when her treatment was so tiring that she'd go quiet for a while, lose her phone and not find it for a few days. I'd learned not to panic. I trusted that she'd appear again to tell me that she was doing okay and that, hopefully, she'd be allowed home for a bit.

Her name had been tagged in a post – that's why it popped up on my timeline. People I'd never met were talking about her in the past tense. My old phone lagged as I searched frantically for something definitive, a clear word of what I prayed wasn't true. It was her sister who had broken the news. Ben was gone. And I was destroyed.

I didn't have anywhere to put my grief. No one in New York knew who she was. She'd been unwell since before I moved and never had the strength, immune system or money to visit. I didn't know who to tell, and I couldn't find words to describe her. I called her mum and tried not to cry as she told me how she'd left this Earth struggling to breathe. I desperately wanted to get back for the funeral, to tell her I loved her and how sorry I was that I didn't realise how long it had been since she'd last responded to my messages. I read the final words that I sent her, the usual exclamation marks and kisses, and I wondered if she'd read them. I was sickened by my failure to notice she wasn't replying. How could I have missed this? How could I not have know what was happening? How do I say goodbye?

The farm was the only place I could bear to be. I took my grief up the stairs and asked the soil and the crops and the blazing sun to hold the unbearable weight of it. I volunteered to spend that day weeding. I leaned into the rhythm of the job, the certainty of getting covered in soil having become less worrisome. It's a task for the determined. For those who trust that their small acts will be of service, that their efforts have worth, even if they're not there to see what comes of them. It is never a job that's truly complete as the weeds will always return but, Sisyphus-like, we persist. Not every job on the farm is as triumphant as the harvest, but the humble and lowly tasks prepare the ground upon which flourishing may take place. Weeding shows us the kind of diligence and faith that is asked for in the process of persuading and enabling plants to thrive – and that the journey is made of more than just glory. It is a good place for new growers to begin.

Her absence moved me in waves. I'd be absorbed in watering, watching the spray of the hose make gossamer rainbows, and then the fact of her absence would punch me hard in the chest. I'd be laughing with someone at the market stand and stop short, ashamed, that I dared laugh when she wouldn't again. I hadn't expected her to die, even though I knew that she might, so I had to realise over and over again, to convince my heart that it was true.

I kept tending the soil in the exhausting, searing heat until I was too tired to keep going. When the sun dipped behind the skyscrapers, the sky turned from blue to pink-violet and my skin bristled from the sunshine it had gathered as the temperature steadily dropped. Lying on the ground, quite filthy by then, I stared upwards for some time; my skin had turned a shade darker. I imagined telling Ben about what I'd found here, and that something was happening to me. That I might have discovered something magical and, if I could, I'd have loved to share it with her. I wanted to tell her how I'd spent my day, lovingly tending crops I couldn't name, and how I'd found a place that was welcoming, new friends to teach me to grow and hallowed ground upon which I might thrive.

She wouldn't have recognised me that day, hands darkened and encrusted with earth, sticky with sweat from the kind of hard graft neither of us had ever thought we'd want to do. She would have thrown her head back, thick black hair flying, and laughed massively, with that smile that showed most of her teeth, because she'd think, I'm quite sure, that I was kidding with all this. And then she would laugh some more, because it would have been funny to see me lying there, dirty and peaceful, if you'd known me as well as she did.

There's a cruelty to mourning under the July sun. I wanted weather that matched my insides, I wanted dark clouds and rain storms. The joyousness of the bright, clear days and the laughter of sidewalk margarita-drinkers were maddening. I wanted the world to realise my sadness and to mirror the gloom in my heart. I would have done anything for just a moment of the heavy darkness of a rainy London day.

We'd never talked about the possibility of her death. Even when a new treatment regime had pushed her to the brink, she never entertained the idea that she wouldn't get better – at least not with me. She endured the brutality of the treatment with defiance, refusing to surrender to its ravage, even when her bones, weakened by chemotherapy, left her too tired and in pain to stand. I chose to believe what she said, instead of what I was hearing and seeing. I saw what I wanted to see and believed what I needed to, because it was too hard to accept the possibility that she might not make it. I was thousands of miles away when she met a wounding relapse with more fight in her heart than I'd ever imagined possible, and from her hospital bed ran a fierce campaign to get more people – especially those from under-represented communities – to sign up to the Bone Marrow Registry. What was left of her energy went into growing that register, for her sake and for all the others caught in the same battle, and the universe paid her back with a match and a transplant in the last spring of her life. All the while I was busy being selfish and trying to protect myself from what it really meant that she was about to have a bone-marrow transplant. I went to yoga classes, found a therapist and ate cheap takeaway noodles while failing to notice how long it had been since she'd last answered the phone.

I worked on the day of the funeral, hoping to distract myself. It was the point in the summer where, usually, the heat would make the air thick and unbreathable, but those first days of August were marked by an uncharacteristic coolness. Time was moving glacially, as it does in the fog of sadness. I wanted to accelerate through this day, but sorrow was determined to slow everything down, refusing to let me bypass what it had to say, and all that it insisted must be felt. Unable to focus, I left the office early and travelled past my subway stop to the end of the N Line and turned left in the direction of the water.

Hell Gate is a tidal strait in the East River and, despite the tumult with which the water flows, and the churning current which has dragged many boats and bodies to the river's bed, it was a key gateway to the Atlantic from the seventeenth century onwards. Those not daring enough to snatch at the slim window of safety to pass through it unscathed would spend time, money and coal going the long way round. At one point around 1,000 ships a year would sink or run aground there. In 1780 a British frigate called the HMS *Hussar*, carrying soldiers, enslaved people and a fortune in gold coins, hit a rock and sank there, despite a man named Swan – an experienced navigator and enslaved man – warning the captain that the vessel wouldn't make it through intact. New Yorkers still search for its wreckage in the hope of finding its lost treasure.

It was to this water system that I felt drawn – not as dangerous as in times gone by, but still turbulent. I was searching for a ritual, something meaningful and comforting, so I sat against an old tree, my back pressing against its rough bark, and I wrote to her. I scribbled silent, frantic feelings through falling tears that landed onto the page and blurred my words together. As the day was ending and the sky was aflame, I put my message to Ben in a small jar and threw it into the water below, remembering how much peace I'd felt when we scattered my auntie's ashes in the ocean off the north coast of Mauritius. I watched as the jar bobbed along, slowly at first, and then, in a sudden whirl, was dragged under the surface. I wanted to believe that the water would take my words to her, but on reflection, it was a foolish idea. An act of pollution that I hoped would ease the guilt I felt for being away for so long. An attempt to say goodbye because I'd missed my chance. It was supposed to bring me some relief and for a moment it felt like a goodbye enough, but I ambled home with a leaden weight in my chest. My throat felt like it was closing. That weight, that obstruction, returns whenever I think of her, even now, years later.

The day after was a Saturday and I spent it at the farm, learning to harvest. I learned how long okra should be, before cutting the pod away from the stem, and what depth of red or shade of lemon-yellow the different peppers that grew there ought to be before gathering them into a crate. I learned how much a tomato should give when gently squeezed, to signal its readiness for picking; and that no matter how many times you return to the French bean patch, there will always be more hiding under leaves, tucked behind stems, as if they grow an inch more whenever your back is turned. I watched carefully and tried to match the speed and diligence of the experienced farmhands as they whipped pounds of produce into crate upon crate upon crate. Even though I couldn't keep up, I was thankful to be part of the process.

More than any date in the calendar or cosmic alignment, the arrival of tomatoes has come to herald the beginning of the summer for me. They flourish when the long, sunny days urge their stems to grow tall and thick. Perfect, yellow star-shaped flowers form and yawn open, ready for the buzz of a nectar-hungry bee or the bump of a clumsy farmer to cause that flower to transform into fruit. The tipping point in the season – the solstice – the longest day passes as the tomatoes start to swell and assume their mature form. More remarkable than the uniform supermarket tomatoes, the heirloom varieties are a parade of beauty, from bright oranges, yellows and purples, to deep scarlet and stripes, forest green fading to deep mottled red, while some, quite remarkably, are nearly black. Rarely a perfect sphere, the more uncommon cultivars refuse to conform to symmetry, growing like miniature pumpkins or plums or pears, bulbous and uneven.

There were rows and rows of them at Brooklyn Grange, some as tall as I am, swaying in formation in the breeze. The most beloved variety was a kind of cherry tomato, tiny pale-orange bursts of candy-sweetness that arrived in their hundreds. But I preferred the hefty golden-yellow heirlooms, kissed with peach on their shoulders and marked with a deep cross on the top of the fruit as though scorched. I'd happily eat them as hand-fruit, with a pinch of salt maybe, but nothing more. Even better when just picked and still holding the sun's warmth. It had been five or so years since I'd visited Mauritius, and it was there that I'd last eaten a fresh tomato as delicious as the ones that grew on that roof. I would long for those pomme d'amour whenever I cut hopefully into a plastic-wrapped, artificially ripened supermarket specimen and was faced with mealy pink-grey flesh, with little flavour and devoid entirely of sunshine. Those rooftop tomatoes were so distinct and miraculous, and they reminded me of Mauritius.

Spending time amongst the tomato beds turned my fingers yellow, then green, then nearly black as the plants I was wrangling wrangled me back and left remnants of their hairy stems all over my hands and clothes. The cherry tomatoes click off the stem with ease, while the weighty beefsteaks are best uncoupled with a sharp tool. Each one has to be placed gently in the crate, not tossed or dropped, lest you blemish their taut and gleaming outsides. Kneeling prayerfully on the ground, I'd nestle them against one another, side-by-side, in layers no more than two deep, to be whisked away to a nearby restaurant and made into Caprese salads or pizza sauce. Should one fall and split, it was no less precious to me. I would carefully transport the most battered back home, like an egg with a small crack, a treasure, and turn it into rougaille.

Tug a little too forcefully, or fail to steady the plant, and a too-swift harvest could tear a branch or snap a stem and inflict a mortal wound, compromising the future harvest. I felt deeply responsible for doing a good job. I couldn't bear to injure these earnest green beings growing in defiance of their urban surroundings, or jeopardise the living of the farmers who relied on them. This work could not be further from 'low-skilled' and it gave me what I needed that day. I needed to nurture something; needed to focus my heart and play a part in the flourishing of something. I needed to peek under dusky-green clamshell leaves to see the purple bottoms of budding aubergines emerging from spiky sepals, then cleave the largest from its branch to take home and turn it into a curry.

When Ben was diagnosed, I ditched a hideous job and a year later I migrated. Now that she was gone, I looked at the path that I – that we – had chosen seven years prior and it appeared more empty to me than ever. I'd done my best to work hard and gain a little status, but after all that striving, I felt desolate. I'd been watching other people, through a camera lens, living lives of meaning; and over that growing season, it went from being everything to me to nothing at all. I didn't see the point in my career any more. I wanted to find purpose following a different path.

The winter that followed would be my last in New York and the first without my friend. Autumn turned the foliage to reds and golds, then brown, and as winter blew the last of the leaves to the ground, the farm closed and I despaired. I felt deprived of the one place that had brought me some peace. While I'd lived my life, thus far, ignorant to the alchemy of plants and unaware of the importance of the natural world, that summer it had saved me – from the gaping hole that was left in my heart, and from the heavy ache of continuing on without her. And it would save me over and over again, as it taught me to savour the cold and await the gift of spring. On that earth, amongst those rows of edible plants, was the only place I'd sensed the possibility of healing. Through this act of growing food, which is so elemental, I was able to start stitching myself back together. In this abundant enclave in the midst of New York City nature made herself known to me and made it clear that she was not going to linger on the sidelines of my life any more.

A year later I left New York. I'd been living there for four years, even though I hadn't planned to stay that long. I was fortunate enough to have an O-1 visa by that point, but it was this document that felt like a limitation on my decisions that I couldn't submit to any more. My hopes for myself had changed. How I wanted to spend my days had changed. I missed my family. And I couldn't face building a life in America knowing that every three years I'd have to convince the U.S. Immigration that I should be allowed to stay. And there was absolutely no way that I could explore working with plants unless I was willing to continue volunteering, and fitting it around the incredibly busy work of making documentaries, which I was no longer passionate about doing. Coming back to Britain presented the possibility that I could make the space to learn more about plants, to train and study and do. Then, if I was lucky enough, to turn the labour and skill of growing food into part of my working life. The logical thing might have been to find a farm in the countryside that would take a passionate novice and turn her into a grower, but it didn't occur to me as an option at the time, since what I'd really fallen for was the practice of growing in the city. I was certain, along with cosy pubs and old friends, that I could find a green space to be part of in London.

By the winter that followed my second season at Brooklyn Grange I was back in my flat in Hackney, catching up with friends and taking in all that had changed; and seeing, with fresh eyes, all that I hadn't noticed of a place I thought I knew. I took long walks around a nearby park and along the canal, pausing by the water to watch the cormorants perched on the willow trees, stretching out their impressive wings. I watched coots making nests and shepherding around their tiny fluffy chicks, and fat-bodied carp surfacing to snatch breadcrumbs from the ducks. It all seemed more alive and beautiful and vibrant than I had ever seen it before. Maybe because I was running too fast when I left for New York, or maybe because I'd never stopped long enough to give it my attention. Either way, this was the first spring in London that had my full focus, and I watched, enthralled, as plump, generous flowers swelled on the magnolias and the ginkgo filled with elegant fan-shaped leaves in the most luminescent of greens.

CHAPTER 4

Christmas has crept up on us. Rain falls relentlessly in the days that lead up to it. The dips in the roads have flooded and the nearby fields look like marshland. The steady dripping sound of water finding its way through the hole in the roof wakes me up most nights. I press my eyes shut and try to hold on to the small slivers of sleep I can capture, but the colour of burnt orange behind my eyelids looks like the discoloured moisture that stains the curtains and plops onto the window-sill. Rust-coloured raindrops soak through the wall and cause it to quietly and steadily crumble and fall apart. The same orange-red as the bushfires that are raging through Australia. How much they must be wishing for the rain that I am cursing.

We cobble together a kind-of Christmas tree from branches of holly and cypress that we salvage from the garden waste, and thread them through a frame that Sam has made from two big sticks anchored onto a plank of wood. Hand-me-down baubles and gifted ornaments now hang precariously on makeshift boughs. It's a little thing, but it's one less tree cut down. We've invited my parents to spend the festive season with us this year. It's because of them that we have this house and this garden, and enough room for more than two people, and all the mince pies I keep baking.

My dad's no good at slowing down. He doesn't know how, but I insist upon it. Even though the roof is still leaking and the outside light has stopped working, I convince him to down tools for a while, and I feel better for watching him drift off in front of the TV with a belly full of food and a small glass of whisky. I found a nearby church so he that could go to midnight mass on Christmas Eve, as usual, but when the time comes, he decides to stay in with us to play cards and eat gajacks together. We're all relieved, because Mum never wants to go with him as she doesn't think God minds where she says her prayers, and I gave up on God when I was a teenager.

'Do you pray?' a good friend asked me recently. 'I just wondered where you get your hope from?' It's a bit of an odd question to ask someone who doesn't believe in God. 'I don't pray in the way that I grew up praying,' I tell her. I grew up Catholic, praying to God and Jesus Christ and the Virgin Mary. I went to a Catholic school and I was baptised, Holy Communioned and Confirmed. I believed, and then I just didn't. My first outrage at the Catholic Church came when I learned of their belief in the sinfulness of homosexuality. I knew myself what it was to be judged and I refused to assume the position of judge, no matter what a priest or the Bible says. One evening

I shouted to my mum, who was in the next room, to tell her that I didn't want to be Catholic any more and the Church's homophobia was why, and she merely said, 'Okay,' because what else do you say to a forthright and opinionated teenager who cries every other day? Neither of my parents swallowed the Church's religious doctrine in its entirety, so they didn't resist when I decided to throw it out of my heart.

It took a number of years before I understood that the mere fact that I was born into this religion was in large part a colonial hangover, and I was enraged anew at the thought that I'd spent my youngest years believing in someone else's god. It was the Code Noir – the document that set out the regulations for slavery in Mauritius and the other French colonies – that forced Catholicism on the enslaved as one of its many commandments. This document outlined what crimes were punishable by whipping, branding or death, and how the children born to the enslaved would be enslaved, too. It proclaimed that the enslaved had to be baptised into the Roman Catholic religion, demanded that they pray for their owners and masters and forbade them from practising any faith or spirituality of their own. It declared that work could not be carried out on a Sunday, not even by the enslaved. It has been argued that there was a measure of humanity encoded into this document, but its principal purpose was to formalise the status of the enslaved as 'chattel', for the purpose of insuring them as *bien meuble*–an asset, property, a 'good'. It was a hateful document, and all the more hateful for what was done under its doctrine. It was hateful in the way it forced its religion onto those who had their own beliefs and gods and goddesses; and hateful to all that was erased in its name.

*

Mauritius, 1962

The expectation that they should go to church every Sunday was passed down to them from their parents who'd inherited it from their parents who'd inherited it from theirs. They were raised to be good Catholics who believed what they were told by the white-skinned, French-speaking priests and knew better than to question the word of God. They sat attentively, anywhere but the front pew, as the service was delivered in Latin and learned how to sound out words whose meaning was a mystery, because if they were good, after the last amen, they'd be allowed to play with their friends who'd also sat quietly through mass.

They were brought up to fear ghosts and spirits and vodou. All the ungodly things that only heathens indulged in. They were taught to be suspicious of those who spoke to their ancestors and left offerings of sliced limes at crossroads. But their aunties waved pouches of salt over their heads to ward off evil, and if they came home after midnight, they would walk into the house backwards to leave the malevolent spirits that might have followed them on the doorstep.

The whole village would come out to watch le comète move through the night sky, its tail hanging in the air, and think of the cursed children born on the nights when it had passed by. They feared the full moon and the tales of lougarou, the half-animal and half-man who prowled around after dark. Every now and then there would be a sighting, and word would get round to be careful at night because lougarou might be lurking in the shadows. It was said that lougarou came from Madagascar and that it was conjured using black magic, so they prayed to Jesus, Mary and Père Laval to keep them safe from harm whenever they heard dogs howling into the darkness.

On clear nights, she would look up at the stars and wonder how God had hung such magnificence in the night sky. On the bus ride back to the city after a day spent by the sea, she would press her nose to the window to watch the full moon rise. She'd look at its rugged surface and feel a terror wash over her at the face that she could see; and before bed, would make the sign of the cross and pray to fair-skinned Jesus and Mary, and an old white-haired God, to keep her safe from it. But she'd go back the next night to see how the moon had changed shape and look again for that face to appear, because she was enthralled by how vast and unknown the universe was and her curiosity and awe would always outweigh her fear.

*

'I don't pray in the way that I grew up praying but I suppose I do pray,' I tell my friend. To sow, plant, harvest and eat, for me, is an act of worship. I kneel to the ground and bow down to the forces and rhythms of the natural world. I honour them with my reverence and I offer them my trust. I trust that the cycles will turn and that, even when they don't conform to my wants or perform as I expect, there is a lesson to be learned from it. It is prayer to move in step with the seasons as they turn and with the weather as it changes, especially in these dark times of the year when memories of light and warmth and verdant growth are hard to conjure. It is prayer to remember and believe that they will return again. It is prayer to trust in the profundity of small acts – of growing and gardening and loving and feeding – and to trust that they are happening in tandem with the many other small acts of wholehearted people, and that they will, and do, add up to something meaningful.

I trust where I sit as being infinitesimal within the great elemental shifts across our planet, a planet that sits within a universe amongst universes, under a sun and moon amongst many suns and moons. I sit within this knowledge and believe it gives my modest acts more meaning, not less. That this knowing shows my existence to be both miraculous and profoundly unremarkable. From this understanding, I feel able to participate in these great flows of energy that move us all to worship at the altar of the forces of nature. So yes, I suppose I do pray. Growing plants is how I pray.

I follow the practices of ancient traditions that looked to the night sky for guidance in tending their gardens. I pay attention to the forecast that charts the wax and the wane of the moon, and I follow the wisdom of those who sensed that the pull and release of the moon's gravitational force would coax seeds to germinate or urge plants to root down, or determine whether a harvest would last after picking. I follow the lunar calendar whenever I can. But when I lived in the city I never witnessed the rise of the moon, let alone sensed the energy she exerts. Now I watch the sea as the tide pulls away from the coastline and witness the power she wields. I grow following the cycles of the moon and this, to me, is a spiritual practice.

As the year is coming towards its end, I stand with my mum, leaning against the fence at the bottom of the garden, looking towards the darkened treeline at the horizon, her in my wellies, me in Sam's. And I watch her as the clear night sky makes her stretch her neck upwards. These days between Christmas and New Year have been a blur of short, brisk walks by the sea, back-to-back cups of tea and bad festive comedies. But tonight is one of those precious nights when the clouds have dispersed, and the moon promises to rise large and luminous as night falls. The parish council has a 'dark skies' policy, which means that external or street lights are not allowed, so the stargazing here is some of the best in the country. I'm certain she'll love to see the moon's largesse, so I wait until it starts to appear over the horizon line – a not-quite-full warm, waxing gibbous – before I suggest that she levels her line of sight. 'I can't believe I've never seen the moon in England like this before,' she says quietly, awestruck. She tries to take a picture of the moon to send to her sister-in-law in Mauritius – a fellow stargazer – but all her attempts are fuzzy and underwhelming, so she abandons the futile task and instead we bask in the sight of a warm orange moon on a dark night. We stand together, shivering and watching as the moon ascends, growing smaller and brighter, losing its warm colour as it moves higher into the cold December sky.

Mum gets her phone and holds it above her head. She's using an app to identify which astrological constellation is twinkling overhead. She does this when she's in Mauritius, too, walking by the sugarcane fields in the warm evening air, arms linked with my auntie, so she doesn't trip over her own feet. If I'd been born in her homeland, maybe we'd have turned our gazes skywards and learned how to find the Milky Way together. We might have done so where I grew up, too, if it weren't for the suburban street lights, security lights and garden lights that drown out most of the night sky's gentle sparkles. Only now have I noticed her deep love for the night sky; and only now that I am here am I finding my own.

Sam has convinced me to venture out into the night, even though the suggestion of frost is hanging in the air. He accepted Rachel and Graeme's invitation to the pub on our behalf, and roundly ignored my annual tradition of refusing to celebrate New Year's Eve. I've agreed to go along for the hour before midnight, to see in the new year in this new place at our new local, only as long as Sam promises not to wander off and leave me alone.

It's a relief to walk into the pub this time and feel adequately inconspicuous. The pub is full of people, and the noise and heat from the cheer slaps me in the face, and the warmth of people talking and drinking and laughing and spilling steams up my glasses. It looks like most of the village is here, and I'm determined to enjoy being here, too. Every few minutes someone pushes by on their way to the bathroom and Graeme grabs them for a quick introduction. 'If you need a tree surgeon, Mark lives just round the corner,' and 'If you have any plumbing emergencies, Greg lives up the road, past the church.' Apparently Joan can make us curtains and, should we ever decide to get married, that guy over there drives a horse and trap and can be hired by the hour. Everyone here is a person as well as a utility. And nearly everyone knew we'd arrived well before tonight.

'Oh, you're the new couple who moved in up the hill.'

'Yep, that's us. He's Sam and I'm Claire.'

Everyone's friendly, most are more than a little drunk and I'm running out of things to say. I have no hireable skills to offer, and I'm starting to think that I don't have what it takes to be a useful addition to the community. No one needs a small-space food-grower with no clue about herbaceous borders, and no interest in using weedkiller or digging up the soil, to help them maintain their country garden. Everyone who wants one already has a vegetable patch. I can't help but feel embarrassed that I've turned up in this village without a real job or a skill that I can share with the people I'm being introduced to. This seems to be the way people operate around here – you're a character and you are a service. But the feeling of uselessness is all in my head, so I try to cast it aside and nudge my way into other people's conversations.

As one of the bar staff tries to squeeze by to collect glasses, Graeme gets his attention and leans in to tell him something.

'These two just moved in up the road,' he says, gesturing to Sam and me, 'and after us and you, they're the fourth and fifth person in the village who didn't vote Tory!' They all chuckle – Sam, too – and give each other knowing, comic winks as I manoeuvre my way back to where Rachel is standing. We spend the last half an hour of the year chatting about chicken-keeping, vegetable-growing and how many mutual friends we probably have who live on boats in Springfield Marina. We belly-laugh together over the village newsletter's lament against the 'Goose Bully' who'd been caught on CCTV driving their car too close to the village flock as they were trying to cross the road. It's not how I'd wanted to spend tonight, but it's not quite what I expected it to be, either. There are people who live here that I can imagine being friends with.

As midnight approaches, everyone pours outside to watch the fireworks display, clinking glasses half-full of cava and wishing each other the best for the year ahead. We don't stay for much longer and are soon walking quietly home through the village, the two of us with Rachel and Graeme and their scruffy dog, Winnie. We all follow one beam of torchlight cutting through the dark first hours of 2020, only pausing to stifle our sniggers as Graeme, fulfilling an annual tradition, climbs into the front garden of the cottage his grandmother once lived in, to steal a sprig or two of rosemary for his New Year's Day roast. I lean over and snap off a few leaves, too, not because we need it for our dinner – we have a bush in the garden already – but because I want to walk with that woody smell of savoury evergreen and commit to memory the sound of our muffled laughter echoing into the cold haze of the first night of the year.

Although I'd done no research into it, I was sure that London would offer more of what I'd found in New York and, as it turns out, the east of the city – where I'd moved back to – was a pretty good place to start. For a number of weeks I explored corners of Hackney I'd not visited before, hopping from one green place to another. Seeking out community gardens filled with spring bulbs flowering, and exploring city farms with pigs, geese, sheep and chickens. Polytunnels, farm animals and herb beds hidden between blocks of flats or towered over by office buildings. I walked around in circles trying to find these places; it's no surprise that I hadn't come across them when I last lived in this city and, back then, I hadn't known there was anything to look for. You have to want to step away from the busy roads, off the tarmac and concrete, to find your way to these little islands of green, where the smell of blossom or manure replaces the exhaust fumes for a while. And it was the hunt that made it all the more magic. Yet the places I found weren't quite the right fit for me. I was looking for a certain something. Somewhere like Brooklyn Grange, where the plants were grown for more than simply their beauty or the joy of the process. I needed to find somewhere that existed to fill plates and bellies, and my search took me to Springfield Park in Clapton on a bright Tuesday in late spring.

The Growing Communities' market garden was brimming with life that day – all shades of green, growing in abundance, spilling over the sides of vegetable beds and onto the woodchip paths. On the left, a polytunnel planted with beans, cucumbers and tomatoes wearing the budding suggestions of flowers and the promise of fruit. On the right, a series of beds with leaves of all shapes and textures and – as I was soon to discover – flavours. Lettuces, sorrel, parsley and chard, chervil, purslane and three-cornered leek. To walk from one end to the other took me past a row of sage, gnarled old branches covered in dusky, soft new growth that offered up its warm fragrance as I brushed by its leaves. Past the shed and wooden bench there was a heavy iron gate that guarded the jewel in the crown – the old Victorian glasshouses. Only one was intact enough to still be in use, so that's where seeds were sown and seedlings were raised. The other greenhouses that lay behind it had fallen into a divine state of disrepair. Large areas had been reclaimed by brambles, nettles and ailanthus that had snuck in, under and through the gaps in the smashed panes of glass. The kind of plants that know how to survive a little too well for most people's liking and will grow eagerly, whether or not they're invited. The entire left side was overtaken by a sea of thorniness and tenacity, growing into every inch of bare ground until it came to meet the paving-stone path, where it had come to a halt. On the other side there was a pond, complete with a little shoal of gold-fish and small wooden arched bridge. The water was flanked by heavy-leaved upright palms and other temperate and tropical plants. A miniature botanical garden abandoned some time ago, but left intact enough to be beautiful. By the water's edge an unlikely citrus tree also thrived, its uppermost leaves reaching the apex of the glass roof and, judging by its size, it had been growing there for many years. Over that season I watched its fruit steadily swell, pale yellow and pock-marked, the shape of a lemon, but the size of a grapefruit. Another volunteer recognised this unexpected citrus. 'It's an etrog,' she told us. It is used in the holy rituals of the Jewish community when they celebrate Sukkot every autumn, to thank God for the bounty offered up by the earth. Pith-heavy and precious, it was growing a stone's throw away from a synagogue.

As I had in New York, I volunteered whenever I could, and would organise my life so that every Tuesday I could take two buses to Stamford Hill and up to the growing site. It was around the same time that I was starting to hear more conversations and more grumbling – on the radio, in the papers and on the TV – about the European Union. It wasn't an issue that I knew much about, but there was something about the debate that felt unsettling. I heard familiar complaints about people 'coming over here', taking jobs and houses and healthcare from those who were less than happy to share their island. Same old story. Every newspaper, every news bulletin, every political panel discussion was talking about the European Union in a way that would make my throat tighten. Although I didn't run into too many of these opinions in person, I felt like I couldn't escape them. While some made an argument for national sovereignty, others argued for a vision spoken through their thinly-veiled racism and xenophobia. A shift was gathering momentum and its familiarity was making me uneasy.

Tuesdays became the lighthouse in my week – it was the

day I would steer myself towards. I was working evenings, and sometimes nights, for a production company in California, to keep my bills paid and my daylight hours free so that I could devote them, as much as possible, to plants. I was straddling the night and day, one foot in my old life working on documentaries, and the other in the hopeful endeavour of working outside. In my oldest clothes and carrying a packed lunch and a flask of tea, I'd arrive heavy with all the energy and anticipation of the past week, ready to discharge it, turning compost, sieving leaf mould, weeding and weeding some more, and then learning how to harvest different salad leaves.

It was a welcoming place where the necessary labour felt gentle. A space for anyone willing to muddy their hands and tick something off the to-do list. The head grower, Sophie, was hard-working and gentle too. Generous with her kindness and knowledge, explaining how to be helpful without interrupting her nimble-footed manoeuvring from salad bed to greenhouse, to polytunnel, to compost heap, making sure all who were working under her gaze had what they needed in order to be useful. The site was tucked away into the corner of a public park, down a quiet path flanked with conifers and rhododendrons, but the gate stayed propped open with a brick so that those passing by would know they were welcome to come and look around. No matter how much we tried, the teenage boys from the synagogue next door preferred to hang out by the entrance and smoke, peering in but staying resolutely on the tarmac path. It was a place that welcomed everyone, even those who didn't want to come in.

No one was bemoaning immigration in the market garden. Not in this place, a short walk away from the road where my favourite falafel and rugelach could be found. A short walk from this unremarkable stretch of shops that I'd heard described as one of the most religiously intense parts of London, possibly of Britain, maybe even of Europe. Not in this place, in a city filled with people and languages and cuisines living side-by-side, not always harmoniously but with an unceremonious acknowledgement that our neighbours had as much right as anyone else to be here. Even though the red, white and black of the tabloids – regularly adorned with the red, white and blue of the Union Jack, overlaid with furious words that declared who was 'us' and who was 'them' in capital letters – would be stacked onto newsagent shelves and gone by the afternoon rush hour, it didn't feel like it was happening here. And it didn't feel like it was happening at all while I was standing under the curve of the polytunnel, as the curling tendrils growing from the bean stalks climbed into an arch overhead, their heart-shaped leaves hanging down and obscuring the stalactite clusters of slender French beans in dark purple. This garden was a place of peace. It was somewhere that the voices of certain politicians could not be heard over the song of the blackbirds, or the firm but kind sound of a volunteer shooing a squirrel away from a freshly planted bed. It felt safe from the sound of poison dripping into our collective well.

That summer I tasted sorrel for the first time. Innocuous-looking pointed leaves that wield a sour sharpness that made my tastebuds and my face contort. And I tried my first Japanese wineberries. Glistening red jewels with fuzzy hats, and they too were startlingly tart. I learned how to pick rhubarb by sliding a thumb towards the base of the stem, gripping firmly and shucking it out of the crown without hesitating; and then, at home, Sam taught me how to stew it gently with sugar and cinnamon, so that my opinion of it could move on from the grim memory of stodgy school puddings. I was offered one of a rare few ripe figs that had swelled and sweetened under the greenhouse glass, and realised that maybe the sun shone here more than I had previously thought. And that summer I happily worked myself filthy, and felt protected and more at ease than I'd ever felt in England before.

I'd been looking for a place that felt like Brooklyn Grange and I'd found it here, where there was joy and laughter and soil and sweat, and what we did meant that people could eat produce that was grown not far from their home. It felt radical. The days that I spent away from the soil I'd read whatever tatty, second-hand grow-your-own guides I could find, trying to piece together the life story of purple sprouting broccoli or greenhouse cucumbers and dreaming of a life spent picking vegetables. It was a time of hopeful imaginings and delicious possibility – such is the domain of the volunteer who has no responsibility for whether the site is productive enough to be considered viable and worthwhile. I was learning how to snap the chard at the stalk just so, unhurried by obligation, and was daydreaming of spending every day like that, without realising that making a living this way would ask much more of me.

Nonetheless, I deployed a fierceness of imagination to conjure up a vision of a life that was meaningful and sustaining, doing work that wider society views as lowly, and it worked. I resolved to return to this place and to train to grow organically the following season.

Come the coldest months, once the overwintering plants had been covered in fleece and tucked in against the cold weather, the growing site closed to volunteers. As the weather grew less friendly and the daylight steadily withdrew, I went back to spending my days walking around Victoria Park and along the canal, and handed my evenings over to working on Pacific Standard Time. By the time spring came around, I'd moved from volunteer to trainee grower, and Tuesdays were reinstated as the high point of my week.

Yet no matter how much I tried to avoid it, the debate about whether to leave or stay in the European Union was getting louder and uglier and, as I saw it, less and less coherent. There was talk of money and legislation, of borders and immigration, of control and power. The echoes of this brand of nationalism and so-called patriotism could be heard ringing out from the other side of the Atlantic, as America considered the possibility that Donald Trump could become their next president. There was a newly invigorated, angry othering taking place, and I was growing less able to hear any of the arguments for 'sovereignty' that didn't appear to orbit around getting rid of people who didn't belong, and stopping any more people from migrating to Britain. The loudest voices were the most bigoted ones and it was causing my old scar tissue to ache.

I've never really been able to separate my understanding of myself from anyone else who finds themselves unwanted by society. I've watched as different races, cultures and ethnicities have shifted along the spectrum of societal disdain. How the dynamics change and yet the machinations remain the same. I heard people talking about the need to preserve British identity, a precious way of life, but I didn't know what they meant. I only knew that they weren't describing an imagined future that included me. Every comment I heard about 'getting our country back', every time someone declared that 'this country is full' and that it was time to 'take back control', it was clear who they were talking about dispensing with, even when the reasoning was absurdly flimsy. I've known for some time that my passport won't protect me while the colour of my skin betrays me.

I had many reassuring discussions with friends and acquaintances who saw the rhetoric and were bothered and worried by it, too. We would tell each other that it couldn't – wouldn't – happen, not here, not in 2016. But these conversations were of little comfort because even they served to remind me that someone like me, perpetually viewed as from elsewhere, would never be free of wondering when their belonging would be up for debate next. We stayed up all night waiting for the Brexit referendum results, but fell asleep before they were confirmed. The clock radio woke us up at 6 a.m. with David Dimbleby declaring, 'The British people have spoken and the answer is, we're out.' My heart sank. I thought it wouldn't happen and it had.

I turned up to the growing site the following Tuesday, body hot from the gently uphill cycle, skin cool against the crisp morning air, and I turned up every Tuesday from then until autumn came. I pushed hardened-off young lettuces – 'Cerbiatta', 'Paris Island', 'Roxy', 'Tarengo' – out of their modules and pressed their new roots into holes dug into freshly mulched beds, each one a trowel's length from the others. While we worked, Sophie would explain why we avoided digging the earth, how the soil prefers to be left undisturbed and that it is so much more than a holding place – more than an inert substance for plants and trees to burrow into. Before that summer I'd never before thought about the purpose of soil. I thought it was made up of the fallen detritus of life. A substance to be walked on, paved over or built upon. Sophie taught me that the soil is an alive thing, constituted of many living things that coexist within it, and through it, while co-creating it. She taught me that soil is precious and our work is to nourish and protect it. As organic, agroecological, nature-centric, sustainable or non-chemical growers – whichever term applies to your practice – our job is to grow the soil such that the plants, to a great extent, are able to grow themselves. This means little more than offering it sustenance and leaving it be, letting the creatures and fungi and bacteria take care of the rest. The soil welcomes nourishment and has a sacred and messy system for assimilating it and so, unless the circumstances are extraordinarily bad, we'd ideally find no need to dig it over.

I trusted the soil that had been nurtured there. There were years of love and dedication in that earth, so many days and hours of acceptance and kindness. Yet at the same time I was coming to feel unsettled by the prospect of devoting myself to the earth in this country, to committing myself to its thriving while feeling that here, on this island, my thriving might not be possible. I wanted to believe it possible to nurture the land of England without surrendering to (or perpetually bracing against) this particular flavour of jingoism. But when connection to land is so tied up with a sense of identity, what does it mean to cultivate the soil of a country that I've never felt truly welcome in?

I crouch down with my back to the radiator, waiting for the heat to spread through my clothes and find my skin. It's comforting here. The washing machine chugs and sloshes rhythmically nearby, and I am listening. The space around my heart feels cavernous, emptied out with an unspecific feeling of worry. The sound of the washing machine, though, is steady and certain. When I lived in New York, doing laundry meant dragging a bag of dirty clothes and bedding down the stairs from my apartment, out onto the street, to the end of the block and into the laundromat. It was a chore but one I quietly enjoyed. I'd sit and listen to all the machines revolving and splashing and, in the warm, dense scent of sugary detergent, I'd feel soothed.

I look through the curtain of condensation that covers the back door. A thick mist settled in the night and remains, hanging heavily over the back field, creeping up and into the garden.

The pine tree is near-invisible, a mere sketch, and all around it are clouds of white. I can't recall what lies beyond that old tree. I can't seem to remember anything of the landscape that is now shrouded from sight. I don't know this place. If I were to peel myself away from this radiator, leave behind the rhythm of the spin cycle, push open the door and walk to the bottom of the garden, into the soupy mist, would I be able to find my way back?

I sit for some time and watch the drips running down the glass, pooling on the door frame. I can almost make out the outline of the empty chicken coop and the sway of the willow. A lurking pigeon sits hidden in its branches and coos. Most else is skeletal, leafless and bare. Colourless, grey on white. Sam pushes a cup of tea across the floor towards me and places a hand over my heart until my shallow breaths slow down to match his. He's found me here before, pressed against a radiator, listening to the rumble of a washing machine in search of security. He's been up and down to London a lot lately, at least twice a week since we moved, and I find it harder to settle when he's not around. Each time he leaves, he gently suggests that maybe I could go outside or take my meditation cushion or yoga mat up to the attic room for a while. All things that have helped before. I say I will, but after he leaves I end up on the sofa, getting so worried about the state of our national politics or the planning application for the back field that I try to disappear into back-to-back episodes of some forgettable TV show. I should be figuring out how I'm going to make ends meet in our new life, but I can't quite bring myself to.

Since we got here we've had people visiting for as much time as we've been alone. His parents, then my parents, siblings and friends at the weekend, then his parents again. We don't refuse anyone and put on a performance of over-generous meals, chilly walks at low tide and sitting by the fire as the sun sets over Battle Woods. I want to appear more settled than I feel. I put on a show so that those who visit believe we made the right choice and, in doing so, I try to convince myself too. And when they leave, I strip the beds and put the washing on and listen to the machine going round and round.

I stay, warming my back, long enough to watch as the mist starts to disperse, backing away gradually down the hill. Where there was nothing moments ago, there is a line of trees and soon there will be another and another until the treeline meets the horizon. I'm paying attention this time, sketching their bronchial outlines into my memory so that, if they disappear again, maybe I won't feel quite so unmoored. As I stare out of the window at the dull, low sky, my phone lights up with an invite to lunch from the only people we know who live nearby. I've been spending my days mostly indoors and hunkered down lately, so I fight my reluctance to go outside, pulling on thermal leggings to help me survive the excursion. Having good friends a twenty-minute drive away is something I'm very grateful for. Even more so because they're the kind of people who offer to cook lunch over an open fire on a brisk January day.

By the time we're heading up their long driveway, the low winter sun is cutting through the heavy clouds and the fire is getting going. In the passing moments of cool fierce light, we eat halloumi and portobello mushrooms smeared with pesto and charred over smouldering chunks of oak, pressed between warm bread rolls, from plates balanced on our knees. With full tummies and cold toes, they lead us across their field, then through a hedgerow before we skid, one after another, down a bank to where trees have been growing undisturbed for many years. They show us where a stream marks the boundary between what is their land and what is not, and where a tree has fallen and dark coal-like fungi – King Alfred's cakes – have begun to emerge. We help each other step over tree roots that have breached the surface, and call out warnings of brambles and ground ivy that threaten to trip us over as we go. They show us where, in spring's dappled light, a wild orchid with pink-purple flowers will emerge from a rosette of thick spotted leaves; and where the ground gives way enough for the water to pool waist-deep and offers the possibility of splashing to cool off when summer comes around. This is what I believed it would look like to find a sense of home in a place. To come to know the rhythms and expressions of the earth and the wild things with whom you share your corner of the world. It's what I imagined and hoped I'd learn to do when I planned our move out of the city. To come to know the undulations of the land that roll out from my doorstep and map them onto my heart. To forge a sense of intimacy and kinship with the natural world that unfolds from where I live and out into the woods.

I've always grown on land that belonged to someone else. I've always grown with the ever-present rumble of fear that the space would be removed from my stewardship, taken back or sold, or that my time there would simply run out. Of course I think that growing food in a city is an amazing thing. The co-opting of one of the most coveted means of wealth accumulation, and using edible plants and flowers to grow it into the site of a quiet revolution. Engaging in the act of growing food – an act that has been so devalued and pushed out of the spaces where wealth and privilege congregate – in this way is a delicious and exquisite insurgency. Yet I've never grown on my own terms, and it is something I came to yearn for. Just a scrap of somewhere that I could care for, and that might care for me in return.

None of the places where I was able to grow seemed to have room for my sustained devotion. I would give my love to a parcel of land and then, soon enough, have to give up on it. That was the agreement I entered into when I grew in London, with no garden of my own. When I grew in a disused plant nursery in Tottenham, I agreed to do so constrained by someone else's ideas and plans. When I grew in Stoke Newington on a piece of land that belonged to the Church of England, I did so at the mercy of the possibility that the land might be sold off to property developers at any moment. I kept putting plants in the ground while hoping that those who allowed me to wouldn't change their mind about the value of my work or the presence of the plants. And I came to crave the space to make decisions of my own. A garden where no one else's opinion held sway. And the only way that was possible was to sell our flat, leave London and find somewhere else to live. So when we decided to move, I was looking for a garden of my own.

I wasn't seeking ownership so much as consistency and commitment. I wanted to dedicate myself to a piece of earth. I wanted to nurture the soil and be around long enough to watch it flourish from that care. It's a strange thing to me, this idea of ownership when it comes to land, and the plants and trees that grow in it. Ownership says nothing of the reciprocity that is intrinsic to the task of growing. It fails to describe the relationship that I was looking for. I want to steward and be in accordance with the land and yet there's no document or transaction that would make that possible as well as certain. It is ownership or nothing, under capitalism, and as much as I dislike that, I saw no other route to find my way to some land, to a garden, with which I could form a deep relationship.

I can see, in my mind's eye, a time when this land, my garden, was touched by no one. I can imagine the time when the land was owned by no one, too. After the Norman Conquest in 1066, William the Conqueror declared that all land in England belonged to the Crown. Over the centuries that followed, the laws that determined land ownership evolved such that the land that was used by peasants to grow food and graze livestock was steadily taken out of common use and parcelled out to the wealthy and powerful. King William placed twenty-one areas of England under Forest Law, which was designed to protect the animals – and their habitat – so that the aristocracy could then hunt. The peasants who relied on the land were prevented from cutting timber, fencing their crops and hunting for themselves, on punishment of anything from fines, to mutilation and death. Over the centuries that followed, more and more land that was grazed and worked by commoners was enclosed by aristocrats and gentry. The steady disenfranchisement of those who once worked the land, but did not own it, underscores the land inequality that persists to this day, such that 30 per cent of England remains in the hands of landed gentry. In fact, the main source of prosperity for Britain's wealthiest aristocrats, the Duke of Westminster and the Grosvenor family, is land and property and their portfolio can be traced back to the Norman Conquest. As for the rest of England, 17 per cent is unaccounted for, 5 per cent belongs to all ordinary home-owners combined and the remaining 48 per cent belongs to companies, those with new money, conservation charities, the public sector, the Church and the Crown.

And yet I bristle at how I participate in this system of seeking ownership, of reaching towards the land and grasping at the deeds. I participate in the legacy of wanting land of my own because I don't know how else to secure a relationship with a piece of earth. It saddens me that ownership is the only way in which I feel secure enough to truly dedicate myself to a piece of land. It feels wrong that it was only by virtue of my financial privilege (created for me by my parents' labour and sacrifice) that I am able to lay claim to a place, and that there are many others who aren't able to do the same, no matter how passionately they want to steward the earth.

Ownership is an insufficient relationship to land. It requires nothing of the owner but to have access to money. It doesn't ask whether you will care for the soil or feed the birds, whether you'll learn the inclinations of what grows there. It doesn't insist that you leave it more vibrant and robust and resilient than you found it, or see it as both your home and home to the other beings who live there, too. When all that is asked of you is to have enough money to transfer on moving day, and to sign the paperwork and pay the lawyers, what relationship to the land can be expected of a landowner?

On the drive back, I look through the bare hedgerows and see the houses that are obscured by leaves for most of the year. Grand buildings with thatched roofs, leaded windows, vast gardens and enormous barns, some painted jet-black. One Tudor house, painted white with black beams, has the year 1509 painted on the outside. Homes that were built hundreds of years ago house families that have lived here for generations. There's a lot of history here and lots of wealth, too. The properties are far bigger than I realised. By the time we get home, the sun is setting and the sky has turned an unexpected shade of warm pink. Our ordinary 1940s semi-detached house – which felt too big when we arrived – seems more modest and reasonable now.

I venture into the garden to peer at the evergreen shrubs and pull up a few weeds. I find what I think is a type of currant, and probably a grapevine. I examine the unwieldy tree that must have been the first to lose its leaves as it was quite naked by the time we moved in. The neighbour's garden persists in trying to climb over the fence. Their thorny olive offers flowers at this ordinarily barren time of year and exudes the scent of honey sweetness. Despite the warm light, the air is still bitterly cold, and I crouch instead of kneel to save my knees from becoming sodden with the moisture held in the clay of the soil. While I'm trying to pull out the creeping buttercup in the lawn, I notice something unexpected: against the grass, dusky green clusters of leaves that are more upright and less inclined to bend in the wind. Not flat like grass, but round like a chive or similar, probably a plant from the same family. I pick a blade and smell the faint but pungent scent of onion. I place the leaf between my teeth and crush it, and feel that familiar sting of allium hitting my tongue. It is crow garlic. The first edible offering to emerge from this piece of land where I now live.

CHAPTER 5

The days have merged into a continuum of rising and falling light. I wake most mornings to the sound of birds, not sure whether it's Tuesday or Wednesday or the weekend. I lie in the half-darkness trying to tune into the call of one species, hoping to commit one song to memory. I'll try to match it to an online recording later so that tomorrow, when I wake at dawn again, I can picture the birds that perch beside the window and call out to each other in the half-light.

I've been reverting to old habits. Watching TV shows about cooking. When I was a depressed teenager, I spent an entire summer watching food programmes, back-to-back, for hours every day. I didn't go outside or meet up with friends, but instead found comfort and company watching other people prepare and cook food. I'd watch the more instructional programmes, learning how to dice an onion and season a pasta sauce, but I preferred watching the chefs who travelled and cooked their way around the world. Walking around markets, they'd squeeze fruit for ripeness and inhale deeply the aroma of fresh ingredients, immersing themselves in a place or a culture – their own or another's – and then cook up something delicious, often rich with story and tradition. I take comfort in food. Not only the eating of it, but also the ritual and dedication needed for dishes that are languished over, imbued with love and embedded in family and the making of home.

The episodes that I liked the most were those that saw a chef finding their way, somehow, into a home where one of the oldest members of the family would show them how to make something remarkable, which took all day, cooked en masse and intended for sharing. There would be an old nonna making pasta from scratch, folding eggs into fine flour and pushing the heel of a softly wrinkled fist into the dough, kneading it until smooth. Or a kind-eyed nainai folding dumplings by hand, every little parcel wrapped neatly and uniformly, lain so that the next snuggles up to the last. It was always about more than just sustenance, though. There was a generosity and a knowing in each one of those nimble movements. Each unfussy flourish transformed a collection of ingredients into something nourishing, carrying with it a whole ancestry of skill and experience – generational wisdom passed down with every flour-covered, sauce-dripping, pot-stirring, oven-roasted minute in the kitchen. They still lived in a time before the act of cooking adopted speed as an organising principle, when you would think nothing of taking hours, even all day, to cook one large dish or many small ones. The process was as much the point as the end result; the hours spent stirring and seasoning as essential as the moments spent eating.

I've taken some soup out of the freezer to defrost. I told myself I'd try to get back into sourdough today, but half the morning is done and I'm back on the sofa and watching a Sicilian pastry chef shape marzipan into the shape of fruit. The chef's inspiration is his island and the ingredients it offers up. His reverence for the dark mulberries he makes into deep-purple gelato is enchanting. It's no wonder that when we speak of our origins, that which made us, we speak of our roots. It is a recognition that who we are is a thing that is deeply connected to and intertwined with the land – and thus with the food – that raised us. Even if that land is not now, and has never been, where we live. To know what grows where you grew, that it emerged from the same soil that created you and your family and your heritage, places that food at the centre of your identity.

Watching people like this chef, and the finesse and devotion of his cooking, is how I came to see how one's ancestry can be embedded through the tastes and techniques that are passed down from one generation to the next. By the side of a fire, or over a simmering three-quarters-full pot, or with spoon poised over a steaming plate, you can come to know who you are. Eating the food of your people is a journey inwards, to the bottom of your belly, to the place that tells you that you belong somewhere. And it is the rituals of the kitchen that can offer you a pathway to homecoming, no matter where in the world you find yourself.

While there's plenty that I learned in the kitchen of my childhood, that long summer of watching food programmes showed me what I was really missing. I didn't have a childhood under the feet of my grandmother, learning the very precise skill of making dal pouri or following my grandfather to the outside kitchen to watch him fry the fish that he'd caught over an open fire. I have gentle memories of the dark red of my mother's mother's floor, as I sat on the porch picking the tiny stones out of the rice before she cooked it in a metal pot; and a warm remembering of how my father's father cut down a stem of sugarcane with a serpe and stripped it, before chopping it for me to chew on, sweet nectar filling my mouth; and that time he cut a potato into thin chips and fried them for me, serving them with a sunny-side-up egg, when I'd had the audacity to turn up my nose at whatever was being served for lunch. But I will never know who I might have been if I'd grown up with them in my life for more than just those moments. If we'd spoken the same language, laughed at the same jokes and been able to tell each other the story of our lives.

There's so much that I'll forever be desperate to learn that is now beyond my reach. I'll never know who my grandparents really were; and even when they were alive and clear of mind enough for me to have asked them, I couldn't speak our language. I suppose that's why I find comfort in the food that raised me. While I may have rejected it many times, felt ashamed and begged for chicken nuggets instead, it remained steady and present, reminding me of the power of knowing that I was part of my family, a culture, our history. It is consistently comforting, delicious and welcoming. I could do a better job of learning to cook the dishes I've come to love and appreciate, but I'm quite certain my dad doesn't really want to show me. He prefers to be the one who's doing the cooking, showing us that the love he conveyed in the many times he cooked for his family as a boy persists in how he expresses his love for us now. Generous portions, hot from the pan, chilli and pickles on the side.

We make marmalade every year in the late winter, around our birthdays. A year after Sam and I first met, we decided to try making marmalade together. He'd grown up in a house that made a batch every year, and I wanted to make the annual ritual one of our own. It was a heated, fragrant, sickening experience of spillage, frustrated yelling and last-minute panicked corrections. Following a vague recipe was our first mistake, and it ended in us using some haphazard maths and tipping all the sugar we could find into a bubbling cauldron-like pot, then anxiously watching it burble dangerously close to the rim. The hot smell of sugar and oranges filled the two rooms of our little flat and caused a frustrated, idiotic row. All this to say that our relationship survived this experience, and our cobbled-together first attempt turned out to be the nicest marmalade I've ever tasted.

The arrival of the oranges for marmalade is perfectly timed. When the shimmer of Christmas has dulled into the background and January's skies are perpetually grey, these bright juicy orbs begin to appear at the greengrocers. With some not-so-gentle persuasion and the help of copious amounts of sugar, they bring an unseasonal burst of sunshine to the dirge of midwinter. Discernible by their pockmarked skin and the way they give under the thumb like an under-inflated tyre, Seville oranges are unlike other citrus fruit. Their bitterness makes them unpalatable to eat fresh (trust me on this one – we made that mistake once and never will again), but ideal for this process of chopping, soaking, cooking, stirring in sugar and reducing until the concoction hits that perfect consistency, and then jarring for the many future moments that you find yourself bereft of sun.

I've come to love this elongated and ludicrously involved two-day process and, this year, I saved it for an especially miserable weekend when I thought we'd need the uplift. There's only a handful of weeks when you can get Seville oranges and we've managed to find enough to do our usual odd recipe. Score, peel, slice, repeat. I lean into the repetition. Seville oranges, blood oranges and lemons. The bright, juicy smell fills the kitchen. I rhythmically drag the sharp hook of the paring knife through the rind into thin slices, held steady by my gradually wrinkling fingertips, the spongy pith pushing back against the blade. The act holds the full attention of my senses, but leaves just enough room for us to chat while I make sure Sam's slicing the rind as thinly as I am. The flesh and the pith and the pips that remain we squeeze until they relinquish, turning their insides out, flesh bursting and juice running between fingers and down forearms towards our rolled-up sleeves. The smell is the headiest at this point. Bitter and sharp and sweet and fresh, a stark contrast with the gloominess of the grey rain falling outside and the wind that's still blowing ferociously. We've never made marmalade on a sunny day. Since we don't have a bowl or pan big enough to fit all of the ingredients into one, I have to do more weighing, measuring and maths. Divide the rind between two bowls, add half the citrus juice and half the gungy mess of pith and flesh tied in muslin, then add water. I cover both bowls and leave them to soak overnight.

We've always made it in two batches, one after another, in a cast-iron casserole dish that I pilfered from my mum. Every year Sam suggests that a deep preserving pan might be worth the investment, so that we can do it all at once. Even though we have the space to store one now, I resist because it's the fussiness that I love about the process, and how much time it requires me to set aside, to ensure I don't rush and I get it right. The attention that it needs from me, the quantities I halve in my head and then going through it all, twice. That's what I enjoy about this process the most and is why I keep coming back to it year after year.

Twenty-four hours of soaking later, it's time to cook the fruit, over a steady heat and into a fierce simmer. The kitchen fills with orange-flavoured mist, I breathe in the warm scent of the coalescence of three types of citrus at the same time. I stir and watch and stir as the rind turns translucent, and I know it's ready when the sharp tip of a knife can be pushed through a piece of orange rind without resistance. Muslin bag full of pulp and pips removed, and in comes the sugar. It's a colossal, tooth-aching amount to look at, piled high before pouring it into the steaming, waiting pot. More than seems reasonable – certainly more than could be considered healthy – yet it is what is called for. No point making something this delectable and skimping on what makes it spectacular.

The content of the pot changes from a bright orange to a deep coffee-brown and the air around it turns sugary. I stir to keep it from sticking to the pan, and diligently skim the foam that rises to the surface while the mixture reduces down. Thicker and thicker, gloopier and gloopier. Sam wouldn't bother with the skimming, but I prefer it when our marmalade is clear instead of cloudy, so I wouldn't risk giving in to laziness this close to the finish line. After an hour or so of the same ritual of stirring and skimming, and watching the hot-sugar orange bubbles roll and crash, we test the set using a frosty plate out of the freezer. We're only looking for a gentle, subtle wrinkle when pushed, because I prefer marmalade with a little more give, wiggly and smooth rather than sturdy and stiff.

We follow our own recipe and now, after four years of dabbling, I'm certain that our specific mix of sugars is just right. The taste is one part traditional, one part whatever we are as a couple. Bitter orange, warm sweetness and a little caramel. The majority of the sugar is white and comes from sugar beets, grown by British farmers, probably in Norfolk near Sam's grandfather's house, or Lincolnshire where his mum is from, or somewhere in the Midlands near where he was born. The last cupful, the sweetness that brings the darkness and the extra flavour that makes our marmalade a little different, well, that's the dark muscovado. Deep chocolate-brown, smelling richly of molasses and grown on the island of Mauritius.

The first of February is the anniversary of the abolition of slavery in Mauritius, but I didn't know this until a few years ago. I want the date to mean something to me, but I wasn't raised to know this day. None of the Mauritians I know talk about the history of the island. My family – blood and chosen – never did. Especially not enslavement or the indentureship that followed it. I remember the first time I realised it was part of our island's history. On a visit there, when I was in my early teens, there was a song being played all over the island. I would watch, mesmerised as, with a sudden intensity, my dad and his brothers and sisters would throw their heads back, eyes closed, and sing these words into the air: 'Disan exklavaz monte desann dan mo lekor.'

I asked him what the words meant, because I wanted to know what made them sing that way, and he translated, 'The blood of slavery flows through my body.' I'd always thought that sega was fun and frivolous and sometimes silly, but that was the first time I'd heard it gesturing towards our history. And those words punctured the illusion that I'd held until then, of the island as a honeymoon paradise.

Sega was the music of the enslaved and of the fugitives who escaped. It was the music of resistance and memories, and of the possibility of joy and love amidst suffering. It was the carrier of stories and the sound of survival, played next to fires lit by the seashore and sung into the darkness of the night. I think of that song whenever my dad picks up the ravann and plays. And I can't listen to that song any more without weeping. I asked my dad to tell me more, and he told me the one story that all Mauritians know about the enslaved who created their nation. It is the story of the maroons – those who escaped their chains and ran up the steep and rugged mountainside of Le Morne Brabant, where they hid in the dense jungle and near-inaccessible caves before forming small settlements at the summit. When slavery was abolished, the uniformed police climbed up the mountain to tell them of their freedom but, on seeing their former captors advancing, the maroons panicked, desperate not to be recaptured and enslaved once more. Rather than lose their freedom again, they climbed to the very top of the cliff, turned west to face their homeland and threw themselves to their deaths.

That's the only story they knew about slavery in Mauritius, so it was all that I was told. When they had nothing else to tell me, I didn't think to ask them why not. As an adult, I've tried to seek out our history, and so often I have fallen short. The story of enslavement is mostly focused on the Atlantic and rarely includes what happened on these islands in the Indian Ocean. A few days ago I found a hefty 750-page book about slavery in a charity shop in Eastbourne, and Mauritius was not referenced at all. I've only found two history books and a few research papers written in English, so now I know scores more than my parents and uncles and aunties do, and far more than my illiterate grandparents were ever told. The British Empire's telling of history – its selective narrative – was embedded into the governance that structured public life and the curriculum that was taught to countless children, my parents included, who were subjects of the British Empire until their teenage years. And my parents are not old, and this was not long ago. It is from this hushed place where our histories have been obscured that a shame emerges, I think, and it keeps talk of enslavement and colonialism out of the mouths of many Mauritians. The very notion of being connected to enslavement is not something a Mauritian wants to concede. Creoles – those perceived to be the most direct descendants of the enslaved – remain at the bottom of their social structure. Better to be anything than that. C'est le malaise Créole.

This is what it is to have your story written for you. To have your story written by the oppressors who would have you believe that the shame of those who exploited you is a shame that is yours to bear. This shame is their offering and they expect us to carry it. They want us to carry it because they refuse to. And we Mauritians have been convinced that it is more shameful to acknowledge the truth of our ancestry than it is to ignore it and disassociate from it, to participate in our own erasure.

History is story-telling and myth-making. Events took place and then were conjured into a narrative that was classed as history. To believe that history, as it currently stands, is an immutable and sacred truth assumes that those who documented it were objective cataloguers, and asks that we accept these so-called truths and preserve them as best we can. But like history, truths are created, documented by spectators who believed themselves unimpeded by trivialities such as opinion or bias or prejudice. Stories told and retold, then moulded by those with most power so they reflected what they believed to be virtuous and self-evident. Western science and medicine, art and literature, psychology and psychiatry, religion and spirituality were created by the same subset of people who constructed language and concepts and values that were presented as objective, too. It's a fine system as long as hierarchies remain intact and power goes unchallenged, so that histories can continue to be retold without context.

Seeking out the stories that exist beyond those that we are fed is as necessary as it is, for some, uncomfortable. It asks that we expand our minds to consider that history is not a singular narrative that we are obliged to accept. It asks that we make space for the fact that multiple truths can exist at once. That what is true for me and what is true for you can be black and blue and still, at the end of the day, both can be true. But one history, one truth ought not usurp another. It is not honest and it is not just. The consequences of privileging one story over another is evident in my family and me, and my kin. It is evident in how we have been held away from knowing our own story, and how we can't find our way to our ancestors' names. We who were raised on a diet of European exceptionalism were fed histories that left out the inconvenient and the gruesome. We learned histories that spoke generously of the victors, while choosing to ignore their abuses. We were taught about injustices that took place at the hands of others, and not the injustices that we carry in our bones. They took our history and tried to convince us it doesn't exist or, if it did, it was inconsequential and we are better off not knowing it at all.

They wrote over my story, and they may have written over yours too, so that you would adopt their version as your own and never wonder about what of your history might have been lost.

The erasure was intentional. It keeps us, the erased, from knowing the true extent of the injustices meted out on our people and those like us. It keeps us from demanding truth and restitution. It keeps us silent and compliant, and heedlessly aligning ourselves with the power structures that haven't stopped exploiting people all over the world. The erasure keeps us from knowing what came before we were stolen. What knowledge and wisdom, innovation and understanding, love stories and war stories, languages and beliefs have been obliterated in the process of erasing us? And the question that looms largest in the space where my heart aches is: had we been left to live our lives without interference, who might we have been? The legacy of colonised peoples holds so much more than just tales of suffering. I refuse to believe that's all that there is; I know there was much before. I know that there was resistance and wisdom and that there was survival. I know this to be true because I wouldn't be here, were it not.

It is this ancestry that I wish I could find. It is what I wish I was taught, or could find in books handed down to me, instead of lost between the cracks of a colonial education system and disrupted legacies. The teachings of my elders slipped away through acculturations and migrations, turning to dust when I abandoned our language to assimilate. Before they were enslaved and colonised, they would have been agriculturalists, growing on the land of their mothers and fathers to feed their people. They would have passed down their skills and their wisdom to their family and their community. A knowledge made of practice, ritual, faith and instinct. A knowledge that confers heritage and identity.

I try to grow plants in this way today, holding the sense of my ancestors near and daring to follow whatever instinct, whatever inheritance I can sense. Paying deep attention to the movement of the weather. Watching diligently how the plants change from day to day. Moving my rhythms to match their needs, providing what is necessary for them to flourish. Treating the providers of life – the soil and water – with respect and never taking more than is needed. Returning all that I can to the earth in gratitude for all that it offers up.

*

Escapee. Fugitive. Maroon. Marronage.

The history of slavery on the island is as much the stories of the enslaved as it is the stories of those who dared to seek freedom. They escaped, leaving behind the plantations and their chains. They planned their escape, sometimes alone and sometimes with others, to run from those who called themselves maître or master. Darting between the trees, they disappeared into the darkness and trusted their lives to the wilderness. They climbed up treacherous mountainsides and descended into ravines, slipping away into the cavernous shadows. They would stop for a time by the banks of the rivers that ran with fresh water to drink deeply. They'd seek shelter from the searing midday heat under the shade cast by the forest canopy, laying their weary heads down for a while on the ferns that covered the ground. They bathed in the pools beneath the crystal-clear waterfalls that cascaded down and through the rugged peaks. They would listen out for the sound of birdsong to return and take it as a sign that they could pause for a while to gather themselves, and to talk to one another as though ease would one day be possible. From time to time they even allowed their minds to drift away from the immediacy of the present, to allow themselves to ache for their past or dare to imagine a future of true liberation.

They slaughtered gone-native cows, caught fat crabs from the sea and the eels that swam in the river. They gathered wild raspberries, coconuts, honey and taro leaves to feed themselves, and grew maize and tobacco in hidden gardens of their own making. They dreamed of the future as they gathered seeds, sowing some straight away and wrapping the rest in small scraps of fabric, keeping them safe for the time being. They collected medicinal plants to prepare remedies to care for each other, snapping aloe leaves to soothe their hot skin. They practised the divination and herbalism taught to them by their elders, noting where the abortifacient plants grew, should the women be recaptured; and where the trees with poisonous bark could be found, should they want to seek revenge. They recruited their plant allies into their acts of resistance. They reclaimed the practices and kinship with the land that had been used to exploit them.

They told the time by watching the sun as it moved through the sky, and the moon changing shape as months passed by. They endured the cyclones that lashed through the island without solid shelter, as heavy rain and great winds uprooted and defoliated the trees and caused the land to slip into the sea. They hunkered down against the devastating stormy weather and waited for the clear blue skies and perfect rainbows to return.

They kept watch, with one eye on the lookout for the chasse des maroons who were hunting them down, and the other looking towards the sea, in the direction of home. They spoke of who they were, of their family, of the communities that they were part of before they were stolen. They spoke of their values and the beliefs they held and hold, and of the hierarchies and codes and stratifications in their own lands. They told the stories and riddles they carried with them that reminded them of home; they called each other by their real names. They honoured their ancestors and feared that they would die far from their homelands and that their bones would not be laid to rest alongside their forefathers. They spoke to spirits in nature, and cast lots in the hope they might come to know what the future would hold.

They kept moving from place to place, desperately and violently grasping at survival, planning raids on the plantations they had escaped from, to steal all the cassava, corn and chickens they could carry. Their presence loomed large and struck terror into the anxious hearts of the colonists, who feared that a lawless band of them would appear after nightfall to attack them and 'their' property. They taught each other how to fight and sometimes they fought each other, and often they fought for their lives. It was not an existence free of brutality. They resisted and were wounded and many died, all so that they would never be claimed as another's property again.

They chose leaders who were once skilled warriors and, as maroons, became warriors again. Sans Soucis was from Mozambique and lived as a maroon for thirteen years. Pedre Coutoupa – from Mozambique, too – led a gang of twelve maroons with the support of his lieutenants: Vincent, who was Malagasy, and François, who was a Creole. They referred to Bellaca as the Chief of Banditti, as he held possession of the mountain of Le Morne Brabant, which offered safe refuge to countless fugitives. They fought for their freedom and that of their followers, and we know their names now because they were executed for doing so.

It was called petit marronage, a lesser crime, when those who escaped did so for only a short time before returning or being captured. Those who absconded indefinitely would be accused of grand marronage and, if proved guilty, would be punished by imprisonment, bodily mutilation, flogging and execution. But death, for some, was preferable to being someone's property.

There were some maroons who, so desperate to return to leur pays, would commandeer a boat or carve a pirogue from a tree trunk and set sail north-west. Steering by the stars and clutching their gris-gris tightly, voyaging in the hope of surviving the 500-mile crossing to reach their motherland. For those who were born on the island – the Creoles, who were further away from a sense of a homeland elsewhere, with each passing generation – marronage was how they resisted. A declaration, even if it was a temporary one, that they could exert some control over their own lives.

*

Sam signed us up to join a beach clean-up and although Storm Ciara has only just moved on and there is promise of another storm coming, we head down to try to be useful, despite the wind picking up along the way. We walk towards the section of beach where the group was supposed to be meeting and spot one person, three breakwaters over, who appears to be wearing gloves and clutching a flapping bin bag. We walk into the wind, barely able to open our eyes, and by the time we reach where they appeared to be, they've gone. There's nothing left to do but run away from the worsening weather. The wind whips against our backs as we turn on our heels, shoving us along as we head back the way we came. The clouds darken and the sea swirls into a shade of dirty green as the waves crash angrily against the shore. We pick up whatever litter we can fit in our pockets – bottle top, a chocolate-bar wrapper, anonymous chunks and slivers of plastic – as we scurry along the shore, praying we get back to the house before the rain starts to hammer down.

It takes a few days for the worst of the storm to move on. There's flooding all over the country and, while the rain has stopped, the wind still insists on blowing. I've lain awake for most of the night, listening to it wailing through the gaps around the windows and doors. When the morning arrives I have a toothache and the pain narrows the focus of my mind. I've been clenching my jaw in my sleep again. I don't have a dentist here yet. I haven't even registered with the doctor's surgery in the village. There are many mundane to-dos that I've been avoiding – things that will make my presence here more concrete.

Sam opens the curtains and leaves me to stare out at the bare oak tree in our neighbours' front garden for a while. Starlings pause in its branches and dart, black and iridescent, onto the wisteria, then up into guttering above the bedroom window in search of gaps to nest in. When I look out of the window over the front garden, I can see pointed tips in surprising greens, pushing aside decaying leaves, breaching the sodden earth. The top part of the lawn is mostly moss, because of the dank shade cast by the tangle of our neighbours' many trees, yet it is peppered with the crinkled rosettes of primrose leaves. The first signs of the promise of spring.

As is the annual habit of the seasonally attuned and climate-concerned of us gardeners, I'm sure I'll soon be fretting over how it's all happening too early, and will try to dampen the spirit of those who are eager for winter to be over. Every season, every month, every day has its purpose. I try not to wish time away. Still, the early months of the year are a slog, and some days are more of a slog than others. I take myself to the back door and stand looking out at the back garden. Not much has changed since I was last here, apart from all the branches and piles of leaves that the two storms have strewn about.

The sky is dull and white and everything appears flattened by it. The sun lies behind such a dense layer of cloud that it's hard to sense the time of day from looking up at the sky. Sam nudges me to step out into the garden. He's right. A little movement, a little air, might help lift my mood a bit, so I pull my musky old dungarees over my leggings and put on an extra pair of socks. These old clothes smell of the days I spent kneeling on London soil.

There's no urgent need to weed today, not really. A few things have started to grow, but it could wait. But I feel called to do something reassuring and familiar. A pledge to nurture this land. So I start by clearing up all the twigs and branches scattered around by high winds, then turn my attention to the tufts of grass and bittercress that have pushed their way into the flower bed. Most of what grows in this garden was planted intentionally, but the plants that have found their way here by other means are starting to show themselves now. There's a healthy oak sapling in the middle of one of the ornamental beds, most likely the work of a squirrel or a jay. Little roses and sedums and beech saplings are appearing between the stones and paving slabs, because of a bird or the wind or gravity. I suppose, to most discerning gardeners, these too are weeds, but some have been here longer than I have and may well be worthy of their space, however misplaced they might appear. I'm hopeful that as spring unspools into summer, then into autumn and the winter that follows, I'll appreciate both the choreographed and the improvised. It might be that these plant volunteers will be wonderful, an unprecedented and pleasing surprise. They might come into leaf and into flower in tandem with whatever else has been planted here and, entirely incidentally, become part of a beautiful, accidental tapestry. So for today I'll weed out the plants that I know can be bullies, who may spread and take up more space than is reasonable. I'll let the unexpected, but not unwelcome, be for this coming season and allow them this year to argue their case.

The sky overhead is full of birds, darting from branch to bush, crying out to each other when their beaks aren't full of twigs and grass for building nests. The goldfinches trill at one another, while the long-tailed tits pull at the blooms of lichen on the oak tree's bark. They have been gathering momentum lately, flitting around with each other, chatting and flirting. One song, louder than the others, pulls at my attention and I stop for a moment to listen. Four notes being sung in a loop on repeat. I look up into the willow to see who is singing out from the branches, but in this dull, flat light everything looks monochrome. Before there is time for my eyes to adjust, the bird tires of singing in circles and, with a quick flap of little feathers, flies up and out of sight.

CHAPTER 6

I was willing to do anything to leave documentary production behind and work outside, so in the same season that I was training with Growing Communities, I took a job working as a bee-keeper. Every Wednesday I'd run from office building to museum rooftop to city garden in a bee-keeping suit, checking on the honeybees of London. I was taught the approach to bee-keeping that teaches keepers to puff smoke into the hive to 'calm' the bees, before cracking it open to look inside, and declares that to be a responsible bee-keeper you must inspect regularly and suppress swarms. I was taught that giving fondant to bees to keep them alive through winter, after you've taken too much of their honey, is an acceptable thing to do. And then on Tuesdays I'd go back to the market garden to study the principles of growing food organically – growing crops through observing the systems of the natural world and avoiding practices that disrespect them.

At first I was captivated by both practices: the felt experience of pushing seedling into soil, and the gentle roar of a steady stream of worker bees flying off to forage. I spent that summer cracking open the propolis that honeybees produce to seal their hive and peering at their honeycomb; picking cucumbers and planting out parsley; and trying my best to discover the names of the plants I was meeting. I was coming to know the difference between this lobed leaf and this crumpled one, and was beginning to call each plant by its name. Coming to know the features, the taste, the inclination of the plants that I was cultivating was like learning to speak a new language. Coming to understand how different plants grow, behave and react, then anticipating their needs and meeting them, was like learning to sing their song. The more plants I became acquainted with and could identify, the more enthusiastic I felt as a new grower. And yet every Wednesday, in my protective suit, I was doing the same thing again and again. Smoke the beehive, crack it open, disturb the bees and peer inside. Dismantle the bees' home to check for pests, for honey quantity or for signs that they may swarm.

The more I understood about these two approaches, the more I could see how they curved away from one another. One told me to grow companion plants alongside my crops to encourage a balanced ecosystem to arise, the other bought queen bees from Eastern Europe that arrived by Royal Mail and were bred for docility and productivity. I couldn't reconcile committing myself to nature-centric vegetable-growing while keeping bees in a manner that felt so unnatural. As I came to see that these 'conventional' techniques put human needs before the bees, I went searching for other ways to keep bees that don't operate from the assumption that humans are entitled to dominate and oppress. So after I made it through the autumn harvest unstung, I quit that job and retrained in natural beekeeping. With minimal intervention, no smoke to disrupt their communication and in hives designed for their well-being. All the while, harvesting and learning the names of all the plants that I could.

Before the eighteenth century the manner in which species were named varied greatly, and the labels given to plants, minerals and animals often differed from naturalist to naturalist. With the influx of plants and animals brought to Europe from all over the world came the need for a more simple and standardised system of labelling, so Swedish biologist Carl Linnaeus popularised a system of classification – the binomial nomenclature system – which simplified and standardised the categorisation and labelling of the natural world. He proposed that his system was based on the 'law of priority', which stated that the first 'properly published' name takes precedence over all the names that came before it.

Central to Linnaeus's work was his belief that to come to know God's creations – to name them and classify them – was a divine calling. He believed that it was the reason he'd been put on Earth. And he extended this work of discerning the 'Divine Order' to include the human 'species' by devising four categories, each assigned with distinct physical attributes and character traits:

Europaeus albus: European white – White, sanguine, muscular; Light, wise, inventor.

Americanus rubescens: American reddish – Red, choleric and straight; Unyielding, cheerful, free.

Asiaticus fuscus: Asian tawny – Sallow, melancholic, stiff; Stern, haughty, greedy.

Africanus niger: African black – Black, phlegmatic, lazy; Sly, sluggish, neglectful.

It was systems like this one (and there were others) that formed the basis for the development of scientific racism, which was used to justify all manner of violent atrocities – including indigenous genocide and slavery – to advance the Western colonial project and, later, that underpinned the eugenics movement. And it is Linnaeus's naming system that remains the standard for the naming and categorising of the natural world to this day.

Without doubt, the act of labelling has utility. That an ostensibly universal system exists that enables us to identify a creature, a fungus or a plant is as remarkable as it is practical. As horticulturalists, we use this information to insert our effort into the lives of plants in order to persuade them to grow in the manner we prefer. But the power to create and assign labels, and to erase what existed before, is one of the many ways that systems of domination are established. It enables those with power to construct and impose knowledge systems that further uphold their belief in their own supremacy, and to assert that domination by writing it into science or culture or history or philosophy. It is how power is hoarded, codified and protected, so that all that falls outside it is regarded with scepticism and deemed unscientific, even when it is that very knowledge that has been co-opted. Instinct and tradition, memory and inherited wisdom, are all left to crumble and disappear. The power to create stratifications and hierarchies has been deployed to justify discrimination and oppression, turning human against human, time and time again. The 'one-drop rule' in the US, for instance, is a social principle that originated during the period of enslavement (and went on to be represented in a number of laws in the early twentieth century), which determines that to have one ancestor of African origin was enough to designate an individual as Black. This conceptualisation of race and 'race purity' (as well as the belief in 'racial impurity') codifies race as a hierarchy, and results in a system of colourism that confers privilege on those who appear proximate to whiteness.

I see the legacy of this hierarchical mindset reasserting itself as I thumb through gardening books and write the labels for my seed trays every spring. The same people and their beliefs birthed the systems of classification that sought to categorise plants by their observable physical attributes, and humans using their reductive and inhumane perceptions of race. And I find myself wondering what else they missed. What is lost when a living thing is named and assumed known, and judged, on whether it presents as what it is 'supposed' to be or not? What is lost when it is assessed on the basis of its 'known' characteristics and whether those are considered preferable or not, deemed valuable or worthless, found to be exploitable or dispensable? What is lost when we make these assessments and, from our narrow view, then decide what is to be welcomed and what isn't?

*

Port Louis, 1965

She spent much of her childhood living in the capital city, Port Louis, a harbour surrounded by basaltic mountains that offer some protection from the strong winds of the cyclone season. Her family's small flat sat over a quiet street in Quart Lascar in a busy part of the city. Behind the wrought-iron gate that guarded the steps that led up to their home, there was a patch of soil where her mother grew some flowers and herbs, and a huge Aloe vera plant whose bitter taste they used to wean babies off dummies. The buildings sat side-by-side, so there was little room for trees to grow, but where the neighbours had some space and some sun they grew pomegranates, papayas and moringa, whose leaves they would cook into bouillon; and more mangoes than she could eat without getting bored of them. She loved guavas the most, though, and would knock on her neighbours' doors and ask politely for a cupped handful when their tree bore fruit.

They grew plants in pots, too, in their garden at the bottom of the stairs. There is a Mauritian saying that goes, 'If you grow your plants in pots, then the house is not yours', and this proved itself to be true when conflict broke out between the Creoles and the Lascars, and the landlord said he didn't think they would be safe living in the Muslim Quarter any more, so they fled south of the city to Beau Bassin.

She returned to Port Louis when the unrest had passed, to live with her aunt near Chinatown, and returned to her old school. She was studious and conscientious and that pleased her strict father, a stern and secretive man who rarely laughed but loved his family fiercely. He was reserved and serious, but she suspected he hadn't always been, because he had the names of two women – neither of which belonged to her mother – tattooed on his body. He was a Creole and proudly so and, like most Creoles, he was a Catholic. Her mother was a Malbar, although she wasn't Hindu as most Malbars were. She was Catholic, too, and was brought up to pray to Père Laval as well.

She had the same first names as her best friend from school, even though her friend was Chinese-Mauritian. She'd walk over to her house to borrow the textbooks her parents couldn't afford and do her homework as fast as she could. After she finished studying, she'd head across the road to her other friend's house and listen to LPs of love-songs by French crooners with thick hair and smooth skin. Her other friends were Creoles and they'd call her melange because her skin was fairer than theirs and her hair was wavy, not curly, but it didn't bother her much because they were always kind and because, at the end of the day, they were all Mauritians.

*

We didn't talk about race in our house when we were growing up. Not that it was off-limits or that my parents were trying to pretend that we weren't different from our neighbours and my school friends; it just didn't occur to them to. Ours was not a household of progressive ideas or radical books or disruptive conversations. I didn't grow up with the language to describe race or its dynamics or its politics, let alone my feelings about it. Being Mauritian was part of our every day, but describing our identity using terms of racial categorisation in English was not. Ours was a family of four, trying to be ordinary.

We described ourselves as Black because forms and surveys demanded that we do, and because the only alternative was to choose 'other' and we refused to tick that insulting box. We describe ourselves as Black because we describe ourselves as Creoles. Although, strictly speaking, all Mauritians are Creoles by virtue of being born on the island, Creole there doesn't mean what Creole means elsewhere. In Mauritius it is a term that describes how at least part of your lineage reaches back to those who were brought to the island as enslaved people, and they came from many places. From Mozambique and elsewhere in East Africa, Madagascar, India, Malaysia and even from the coastal regions of West Africa, which is 5,000 nautical miles away or more. Creoles carry the bloodlines of the enslaved while almost certainly carrying the lineage of the enslavers, too, as well as any number of migrations that brought people to our island. So a Creole in Mauritius truly is a Creole. It is an identity that acknowledges that there were, and are, new identities being formed amongst and between those who were born on the island. Nonetheless, to be labelled a Creole is synonymous with Blackness – a connection to a Black ancestry, both real and symbolic.

When my parents got on a plane for the first time and moved to England, along with others from the same small island, they relinquished much of their nuanced ethnic identity and became simply Mauritian. But there was no box on the census that reflected that identity, so they ticked Black, while most of their friends and colleagues ticked South Asian. We call ourselves Black even though my dad's fair skin has had him mistaken for Tunisian or southern Italian, and the texture of his hair – inherited from his mother, not his Tamil father – speaks of kinky-haired ancestry and he gave those curls to me. We call ourselves Black even though my mum's hair is wavy and my auntie calls her Malbar, because we know that her father was a proud Creole, despite knowing nothing about his parents. We call ourselves Black because the largest ethnic group in Mauritius is the Hindus, speakers of Indian dialects as well as Kreol Morisyen, who look to India as their motherland, and we know that India is not a place that we could call home. We were brought up Catholic, speaking only Kreol at home, and not knowing what mother country to call our own. Some might say that we are mixed-race, but our sense of ourselves is not constructed in a way for that to make sense. We know who we are because we know who we are not. We are Black and we are Mauritian.

There have been more times in my life than I would care to count when people have asked me where I'm from. When I was younger I'd occasionally invite these inquisitors to guess, knowing they'd likely be wrong. At other times, people have made uninvited assumptions about what they think I am. Dominican, Ethiopian, Brazilian, Sri Lankan. People see what they want to see in me, whether it's themselves or their family, or their assumptions and wants. I once frustrated an older white man, a Vedic meditation teacher, who refused to accept that I don't describe myself as Indian. He so badly needed his ethnic assumption about me to be correct that instead of accepting my explanation, my complexity, he told me that I was in denial. To him, I didn't fit into what he believed to be Blackness, despite how narrow his understanding clearly was.

If I'd grown up in Mauritius, I'm certain I'd have experienced my identity quite differently. I'd have learned to use other terms – such as Lascar, Tamil, Madras, Hindu, Chinois, Francos – and more specific understandings, because Mauritius is as carved up by ethnicity as anywhere else, and its racial hierarchy echoes the divisions, racism and colourism present in the societies that have been altered or created by colonialism.

'When I was young, the pews that were closest to the altar in church were reserved for the white man,' my dad tells me, 'and even if there were no white people there, you wouldn't dare sit in their seats.' The white Franco-Mauritian elite – descendants of the French colonisers – remain the most socially privileged and economically powerful people on the island, despite making up only 1 per cent or so of the population. Unsurprisingly, I've never encountered a person who belongs to their class on my visits there. I'd always assumed that the white people I saw in Mauritius were just tourists and honeymooners. I only know of their existence from the second-hand stories I've since heard. Despite how the walls around their private lycées, executive offices and gated communities obscure their presence, their association with wealth and power positions them (and thus whiteness) as the aspirational (and mostly unachievable) standard for other (non-white) Mauritians.

But if I'd grown up with these labels, maybe my race would make sense to me in a way that it never has while living in Britain. Maybe I could make more sense of the multitudes that I embody and feel more at ease with who I am. Yet I prefer to believe that I'd have found the groupings and terminology as troubling as I do the classifications that I feel obliged to use here, because, ultimately, all racial terminology insufficiently depicts who we are. These words do not capture the depth of our identities and they fail in their attempts to compartmentalise us along discernible lines. After all, none of these terms describe something that is categorically or intrinsically true, let alone biologically real.

So I've set up camp inside a Black identity as the closest thing to a sense of coherent racial identity that I can find, even though I've always feared my water's too muddy to claim it as my own. But to believe in an essential Blackness – of which some cannot be part – plays into the hands of those who constructed race to categorise and divide us all up, and to keep us from one another. I tick the box that says Black because it is so often asked of me. I describe myself as Black because it is a requirement of those who seek to describe my identity. I use this word because, more often than not, it is empowering, but still it fails to capture the truth of who I am. The insufficiency of these terms comes from how they were created without our input or our consent, to describe us, and not for us to describe ourselves. So I realise now that to deny my complexity, my known unknowns, and to collapse myself into a limited construction is to endorse this system based on lies. These terms imply that there's such a thing as purity, when that's a fallacy of the highest degree. We are all more complex than we are allowed to believe, and contain much more intricacy than we will ever know. We are so much more than we have names and labels for. Nothing about my bloodline is linear, nothing inside me is 'pure'.

The more I learn about the diversity of Mauritius and all those who make up what it means to be Mauritian, the more I realise that Westernised, anglicised conceptions and language around race will always fall painfully short. And I'm certain that this is not unique to our island. With each migration and love and union that vaults over and transcends the boundaries drawn between nations, cultures, ethnicities and races, we are asked to reimagine how we speak of and understand ourselves and each other. How we behold and honour one another, as we must. Being Creole and what that signifies is a gift to me. After many years of trying to find a steadiness within a racial identity, I realise that the one I was offered by my Mauritian heritage is the one that honours the truth of my complexity. It offers me an identity that makes a little more sense, and that could actually operate as the expansive and nomadic understanding of identity that I need.

The sound of something crashing down the chimney startles me awake. I put on my glasses in time to see a cough of brick dust come out of where a fireplace used to be, linger in the morning light and settle on the floorboards by the end of the bed. My first blurry thought goes to the roof. The leak is fixed now, but maybe the wet winter has done more damage than we realised and another piece of the house has fallen down. The bedroom wall looks the same – discoloured paint and crumbling plaster. No more disastrous than it was yesterday.

I get down on my knees, torch in hand, and shine a beam of light through the small gap left by whoever blocked the old fireplace with concrete. Standing there, I can see a pair of spindly legs inside the chimney, beneath some oily black feathers. 'There's a bird in there, and I'm pretty sure it's a jackdaw,' I tell Sam as it lets out an annoyed squawk. I got to know the call of this species of corvid after spending some weeks in the company of a tame one on a farm. She would stand outside my caravan and make that exact noise until I came outside to give her some seeds. In the torchlight I catch a glimpse of one of its eyes, black and ice-blue, and the crest of soft grey feathers on its head. I don't know what to do with this bird. If it could fly out, surely it would have done so already. It stays where it is, surrounded by dust and detritus, quiet now and keeping still. I stick my hand into the gap to see if I can make it wider and more escapable, but the bricks are intact and all I do is make more mess. Sam fetches some of the mealworms from the shed, which the last owners of the house left behind when they rehomed their chickens. We sprinkle a few on the floor and leave a trail of them that leads to the open window, then we leave the bird in peace to figure out its escape. The first hint of spring warmth wafts in and I'm convinced that this bird will go towards it.

In the back garden the whippy willow branches are lime-green with fresh growth, and flurries of goldfinches pull at the new buds as they break. All over the beds there are flower buds on thick stems pushing up and out of floppy rosettes of leaves, where only a few weeks ago there was nearly nothing, so soon there will be narcissi and tulips and muscari. I've never been one for spring bulbs. I find the smell of daffodil pollen a sickly reminder of sitting through the Easter church service. In a shady corner of the front garden there's a more exciting arrival. Wide, flat spring leaves with a finer scent have emerged. Wild garlic, which has made its way into this corner that echoes the woodland, is filling the air with its familiar and delicious smell. I finally have some work – an article to file, and a workshop to plan – but the freshness of the morning is irresistible. Armed with the comfort of a belly full of tea, I pull on my old boots and warm coat and head out for a walk with Sam to explore the country lanes, where the spring wildflowers have begun to appear, and I want to go out and meet them.

We're often told that the purpose of time spent outdoors is to escape our screens and the pressure and stress they rep-resent, so to go out into the woods with my phone in my pocket feels like something of a failure. While it's true that screens can be an obstacle to feeling present and immersed, I find the presence of my phone reassuring. With it by my side, if I dare to stray from the path in search of something intriguing or lose Sam along the way, I can find my way back. While technology has pulled us away from the natural world, and for many it is the abrasion for which nature is the balm, my phone helps me to feel more at ease. There is an app that can decipher a photograph of a leaf or flower or bark and tell me what the plant or tree is. Another that can trace the outline of a fungus and tell me what it is called and where it prefers to dwell. I squat down and take pictures of the flowers on the woodland floor, the trunks of 100-year-old trees, the leaves that creep over the stone walls of cottage gardens. And this is how I've come to know that the thin stalks topped with soft lilac clusters are the cuckooflowers, named after the bird who calls at the same time as they appear. And that the pink-white wood anemones will turn their faces towards the sunlight, then close them against the darkness, and that their presence is a sign that the woods are ancient and undisturbed, their root systems having deepened over many, many years. It allows me to discover the superstition that to pick the star-shaped flowers of the greater stitchwort risks inviting a thunderstorm or an adder's bite. And after all this, if I'm a little disorientated, I can use my phone to make sure I don't trespass onto private land and that I can, safely, go back the way I came.

Perhaps it's not important to learn the names of these wild-flowers or their ways and stories. Perhaps it's enough to walk by, simply marvel at how pretty they are and breathe the wood-lands in. Perhaps it's more sublime to follow my nose, let myself get lost and, without technology, hone a wayfinding instinct that can lead me back to the path. But I can't do it yet. I'm still getting to know this place. Coming to know the plants and trees feels as necessary as walking these lanes and paths, following the tracks and getting to know the boundaries that mark out which fields I'm forbidden from walking through and skirting around them. I am making the land's acquaintance, and my phone is helping me do it. I'm learning the names of these spring wildflowers as I'm learning the names of my new neigh-bours. I'm getting to know their faces, in the hope that I'll still be here when they return next year. And I'm thankful, in this moment, that I've been able to learn the names of these plants today, and that alongside their labels came their stories. I won-der what else there is to discover about them.

As soon as we get home, I pull off my boots and hurry quietly up the stairs to the bedroom, opening the door as gen-tly as I can. The air is cool and the worms are right where we left them. I shine the torch up the chimney once more and see those thin little legs are still there but, in that moment, pos-sibly startled by the light, the jackdaw caws and flaps its way up and out of the chimney. It could have escaped, on its own, the whole time.

If I'd committed to getting stuck into the garden straight away – if I'd been better organised – I might have ordered com-post to arrive at the same time as we did. I might have carved beds into the grass and mulched them shortly after we unpacked. Instead I resolved to watch the garden unfold for a year, giving it space to show itself as I sat by and watched. Some tidying maybe, some pruning for health and vigour, but, ultimately, getting out of the way to let the soil and the plants that grow here express themselves without interference. But now, a little late off the mark, I watch as flushes of new growth appear, and how the landscape becomes greener by the day. I'm allowing myself to imagine what this season could be, and it feels impossible to resist. As the mitochondria in the plant cells sense the lengthening days and ready themselves to reach skywards, I can't help but greet the coming warmth by taking my seed box – an oversized shoebox, now covered in spiders' webs and winter dust – out from its cool hiding place and peering inside.

There's plenty here from the last few years, left over and saved, swapped and gifted. A vigorous kind of climbing bean, saved on an allotment in New Cross; a film canister of collected nasturtium seeds from a good friend; a paper bag containing a parasol-shaped seedhead of dill. Looking over this collection of brown envelopes and small jars, filled with the potential for life awaiting the nudge to germinate, I see that here – in this box – is the garden I'd been imagining, waiting to emerge. This box is filled with the diligent work of generations of gardeners and seed guardians, and their stories will write their next chapter here with me.

Although I've never before had a garden of my own, I've been collecting and safeguarding these seeds in the hope and belief that one day I would. Surely the way that a food grower begins the real task of making a home is to trust the soil with the seeds that they've gathered through the seasons and carried with them to a new place. Many times I've sketched my future garden in my mind's eye, letting myself dream about what I might grow there. I fantasised and planned what plants I would nurture by my side. And this is how I will, as a grower of plants, let this place know that I'm here to take care of it and that, if it will have me, I'd like to call it my home. All the arranging and rearranging and painting and decorating in the world couldn't make me feel settled in the way that growing something to harvest would. So today I dig into those garden dreams again, but this time I have land upon which to make them real.

On a scrap of paper I sketch out my plot. Five rectangles side-by-side. I'll create a bed for beans and peas, with enough room for them to root down, and some sticks or canes for them to climb up. Next to it will be where I'll plant courgettes and my first winter squash. And by their side I'll grow some tomatoes – maybe the ones that I'm hoping are stripy, if the saved seed is still viable. There will be a brassica bed, too, because if I had a favourite family, that would be it. And, of course, a bed for all the others, for the ones that don't quite fit anywhere else – a motley gang of lettuce and beetroot and leeks this year. The bed I'd be growing in, if I were a vegetable.

The back field hasn't been used much for some time, as far as I've heard, but the strip that runs behind the houses on our road belongs to Rachel and Graeme, and they're allowing me to turn it into a vegetable patch. Until now it has been kept as neat as a cricket pitch, by a neighbour down the lane who enjoys the monotony of pushing a mower back and forth. These regular haircuts have kept all that was growing there tidy and somewhat lawn-like, and while I am tempted to simply lay down some cardboard and pile compost on top, I suspect there is more going on below the surface than I can see.

The soil is a clay one, and after months of taking on water and holding it in the spaces between its tiny particles, it is wearing its less desirable qualities. An entire winter of rain and snow, frosts and more rain has fallen and accumulated in the soil where I drive sticks into the ground to mark out the beds, one metre by four, give or take. Cold, heavy and sticky, the soil resists the cut of my spade and pushes back as Sam and I attempt to remove the top layer of grass from the earth. The work is jarring, slow and little fun, but I relish it nonetheless. I find the bright white tentacles of the perennial weed, couch grass, snaking and burrowing through the clay. With its tendency to grow rampantly and somewhat thuggishly, it's a discovery that justifies this one-off disturbance of the soil. I'm breaking up the clods with my gloved hands, lumps of clay grabbing me back while I pull at its vast underground network. I try to extract each long root without it snapping, but more often than not I fail. Every piece I leave behind, I know I'll meet again in the near future, and it will have grown longer if I miss it this time. Spade by spade, we upturn the soil, draw out all the couch-grass roots that we can find and level the earth, ready for a layer of cardboard – to suppress the other weeds we can't see – followed by a thick blanket of compost.

It's a bit of a chore, as are so many of the jobs that prepare a garden for the growing season. I've spent the last six winters and springs in full waterproofs, thermals and wellies, cold on the outside and warm on the inside, moving compost from where it was dumped to where it is needed. It's the annual job that upholds all that comes after it. The point where a cycle renews, where death touches life and makes another season of growth possible. I imagine most people would consider it a filthy and boring job, and I suppose it is – but at the same time even its mundanity has a hopeful rhythm. I've moved many wheelbarrows of compost before, fed the soil and had to leave it behind. The man who delivered the dumpy bags in the front garden said, 'See you in a year,' and I'm really hoping he will.

I set to shovelling. Thudding the wheelbarrow down the steps that lead to the path that runs through the front garden and down the side of the house. A blackbird walks up ahead of me and, when I reach him, he flies off, orange beak wide and shrieking with dismay. At the bottom of the sandstone steps in the back garden I whistle for Sam's attention, and he comes to help me carry it over the lawn and the decking, to drop down into the field where our vegetable patch is coming into being. I tip each barrow-load onto a bed, and soft black compost hits cardboard over grass and clay. I smooth it out with my hands, the heat gently radiating through my gloves. It smells sweet and earthy and reassuring.

The first time I shovelled compost it was a blistering New

York Saturday in July, and a truckload had been dumped in the loading bay of the industrial building on top of which Brooklyn Grange sits. It all had to be moved that weekend, so a troupe of volunteers filled wheelbarrows and crates and buckets and hauled it to the lift and up to the eighth floor. By the end of the day my hands were covered in blisters and wrapped in plasters, my clothes were filthy and my skin was saturated with compost stuck to sweat. The next day my arms ached so badly I couldn't raise them over my head to tie my hair, but I felt truly incredible. I'd never done a day of work quite as satisfying as that in my entire life.

On the fourth or fifth barrow-load, I pause to catch my breath and watch a bee-fly forage from the pale-blond primroses that have opened amongst the uncut grass. The sky is clouding over and soon it begins to rain. Fat, sloshing drops run down my neck and gather on the tip of my nose. 'I'll finish this run,' I tell myself, 'and then I'll scuttle inside for some tea, maybe call it a day,' but as I tip the last load on what will be the legume bed, the rain eases and the sun pushes out from behind the clouds. The spring rain now smattered across the green of fresh growth glistens in the new season's light. The leaves of the arriving spring bulbs, the crocodilian garlic mustard and the yellow flowers of the lesser celandine are all covered in fresh rain and the smell of life is returning. A newly awakened bumblebee buzzes loudly by, as the rain hasn't stopped her from getting on with her day. I have no excuse now that the sun's out, so I carry on with my task. Load upon load, peering through rain-speckled glasses, I make the journey from the dumpy bag of compost to the vegetable patch. I look forward to the work of compost-moving every year. It's a full-body undertaking and a mucky act of love. An offering-up of what is needed and nourishing. It's a feeding – a satiating of the soil's hunger so that, in a little while, it might satiate mine.

CHAPTER 7

We've cancelled our train tickets and it's the right thing to do, I think. It's a just-in-case, as I've been texting my cousin in Milan who's already in lockdown and the news about the inevitable arrival of the virus is sounding more ominous by the day. It would be less than ideal to find ourselves stuck in Cumbria with the bare minimum of things. But Sam is disappointed. He's been wanting to visit his parents as it's been more than a year since we last travelled north, and I can see there's a part of him that aches for the place. He craves the mountainous landscape between Oxenholme train station and the small village where he did most of his growing up. It's affecting there, with a ruggedness that is noble and imposing. I remember seeing it on our first trip up together, nearly five years ago, and feeling embarrassed that I hadn't known such a place of beauty existed in England. I can't recall that visit to the Lakes with my family, because I was only four.

Sam's relationship with where he grew up was somewhat fraught, though. The divide between the North and the South played out in him, as he felt pulled towards London then returned home to endure the jibes and mockery of the locals in the pub that he'd worked in since he was fourteen. For every drunken art-school anecdote, there are many other stories of nights spent fishing on a lake, setting up camp in the snow and getting to know the ghylls and pikes and fells. In another life, Sam might have stayed; become a drystone wall builder and we would never have met. The landscape lives within him, even though he's chosen a life in the South with me. He misses it. And he aches for it in a way that shows me I've never known a feeling like it.

I don't think it's possible to yearn for the suburbs. I don't miss where I grew up at all. Of course it is possible to feel nostalgic about aspects of it. A park, a walk, a spot where happy memories were made. But as a space, the suburbs are unaffecting. Built of parallel lines and replications, of function – necessarily so – but ultimately uninspired and uninspiring. They evoke no strong emotions in me, no deep attachment, no sense of self as part of a landscape. An in-between place that has never pulled at the strings of my heart.

I spend the time that we would have been on a train sowing seeds. A bit of a late start for the first ones of the year, but I've checked the lunar calendar and it's a good enough time. Sowing a seed, in itself, is a simple thing. It takes place every day without human intervention, out in the world wherever there is room for a seed to sprout. Along the side of the motorway, in the exhausted soil near the railway tracks and in small cracks in brick walls. There are plants growing all around.

Seeds find their way and plants grow. They make it seem effortless.

Sowing the seeds of edible plants is a simple thing, but not an easy thing. We ask these seeds to grow into plants as we wish them to, with our future yield in mind. It is, necessarily, a wilful endeavour, but is best not left to chance. We often ask our seeds to grow where they might not otherwise. We offer them what they need to get started when the conditions outside are unfavourable for them to survive alone and, in return, we hope for a harvest. To be in with a chance of succeeding, our actions need to be considered and well-timed, when the light is adequate and the temperature just right. Tomatoes, for example, need an early start here, because our springs are changeable and our summers not as long as they need, so we sow them when the mornings still feel wintry – somewhere warm and bright enough to remind them of their ancestral home in the Andes. The chillies and aubergines are also first to be sown, as they need as long a growing season as possible to bear their fruit. Without adequate light from the moment they appear, these seedlings will strain upwards and stretch themselves weak. I've watched it happen many times and I've wasted many hours fretting over how to save them, and whether to start over with fresh compost and more seed, a little later, in the hope that this time they'll grow stronger. Over the following weeks, with the lengthening days and stronger light, I'll sow the next round of seeds and there will be plenty whose time has come. Beetroot, parsley, rocket and kale, lettuce, sorrel, dill, fennel, kohlrabi and spring onions. Tray upon tray I sow, label neatly and water gently but generously.

Last night we watched the Prime Minister announce that we're going into lockdown. Our work has been shrivelling up for a couple of weeks, so we knew it was coming. When Sam felt unwell, we decided to sleep separately, just in case; and a few days ago I spent hours stuck on hold to the Foreign Office and the embassy in Chile trying to help a friend get back to London in case her flight was cancelled, because there were rumours that border closures were on their way. It's been a disturbing few weeks, so the lockdown has come as no surprise.

We wake up before dawn after a scattered night's sleep and decide, instead of listening to the news and fretting, to take a walk at low tide. To the sound of the dawn chorus, we scrape the thin, close layer of ice off the car windscreen and set off into the dwindling darkness. We pass a car or two, but the roads seem eerily empty, although it's possible they always are this early in the morning. Reflected in the rear-view mirror, the sun nudges at the horizon as we drop down towards the coast. By the time we arrive, the line where the water touches the land is pulled right back, leaving the lunar rocks and petri-fied wood of this in-between space exposed, the sand rippled into shimmering dunes by the retreating surf. Turning east, we walk with the wind blowing into our faces, looking into the sun as it rises, the sand merging into the dawn sky. Warm apricot fading to nigella blue, and the cold so fierce and sharp that my teeth ache and my eyes stream. I pull my scarf more tightly around me, trying to cover where the cold wind has found exposed skin. The sea air is cleansing – a blast of saltiness blows through my hair and clears my tired early-morning mind.

When we came to visit this bit of coastline for the first time, nearly four years ago, I'd booked the cheapest holiday let I could find, and we dragged our overstuffed backpacks and bikes down on the train. We spent four warm early-autumn days cycling up and down from St Leonards to Hastings, and eating soft ice cream and bags of chips on the pebble beach while the sun shone over the Channel. We allowed ourselves to dream about taking the life that we were building together and moving it towards the water.

We came back a year later, and again a couple of months after that, and just kept returning. One day, while walking near the sea at Bexhill, I saw the corner of a page torn out of a magazine with the word 'Mauritius' written across it. I tucked it into my purse and took it as a sign. A year after that, we moved into our house. If it weren't for the challenge of growing vegetables blown about by the sea breeze, we might have chosen to live closer to the shore. Instead I check the movements of the water and time our walks for when the tide is as far out as it will go, and I walk until the salty air clears away my emotional debris. Something in me feels called towards the sea. Mesmerised by its power, but untrusting of the way it flows.

I follow Sam as he explores the rock formations – deep oranges to ochres and dusty reds – undulating into small canyons, pockmarked by shelled creatures and worn smooth by the back-and-forth of the tide's steady abrasion. Clusters of iridescent blue-black mussels peppered with tiny barnacles hold tight to the surface of the rock, next to the clinging limpets and stripy-shelled whelks hiding amongst them. I pick the pristine white shell of a common piddock out of a rock pool and trace my fingertips along its ceramic surface, following its ridges in concentric circles, and then put it, sandy and wet and cold, into my pocket as we turn around and let the wind blow us back the way we came.

*

Trou d'Eau Douce, 1966

He was named after the patron saint of England, but he grew up by the sea with the taste of saltwater on his lips. He grew up in a village called Trou d'Eau Douce on the east coast of the island, where the fresh water meets the ocean, where his mother washed the family's clothes. He would walk down to the shore at low tide with his auntie and they'd dig for clams, which they'd take home to scrub clean and cook for dinner. He loved to go fishing and, after he'd finished his studies, would be allowed to join his father on the boat. It was where he felt happiest, where his older brother got to spend his days, but he was told he was too clever to be allowed to spend too much time fishing.

His father was well known amongst the other fishermen for being able to navigate the coastal strait that ran alongside Trou d'Eau Douce without instruments. He could steer his boat through the narrow opening in the coral reef to where the best catch could be found. He could read the currents and guide a vessel along the route that goes east and then north-east, where the passage is obstructed by rocks so big and jagged that they could destroy a boat's propeller. He could guide a boat out to the deep water and steer it back safely, where many fisherman before him had died trying to return. When heavy clouds would start to gather overhead while he was out at high sea, he would turn towards the land and sail back to shore using the mountain peaks as his guide. All this, his father could do by heart.

Over the school holidays he was allowed to head out to sea by his father's side. He'd wake up in the early morning and they would set sail together. He'd watch as his father wrapped the rope of the épervier around his wrist, then throw a section of the net onto his shoulder and prepare it for casting. With one swift move, the net would fly through the air and land, fully extended, with a plop in the water. Then steadily, hand over hand, they would pull in the rope, dragging a net of flopping grey mullet and cordonnier, and occasionally, jackfish into the boat. With the day's catch on board, his father taught him how to swim by throwing him out of the boat 200 metres or so before reaching the jetty. If he had managed to catch any fish himself, he'd be allowed to keep one to bring home, but he'd sell it to the fishmonger instead for two or three rupees, then buy a bottle of Coke and some chocolate, which he'd gobble down before he got back so that he didn't have to share with his siblings.

He still loves to fish on the rare occasion that he can, but he uses a rod and line to catch mackerel now. And if the water is warm, he still swims, all thrashing limbs and splashing, like he's swimming for his life through the turquoise lagoon, 200 metres away from the jetty.

He was named after the patron saint of England – one of a few names he was given at birth. But some years later, when he'd actually moved to the land of his namesake, he'd take on a nickname that was easier to pronounce. He grew tired of listening to people get his name wrong.

*

The next morning's early-spring sky is cloudless and clear, and the kind of blue worn by the tits who, along with their early-to-rise bird neighbours, call me awake before sunrise. We've made a plan to spend the morning outside, taking down the old shed, but I'm waiting for a friend to call from Japan first. I've got no work and no emails to reply to, so I scroll through social media, hoping to distract myself from the uneasiness that is bubbling up as the reality of lockdown settles in. Alongside the words of worry, there's a rhapsody of gratitude for the grace of a warm spring. Pictures of tulips and wild garlic and magnolia flood my screen. There's a sense that if the days are warm and the sky is clear, seeds will germinate and baby birds will hatch and we'll watch spring progress while we wait this thing out. There are photographs showing how the sediment has settled in the canals of Venice, so now the water is clear enough to see fish swimming by. The world is marvelling at what can happen when humans are compelled to slow down. We're all grasping at anything that looks remotely hopeful.

I smiled at those pictures too, at first, but the captions that run alongside them are worrying. 'Nature is healing' sounds like a good thing, but the implication that human beings are an inherent threat to the natural world (and thus not part of it) gestures towards a menacing ideology that slithers amongst the conversations of some environmentalists and conservationists. A video of dolphins pings into my phone for the third time and I can't help but wince. I don't want to be the miserable one who pours water on a rare glimmer of joy at a trying time. I don't want to be the one to explain to my auntie that humans are part of nature, too, and that to suggest that at least the virus is good for the natural world implies, albeit somewhat obliquely, that the death of many humans is an acceptable consequence as long as the natural world benefits. I don't want to have to explain why this is something that an ecofascist would say.

It's an unlikely collaboration of ideas. Ecofascism. Two words that sound incongruous pushed up against one another. It is a long-standing ideology in which a desire to protect the environment coalesces around a sense of national identity connected to the land. It marries genuine concern about the destruction of the natural world with totalitarian solutions like limiting population growth, curbing immigration and preserving the borders of nation states. It seeks to preserve fallacious notions of purity that start with plants and wildlife, and then extend to encompass human beings. Its ideas move seamlessly from saving the planet into saving the planet for some and not for others. And in the space where the urgent need for action over the climate crisis coalesces with far-right politics, it is undergoing something of a revival.

A notable example of ecofascism is the doctrine of 'Blood and soil' that was championed in Nazi Germany and asserts the belief that belonging to a place can only be conferred by blood descent. To this end, the Third Reich's Minister of Food and Agriculture, Richard Walther Darré, described the Jewish people as 'weeds'. In 2017 'Blood and soil' was chanted by torch-bearing white nationalists as they marched through Charlottesville in protest against the proposed removal of statues that memorialise Virginia's Confederate past. By gesturing towards this particular Nazi ideology, they declared that America belonged to them and those like them, aligning themselves with a legacy of European settlers who choose to ignore the fact that America is a land that was stolen by way of colonialism and genocide of the Native Americans. This vital part of the American story is often conveniently ignored by the nationalists who remain devoted to the settler colonist's mythology that America was *terra nullius* – the land of no-one – when their ancestors arrived. A specious colonial justification for land grabbing which was deployed in parts of Africa and Australia in the nineteenth century. One such person was the environmentalist John Muir (founder of the environmental organisation known as the Sierra Club and 'Father of the National Parks'), who, while not ignoring the fact that Native

Americans had lived in harmony with the land before being forcibly displaced by Europeans, deplored them as unclean and savage. And although his perspective evolved into a more generous view over time, he nonetheless failed to acknowledge that the landscapes he so coveted and wanted to protect had, for thousands of years, been tended by the very people he once denigrated.

This belief in protecting the land for some, but not others, was expressed clearly in the manifesto written by the twenty-eight-year-old Australian shooter who, in March 2019, walked into two mosques in Christchurch, New Zealand, murdered fifty-one people and injured many more – at the same time as hundreds of children were gathering together for the School Strike for Climate. He titled his manifesto 'The Great Replacement', referring to a conspiracy theory of white genocide. This eighty-seven-page document repeatedly describes anyone who is not white in a white-majority country as an 'invader', agonises about the low birth rate of white people in contrast to the supposed high-fertility rates of immigrants, and declares immigration to be 'environmental warfare and ultimately destructive to nature itself'. And he openly identified as an 'ethno-nationalist eco-fascist'. His solution to climate change was to 'kill the invaders, kill the overpopulation and by doing so save the environment'.

This was not so dissimilar to the posters that bore the Extinction Rebellion logo and were put up around Brighton in January 2020 stating, 'Sink the boats. Save the world', referring to the dinghies carrying migrants that irregularly land on the south coast. While Extinction Rebellion said they had nothing to do with this stunt, the posters demonstrate the ease with which environmentalism can be co-opted by those with racist or xenophobic agendas. It is more than merely a position of prejudice to adopt an anti-immigration stance while claiming concern for the natural world as your reasoning. It is a refusal – whether knowingly or not – to acknowledge that the countries that amassed their wealth through oppressive systems like colonialism and enslavement use immigration controls to retain that wealth within their borders, while choosing to ignore the many reasons that led to thousands of people becoming displaced (conflict, poverty, climate change, historical extractivism and underdevelopment) and bearing (at least some of) the responsibility for it.

The Christchurch shooter's beliefs about overpopulation are far from uncommon. Up until 2004 factions of the Sierra Club were using the overpopulation argument to prop up an anti-immigration agenda; while far more recently, in 2018 – the same year that he was rated the most-trusted celebrity in Britain – Sir David Attenborough stated on BBC's *Newsnight* that 'population growth has to come to an end'. In this interview he delivers this statement as though it is enough to say that having fewer people on the planet will save it – and, on the surface, that might appear to be an uncontroversial statement – but where the movement for population control goes, along with it comes racism and xenophobia. No matter how fervently its proponents insist, historical efforts to limit population growth suggest otherwise. In 1968 entomologist Paul Ehrlich's book *The Population Bomb* argued that if the world's population was not brought under control, it would be the cause of millions of people starving to death. The first chapter, entitled 'The Problem', opens the book with a description of the author and his family driving through Delhi at night in a taxi. His depiction is written with a barely contained disgust at all the people he saw eating, washing, sleeping, arguing and begging: 'People defecating and urinating. People clinging to buses. People herding animals. People, people, people, people.'

While the book is ostensibly concerned with preserving the planet for all, the contempt Ehrlich expressed for the Indian people he observed through the taxi window that night went on to be mirrored in the global policy that was instituted a handful of years later, which would be responsible for a cascade of human-rights abuses. In 1968, under Robert McNamara – a proponent of population control – who resigned as US Secretary of Defense to assume the presidency of the World Bank, loans to low-income countries were made conditional on their agreement to inflicting population-control measures on their citizens. In India, during a national emergency in 1975, the Indian government undertook a grotesque campaign of forced sterilisation in order to secure loans from the World Bank. Access to water, electricity, allotments and medical care was made conditional on submitting to sterilisation. Homes were demolished and citizens seized by armed police, before being sent to forced-sterilisation camps. In just one year, eight million Indian men and women were sterilised and, unsurprisingly, it was the poor and underprivileged – especially the lower-caste Dalits – who were targeted the most. And this is far from an isolated story. Population-control measures have perpetrated human-rights abuses against people all over the world – from Australia, the United States and Kosovo to Kenya, South Africa and Haiti, from Sri Lanka, China and Indonesia to Honduras, Peru and Venezuela, and then some. And it was often the case that those who belonged to a minority group within the population were disproportionately targeted.

If the Christchurch shooter is right on one point (and the data supports it), it is true that the populations of many Western nations are not growing as quickly as in other parts of the world. But the lifestyle of one person in America or Australia emits the same amount of carbon dioxide in fewer than three days as someone who lives in Mali or Niger does in a year. The world's richest 10 per cent of people generate more than 50 per cent of the world's fossil-fuel emissions (driven by individual consumption), while the poorest 50 per cent generate only 10 per cent. And the majority of that half of the global population live in the places most vulnerable to the effects of the climate crisis. It is a fact that over-consumption is more responsible for environmental degradation than overpopulation, demonstrated by the industrialised nations, like Japan and Germany, who are amongst the top emitters of carbon per capita despite their low birth rates.

In 2019 geographer Richard Heede of the Climate Accountability Institute calculated that one-third of all manmade carbon emissions are down to the actions of twenty companies. Destructive, extractive industrial practices that release greenhouse gases, pollute the waterways and oceans and deplete the soil are responsible for mass deforestation and cause catastrophic biodiversity loss; they are what is responsible for the decimation of the natural world, not any one (average) person. Focusing on overpopulation and personal responsibility for emissions is a convenient deflection peddled by those who are most responsible for it. In 2004 BP began pushing the idea of the carbon footprint, to transfer the responsibility of lowering carbon emissions onto individual consumers, while a number of fossil-fuel corporations worked with conservative think tanks to fund a communications campaign that was designed to shed doubt on the science that connected their actions to climate change.

The focus on curbing global emissions is a mainstream position, and while it would be wrong to dispute its necessity, I feel compelled to question the disproportionately loud and ahistorical demands coming from wealthy nations, mostly in the West, telling emerging economies such as India to lower their emissions. Currently India is the country with the third-highest emissions in the world (behind China and the United States) and yet, while this is something that I wish weren't so, when viewed through the prism of equity, is it just and reasonable to suggest that a country that was bled dry by Britain's colonisation ought to curtail its own economic development? If we were to calculate the emissions of each country in a way that encompasses their historical carbon debt, wouldn't we have a more accurate and principled spreadsheet of climate-change culpability?

Britain might comfort itself with the figures that show that emissions have fallen here for the last thirty years and – with our politicians who un-ironically portray this country as a leader in addressing climate change – believe it reasonable to pressure other nations to follow our lead. Yet a 2020 report released by the charity WWF found that the true carbon footprint of Britain is double what it purports to be, with the emissions generated by the production and transportation of goods made overseas and imported having been left out of the calculation. It will surprise no-one that multinational corporations – with their billionaire CEOs – seek to meet demand in the most profitable way, and this drives a system of production that pollutes, degrades and destroys the environment, as well as exploiting (disproportionately Black and Brown) people in its ravenous pursuit of wealth. So as those who fuel said demand, is it not essential that we scrutinise how our consumption incentivises polluting industries to keep producing and exporting, while dismantling the problematic expectation – of which I have been guilty – of an endless supply of ever-cheaper goods?

These vast, ugly, urgent and seemingly unconnected issues might seem like an enormous leap away from being amused by internet videos of wild animals striding out of the woods into quiet, locked-down villages. But at the root of it, at the core of the message, is a troubling anti-humanism that is grounded in contempt for 'the other'. This Malthusian inclination, this focus on the sheer volume of human beings – as opposed to the activities of industry, and the destruction that results from the endless pursuit of growth and unbounded consumption – will lead, as it always has, to exploiting those with the least power; and they are already experiencing the most brutal impacts of climate change whilst enduring the dual injustice of having been historically deprived of the resources to withstand it.

None of this is straightforward. None of what it takes to address the urgency of the climate crisis, the loss in biodiversity and the many connected consequences is simple. While some believe that the pragmatic approach is to do whatever it takes, others argue that our endeavours ought not further embed the injustice and inequality that carve the world up into who is, and who isn't, most likely to survive the upshot of global temperatures rising. I don't know which approach is most likely to succeed, but I do know this: ecofascism is not the answer.

The phone rings and snaps me out of the deep internet hole I've burrowed into. I'm grateful to hear an old friend's voice. It's safe and familiar; his tone and laugh are reassuringly steady and we talk about the virus in the abstract, even though he's sitting in a park eating sushi and I'm not supposed to leave the house. He asks me how I am, so I tell him and try to explain what ecofascism is, without losing my temper. I try to explain how the poster I just saw on Twitter that declared, 'Corona is the cure. Humans are the disease', suggesting that humans are a problem that a contagious and sometimes fatal virus could fix, is an idea that fits neatly into ecofascist ideology. We talk about other things – what he'll do if there's a halt put on international flights; what I'm working on; what he's got planned – but the flush of rage won't leave my cheeks. Sam's in the garden, taking a crowbar to the roof of the old shed, and I'm itching to join him.

The cold air and fierce sun against my face are a relief, and so is unfurling myself from the angry hunch I stiffened into over the computer keyboard. I've mentally exhausted myself, whiplashing between the arguments of ecofascists, then those opposing them, and then those who'll jump on any opportunity to accuse lefties or environmentalists of being unrealistic, unreasonable or hypocritical. Sam's taken off the roof intact, so that we can use it to fix the tool store, and we remove the last windowpane together, shooing away the sleeping woodlice and disturbing the hiding spiders to save them from getting squished.

He can see that my morning has left me frustrated and I don't want to talk any more, so walks over and hands me a mallet. There's nothing left but the disintegrating skeleton of a rotten shed, and it needs to be brought down. I swing and hit it once, but my first attempt is pretty useless. The impact jars my wrist and the wall barely moves. I'm tentative and not adept at being destructive, and the rusty nails seem to be stronger than I am. 'Bend your knees and put your body into it,' Sam suggests, taking a step backwards. I swing my arms back further and lean into it a little, throwing my weight behind it, and this time the mallet makes contact solidly and a plank of wood bursts free from the joins with a satisfying thud and spins through the air, before hitting the ground. It feels like a colossal exhale. I keep swinging the mallet back and smashing it into the wood, each crash a cleansing discharge of energy, warmth rushing into my chilled fingertips. I smash and smash and smash, from the planks above my head, and work my way down. Some planks split and crack and need yanking off the hinges by hand, while others fly off and then fall crashing to the ground. This structure has clearly stood here for years and been left to decay. The closer I get to the base, the more rot there is to be found, and the easier the last few planks are to dismantle. Most of this old wood will be fine for the log burner. One day, after it's been left to dry, we'll set fire to it and warm ourselves by its flame.

The next morning, stretching my aching arms, I slip into the conservatory first thing to check on the seedlings as the kettle rumbles to a boil. I can't help but check on their progress when I come down in the morning. The lockdown days have begun to feel slippery and indistinct from one another, and this ritual helps me to anchor the day. I check the labels and search for the first signs of life. Sam laughs and tells me that I'm addicted to looking at them. 'You're binge-watching them,' he says, as he sets a mug of green tea on the floor next to where I kneel on a cushion, dropping my eyeline to soil level to gather notes on their progress.

It takes a great leap of faith to make plans when the future seems uncertain and unsettling, as it does now. Yet it is what gardeners do, season after season. We don't know if this will be another year when the rain does not fall for months on end, when the streams and brooks will run dry and our plants will wilt. We can't know if this year early spring will be warm, but the last frost will be late and the apricot blossoms will be knocked to the ground, and it will be a year like the one that produced only a handful of freckled fruit and the squirrels got to them before I could. We pray to the heavens that the frost and the scant snow were enough to keep the population of slugs manageable, so that our newly set-out lettuce and courgette seedlings won't be eaten to the ground on their first night outside. And while fraught with uncertainty, the endeavour is the point. The harvest is a reward worth striving for, but it is not the only goal – at least for those whose living does not rely on it. The journey is the reason, the quest is the grail, the adventure is why every year, in hope, we sow our seeds again.

We, as a species, have come to hold erroneous beliefs that, if only we have the means, we can shield ourselves from the uncertainty that is intrinsic to life. We build homes to protect us from the weathering of storms, and turn away from the notion that our loves might not last. We take comfort in that which denies the march of our ageing, and lament even the mention of our loved ones' mortality, for fear that to speak of it risks inviting it. When, in truth, there is nothing we can truly do to make certain that, in a week or a month or a year, all will be steady and well. Growers and gardeners know this. We are expert in making plans and acting on them from a place of faith that what comes will have something to teach us. And with reflection and acceptance, that wisdom seeps out into our lives beyond our garden's edges. In this strange moment of lockdown,

I hold these lessons close and hope it won't last too long. I hope that by the time these seeds have grown, I'll be gathering a harvest to eat with my friends and family by my side.

I take deep comfort from this understanding of change. While it ensures we have to accept that all we covet and adore will cease to be, no matter how much we wish otherwise, it also assures us that suffering, too, will transform eventually. Even in the hardest of times, knowing that change will always come means that this present moment of suffering will not feel like our prison for ever. And just like the plants and creatures of the natural world, we ourselves are not fixed entities. We are always in a state of becoming. Like the emerging of a leaf, a shoot or a flower bud, we are in constant flux. We move through what is no longer necessary and, with the dawn of each new day, again, we grow.

CHAPTER 8

The mornings are mild enough now that I'm able to sit at the bottom of the garden as the sun comes up. The beds in the vegetable patch lie in a row like fresh graves, covered with dark, rich earth. I watch as an orange-tip butterfly flits amongst the cherry-blossom petals that swirl on the breeze and scatter themselves gracefully all over the ground. The pea and radish seeds that I pushed under the surface of the earth are yet to germinate, but I like knowing they're there, waiting. There are small plants growing on the windowsills of the house, but they need a couple more weeks of shelter to grow, before I put them outside to brave the cool nights. The robins and goldfinches and great tits call out news of broken eggshells and new birth, and of the yolk-yellow young beaks that demand to be fed. I watch a pair of buzzards over the field, circling, and wonder what they can see from up there. I've been told that there are dark-furred rabbits living amongst the gorse and bracken where the field slopes away towards a stream. The buzzards might be watching them even though they prefer smaller prey, or arguing with crows over carrion. We have to watch for the rabbits, too, so we put up a wire fence around the beds to protect our plants from their unavoidable hunger.

The clouds move to reveal the sun and it offers up an unseasonal warmth, and I turn my face towards it to bathe in its comforting glow. When the arrival of spring is cold and ungenerous, I watch how the weather moves through the day, checking the forecast and trying to predict the future. But when the weather is unexpectedly good, like it is now, I thank the universe for what feels like a gift. I bat away nagging thoughts about how the climate is changing, and how the weather shouldn't be so warm this early in the year. I try to ignore the rumbling feeling that perhaps I should be more worried than I'm allowing myself to be.

Before breakfast I sow more seeds. Larger ones this time. All cucurbits: two kinds of squash, two of courgette and three varieties of cucumber. The squash seeds are pleasingly chubby. I haven't grown them before. Most varieties take up a lot of space and are in the ground for much of the warm growing season, bearing only a few fruit. In the small spaces where I've grown before, I couldn't afford to give them so much precious room. These courgettes, on the other hand, are fairly compact and upright, and once the fruit start coming, I hope to be harvesting most days. And the cucumbers are hard workers and climbers. Smaller, slender seeds that transform into handsome vines and, if all is well, will produce enough fruit to share with my new neighbours.

Last night I cried. I'd picked up a prescription for a woman in the village and delivered it to her doorstep, where she told me about her brother-in-law who caught Covid and died quickly. She told me of her worry about her sister, who is grieving alone in her house in the North of England somewhere, with no one to hug her while she weeps. The evening news told the story of the first four doctors to have died of the virus while treating the patients who probably infected them. They were all Black and Brown and, as I looked into the faces of these NHS staff who remind me of my parents, my aunties and uncles and elders, I imagined how easily it could have happened to one of them, too. I cried for all of them and their families, and for all who are mourning, especially those who are doing so alone and uncomforted. I cried because I have a skill that is at last deemed essential – I know how to grow food – but the memories of those harrowing days and nights that I spent gasping for air after my asthma finally landed me in hospital have scared me into hiding. I know I could never be as brave as those doctors were and, feeling ashamed, I cried for that, too.

After breakfast Sam hangs the bed sheets on a makeshift washing line that he's run from the corner of the chicken coop to a stake he's hammered into the ground. Then we make our way to the woodland that we've been getting to know, towards a spot that promises blankets of bluebells. We weave through the trees covered in lush new green and onto the path that leads to that wide and silvery tree. With spring and all its life, its leaves have appeared. Deeply ridged and brilliant red, its leaves catch the sun and dance a rubied light-show onto the carpet of star-shaped moss that covers the ground below. Sweet purple-faced violas with heart-shaped leaves are grow- ing from the nooks where its great roots rise, and then push back down into the earth. What was entirely bare the last time we were here is now a crown of glorious red. This copper beech has revealed itself in all its fiery majesty, with centuries of expansion and contraction, all held firm in this impressive trunk. Fingertip touched to fingertip, we wrap ourselves around the circumference to measure its girth and guess at its age. Two of my wingspans and two of Sam's. About six-and-a- half metres around makes it near enough 400 years old. Where might I have been if I was born when it germinated? The Dutch were yet to bring the first enslaved Malagasy people to Mauritius, so wherever my ancestors came from, before they were stolen across the sea or sold a delusion to migrate towards, that's where they would still be. Zanzibar, Tanzania, Sri Lanka, Guinea or somewhere else entirely.

A few winters ago my dad gave me some seeds and asked me to grow them for him. His favourite vegetable from back home: the Mauritian cucumber. An eggcup's worth of smooth oval seeds, wrapped in a thin piece of plastic and folded in an enve- lope, addressed to him in handwriting that looks exactly like my mum's. Her sister, my auntie, had sent him the seeds to give to me. It was the first time he'd asked me to grow something for him, and the first acknowledgment that he could see it was more than a passing phase. And it was the first time that I could see a way to honour him through the work I'd found my way to, and to show him that it was more than just manual labour. He pressed the envelope of seeds into my hand and, with them, I had a chance to make him proud.

I tucked the envelope into my pocket and, come spring, packed up the seeds with my work clothes, wellies and one of each of our home-made jams and moved to an organic vege-table farm in Gloucestershire, where I was set to spend the growing season working. It was a bit of a leap. I'd reached a point where I needed to get more farming experience on a larger scale, to develop the skills I needed for the grower jobs I hoped to graduate to in London. I'd been cobbling it together for a while – running workshops in community centres, rescu-ing the donated plants after the Chelsea Flower Show, establishing bee-friendly planters on train platforms and teaching gardening in schools – pivoting from one role to another from day to day, to make ends meet. I was doing any job I could that enabled me to be in close proximity to plants, but doing what I loved more was the hardest to make work – growing food in the city is a challenge. Finding an available parcel of land with a good enough aspect, decent enough soil, access to water and a nearby market that will buy your produce for a decent price is a tough formula to crack. Growing food in the city is a labour of love, an incongruous undertaking and a fairly awful way to make a living. Nonetheless, I was sure about being a food grower by then, and I was willing to do whatever I could to devote myself to it, and that's what had me dreaming about leaving the city to find a way to be growing every day.

I wanted to give rural life a go. What once would have

seemed unthinkable had become a hope and a dream. And so, after a flurry of searching emails and enquiries, a video call with a farmer on a tractor and a bitterly cold trial day in February, squelching carrots out of dense, wet soil, I was offered a trainee position for the summer. I was ready to learn about farming on a larger scale while sowing the seeds my dad gave me, in the hope that they would grow and bear fruit as I worked over the following months.

The spring was late in arriving and so was I. I'd been visiting my family in Mauritius for the first time in almost a decade, and so I had to ask for a little leeway with my start date before I'd even harvested my first leaf. There were four workers on the farm that season, and I was the last one to arrive on a freezing day in April, moving into an empty caravan not designed for cold weather. I turned up still carrying the warmth of my family and the subtropical sunshine, so the chill when I got there felt shocking. In the terrible cold of that spring I'd go to bed fully clothed, placing my heaviest books wrapped in towels and old blankets over the caravan's vents to stop the freezing wind from whistling through in the night. I shared the place with enormous spiders who'd made their winter home there and would scuttle out from behind their gauze-like webbing whenever I turned the electric heater on. I missed Sam, and how much warmer and more comfortable I felt when he was nearby, but I was excited to be there. It was an adventure and I wanted to spend my summer learning and growing and figuring out living in the countryside.

But the first few weeks were tarnished with a quiet,

rumbling panic. The asparagus – the crop that keeps the farm afloat – was late to appear above ground and the worry was palpable and contagious. It set the tone and the pace, which was fearsome in both cases. Each day was a cycle of the same duties on rotation. Harvest, plant, weed, then weed and weed some more. Crate after crate of salad leaves, picked and washed and bagged. Field-sized swathes of mesh, heavy with a week's worth of rain, would have to be dragged off the rows of cauli-flowers that awaited beheading and collecting. Thousands of seedlings of onions and beetroot, and four varieties of summer lettuce, were pushed into trenches furrowed into the ground by a tractor pulling tines. In the polytunnels the soil was ploughed and compost churned into it with a rotavator, then dragged over with a chain-harrow, before the young French beans and tomato plants were firmed in. Most of my hours were spent wrestling the deep taproots of docks out of the ground, and teasing endless tangles of couch grass roots from the earth, cursing them when they snapped. I spent hours pulling waist-high thistles out by hand, their prickles pushing through my gloves and drawing blood. With every day that the asparagus failed to surface, frustration gathered around the farm, and for the time we would have spent harvesting it, we just kept weeding. The tales of the heft of last season's yield were starting to seem hyperbolic.

I couldn't seem to get anything right. Even when I thought I was doing all right, for a trainee, correcting my mistakes and learning on the hoof, it was made clear that I wasn't. I wasn't fast enough or deft enough, and my newness and inexperience were not excuse enough. I should be keeping up; I should be able to think ahead, but no matter how I tried, I was always a step or two behind. The other farm workers had been there longer and all knew what to do. I badly wanted to ask them questions, but didn't dare to be seen wasting time. Instead I tried to follow their lead, to mimic their actions and disappear into the team, but there was a hostility that had descended over that piece of land and it was causing me to come undone. I started to doubt myself and whether I was cut out for this work. I started to forget what I knew about plants and soil, about water and time. I kept forgetting what day it was, as each one blurred wearily into the next. My memory loosened its grip, such that even the scant pieces of information I was able to glean refused to remain in my head for future use. My consciousness was trying to detach itself from my body, unwilling to stay present while I wilfully wrecked my physical and emotional self. But I had upended too much of my life in London to take this leap and then to give up on it so quickly. I wasn't ready to accept that this job that I wanted was more than I could bear, or that I wasn't strong enough to withstand how punishing, brutal and relentless this work could really be. And so I resolved to keep going and to work as hard as I could to keep up. I willed my body to do more than it had ever managed before.

April turned to May and, quite suddenly, the warmth that had been missing appeared. Every day that week was a few degrees warmer than the last, and by the seventh day – the hottest bank holiday on record – the first spears nudged their way into the light. From nothing to forty kilos to 200 kilos of asparagus appeared in a matter of days. The speed of the harvest, the weight of the heaving baskets, the bruising of my hands and the darts of pain between my shoulder blades. The velocity was staggering. Every day, before the morning fog had time to disperse, we'd be out bending and cutting, and bending and cutting through two acres of asparagus and then hauling the baskets in for sorting, bundling and packing. Asparagus grows at such a speed that it has to be harvested every day and, on really hot, sunny days, sometimes twice. While we were out there, panting and sweating, the farm seemed to be able to breathe again, relieved to be back on track.

Time off during asparagus season was rare and precious, and I spent my days off grasping at sleep. The exhaustion was bewildering. My right hand was so haunted by the strain of twisting my wrist to sever the stems, and haul the baskets, that it would contort into the shape of a claw in the night. The buckling muscles in my fingers were so agonising they would wake me, no matter how deep and fatigued my sleep, and I'd have to massage my gnarled hand until the cramping subsided enough for me to rest, before another day of the same. My boots fell apart. New gloves would only last a few days before holes large enough for my fingers to poke through would appear. The parched earth would dry out my hands, skin splitting at the knuckles, and my nails would chip and break against the stones in the soil. My mind remained dull and foggy but there was less to figure out, now that I was duelling with asparagus spears every day.

On the afternoons when I was sent to weed in the fields at the edge of the land, I'd be grateful for the mental space and the simplicity of the task. I knew what was expected of me there. But the fields were huge, and the weed burden was heavy. Years of leaving it a bit too late, letting flowers turn to seed and, once uprooted, left in the path to desiccate in the midday sun, had caused certain areas to become swamped with unwanted plants. It wasn't how I'd have done it; leaving weeds to set seed merely kicks the can down the road. But I was in the habit of following the lead of the other workers by this point, so I did what was asked, despite knowing I was making the problem worse – or, at best, shunting it along to the following season for another farm worker to tackle. Hoeing or digging or pulling with their hands, they would tear up and down each row, leaving behind the first fronds of parsnip or carrot, and I'd race along behind, perpetually trying to keep up.

The work was necessarily monotonous – somewhat more so than I'd expected. If I could, I'd listen to music and lean into the beat to maintain my momentum. And I picked up an unexpected pastime that turned the endless weeding into a treasure hunt. The farm was situated on top of a Neolithic site, the remnants of which were hidden in the earth, so as I worked I searched for pieces of flint that bore the markings of life from 10,000 years ago, of stone struck against stone. The possibility of finding something remarkable held my attention on those long, tedious days. Every evening I'd return to my caravan with pockets filled with shards of flint and wash each one carefully and examine them by lamplight, hoping to find a little ancient history. Most days I'd find a distinct marking and would occasionally come across a piece worth keeping hold of. After weeks of digging and looking, I unearthed a small hand-axe that fitted satisfyingly between my thumb and forefinger. Perfect – I'd guess – for skinning a small animal.

That summer's heat was astonishing. Searing and relentless. The pond by the caravans that was home to a pair of moorhens and their fluffy babies in the spring was drained empty, to water the plants, and then baked dry in the unceasing sun. The frenzy of the asparagus harvest was displaced by the challenge of keeping the plants from wilting to death. As an ordinary summer became a heatwave, the soil turned to arid, scorched dust. The heat was dizzying, so that working in the open fields was nauseating and I could barely catch my breath. For every task completed there were ten left undone, and every sweaty day ended with trying to forget about what had been neglected. No grower's work is ever done, and the to-do lists there were painfully far from complete.

There were good times, though, outside the working days. I was closer to the natural world than I'd ever been, and there was so much of that to adore. After a day's work, I'd lie with the other farm workers on the grass to recover, holding peeping baby chicks and ducklings or watching red kites flying overhead, swooping low enough to show off their forked tails and patterning, before diving in pursuit of prey. Some mornings I'd wake to the sight of a deer grazing under the eucalyptus trees by the caravan window, and I'd make breakfast as quietly as I could, so that we could eat our first meal of the day together. A mole burrowed under a piece of weed-proof membrane, and the farmer's daughter caught it before their border terrier could. Before setting it free, we stroked its velvet-soft fur while it tried to burrow through her hands with its powerful claws. A tame jackdaw was brought from Wales to live on the farm and would spend the evening sitting on our shoulders. She would pull at my glasses and squawk in my ear until someone gave her a sprinkle of mealworms. I even became part of the farm workers' Monday-night ritual of cooking dinner for each other and watching TV. But the next day would come, and the quiet competitiveness would inch back in and prise me steadily away from them. I was still the weakest of the pack.

I was too nervous to go exploring alone. I was deeply afraid of getting lost and having no one to call for help. On the weekends when Sam couldn't visit, I'd withdraw into my caravan, only leaving occasionally to drive to the nearest town and walk down the high street to be near ordinary people doing ordinary things. When Sam could travel down to stay for a few days, we'd walk to the edge of the farm and into the quiet woods and through fields of sheep grazing peacefully. I wanted to venture further, but an uneasiness had settled into my body. While the farm didn't feel safe, somehow the countryside beyond it felt even more unnerving. I was conspicuous there and knew I was being looked at. The heads swivelling at the pub, the glances that lingered a moment longer than was polite. I put up with as many as I could, before conceding defeat. It was just easier on my heart to wait out my time in the caravan, wondering why my dad's cucumber seeds wouldn't germinate.

My time on the farm was short and ugly. It marked me more than you'd imagine three months could. I kept hoping it would get better, but every day was more of the same. More unkindness and antipathy. More rejection than I could bear. I'd been so determined to return to London with a summer's worth of proper farming experience that I hadn't noticed that what was happening was intentional; and by the time I handed in my resignation, they were waiting and hoping for me to quit. I counted down the days until I was able to leave. I counted in hours, in minutes, in cycles of Beyoncé's last album on repeat. I rushed my goodbyes to those who had been nice to me and drove away too fast, hoping they wouldn't notice me leaving with hot tears pouring down my face. I left bloated with shame and relief.

Those months were a stark lesson in the reality of farming. I was familiar with how laborious the physical work could be, but was unprepared for the cumulative erosion of doing it every day. I knew that whether people were willing to pay for organic produce, and at what price, was the fine line between a viable business and a failure; and it was on that fine line that the mental and physical health of those who work the land hangs. I knew there was a tipping point somewhere between how much land needed to be cultivated and how many plants would need to be grown, between the amount of work it took to do that and the cost of labour to do so. And that midpoint, more often than not, does not lean in a farmer's favour. It must have been heartbreaking to do so much and for it to always be so hard. To be forever on the back foot, no matter how good you are at the job that you once loved. If it was my farm, I would have been angry too, and I would have been terribly, terribly sad. I watched the arduous but tranquil image of rural life that I'd hoped to find disintegrating into what I'd suspected it would be in reality: unwelcoming, hard-hearted and with no space for me.

*

You ask me... why I will not work in that field, I will tell you: In that field my father worked as a slave, and was lashed as a slave, and do you think that I would work upon a spot that I cannot think of without pain.

Reverend Patrick Beaton, *Creoles and Coolies; or, Five Years in Mauritius*, 1859

After slavery was finally abolished in Mauritius – it was the last of the British colonies to do so – the formerly enslaved were forced into a period of apprenticeship that enabled their former masters to continue to take advantage of their labour while they 'learned how to be free'. Once this period had expired and they were allowed to leave, many of those who'd toiled in the sugarcane fields left the plantations behind. What they were seeking was land of their own, and to finally live a life on their own terms. Those who could do so, obtained land, while others made agreements with landowners to trade a portion of the produce they grew as rent, and the rest squatted on small pieces of rugged land and sowed seeds into it as though it were theirs. Petit morcellement. The subdivision of land into small plots. They would take a marginal plot of uncultivated land and coax it into fertility and fruitfulness. Growing vegetables like manioc, sweet potatoes, bred malbar and maize, and raising livestock and poultry, they produced enough for themselves and their families to eat and hoped to have some left to sell at the bazaar. Those close enough to the coast would also fish using the techniques and skills taught to them by their elders, passed from one generation to the next, and carrying with them echoes of past lives and homelands. These former apprentices – those who'd been enslaved – were obsessed with the pursuit of land for themselves. Owning land meant the ability to own their own labour and work at their own pace, to determine their livelihoods and run their lives independently. Land, to them, was freedom.

Despite the importation of thousands of indentured labourers from India to replace the formerly enslaved, a labour shortage loomed and, in response, the British Colonial Government attempted to set up industrial and agricultural institutions and introduce instruction in horticulture and gardening into primary schools. This was met with disgust and suspicion by the now-free people who were forging livelihoods on their own terms, at last, and were able to send their children to school. They interpreted the government's actions as an attempt to push them and their children back into the plantations, furthering the dominance of the white man as 'master' while denying the workers the chance to strive for the upward mobility that they witnessed being afforded to the bourgeoisie of the island. If the parents of these primary-school-age children heard about a teacher showing their class how to cultivate the soil within the school walls, they would keep their children at home and, if enough of them did so, the school would be closed down.

> It is a notorious fact, and one susceptible of an obvious mode of explanation, that the class of ex-apprentices in this colony, entertain a strong prejudice against any sort of occupation connected, in their minds, with their former mode of existence–the least semblance of compulsory labour being sufficient to excite the most unequivocal symptoms of repugnance.
>
> Hence the violent outcry and opposition raised by most parents, whenever any teacher has attempted to initiate their children into some of the simplest, easiest, and most trivial elements of gardening operations.
>
> Third Report of the Mauritius
> Education Committee of 1847

Mauritians watched as certain people accessed a sliver of social mobility by conforming to the standards set by the British colonial institutions. That way lay power and prosperity. And so, in Mauritius – as in countless other countries throughout the world – their society came to view labouring in the field as lowly, and to see intellectual labour as the highest of aspirations.

*

Even though I was certain I knew the answer, I once asked my dad, 'What did you think of me giving up my career and growing plants instead?'

'Well,' he replied, 'when we dreamed about what we wanted for our children, it wasn't to go out and work in the fields.'

I've always known this. My parents made choices and sacrifices to give us – my brother and me – the experiences and opportunities that they didn't have. They wanted to create for us the chance of a good and steady life, and to choose what that looked like for ourselves. They felt that the measure of my success – and theirs, as parents – was achieving a degree and moving on to a career, one that was professional and respectable and secure. And while I worked in television, they were proud to tell their friends when to look out for our surname rolling up the screen in the end credits. Less so now that I'm just growing vegetables. 'Why is she giving up a successful career?' they asked each other. They didn't understand why I'd quit a good job. They worried that I'd regret it, and they worried I wouldn't be able to make a decent living. That's always been my dad's main concern. He values steadiness over anything else. Aside from the enormous leap of faith he took in moving to England at eighteen years old, he has always chosen the least-risky path. I imagine if he'd been graced with the kind of opportunities that I've had, with the brain that he has – able to teach himself to rewire a house, plumb in a new boiler and fix every car that there's a Haynes manual for – he would have gone to university and become an engineer of some kind, or trained as a pilot, if he could. But, unlike me, he would have stuck with it as he did with nursing, paid into a pension every month and saved up all that he could, so that one day he'd be able to help my brother and me to buy a home. He would never have been tempted away from a reliable job, even if he had a strong suspicion that it could have made him truly happy.

'But I'd never seen you quite as happy as when you took us to the farm in New York,' my mum tells me. I remember that day well. They both got stuck into the weeding and harvesting while I proselytised about my love for the place and my infatuation with the vegetables that were growing up there. My brother meanwhile spent the day looking out from that high vantage, across the river at the Manhattan skyline. He's turned out more as my parents expected, I think. Proper job, good salary and a baby on the way.

At the start of this journey, at Brooklyn Grange, I quickly came to appreciate how little we value the work of growing food. It is rarely spoken of as an aspiration by people who dream of a future of meaning, worth or wealth. It is demeaned and denigrated, and has disappeared from our view despite being the foundation of all that we do. We don't value, as we should, those who grow our food. I sowed a seed for the first time as an adult. Watching the seeds that I've sown germinate and grow, struggle in some instances through my lack of knowledge, and then thrive in spaces better suited to their needs, I realised how little I understood; I realised how I'd steered my life towards endeavours that caused me to drift further and further away from the understanding that nature is not an externality or a backdrop, and far from an irrelevance. I realised that powerful systems, far larger than I, benefit from encouraging us all to believe that this work is degrading. But they are wrong. Growing food is everything.

As I seek to learn about who I am and what made me, and what it means to call a place home, I'm quite certain that my searching would always have led me to the earth. While I find it excruciating to contemplate how it was this very work that confined my ancestors to lifetimes of exploitation, it is this work that has come to mean everything to me. This work is integral, essential and ancestral. It is an act of reclamation to find dignity in growing the plants that feed people.

In the moments of steady and gentle repetition, carefully taking each tiny seed from the creased lines in the palm of my hand and softly nudging it under moist compost with my fingertip, I see myself dancing the same peaceful dance of my ancestors. The sway of placing hopeful seeds into welcoming soil is a tiny gesture, a tender offering, that has upheld humanity for the longest time and will be repeated until we cease to exist. In stepping towards this work and calling it my own, I know I am singing the same song that my ancestors sang when they committed themselves to the earth in service of their family, their community, their people and their land, and in service of the natural world that would meet them, with the same generosity and commitment.

No matter the challenges of the seasons before, as soon as the weather gestures towards the possibility of spring I return to my box of seeds. Each seed is the accumulation of generations of pollination and reproduction, selection and adaptation. Each seed contains all that I need to start anew, wherever I find myself. Within its DNA are the imprints of the lives of those who cultivated each plant, and the way that seed was passed from parent to child, from grower to neighbour, from friend to friend; and it's through this succession of cultivating and sharing that we have this precious inheritance. The work of growing food is a precious inheritance, too, one that I have taken up with my whole heart. Where once I would have been ashamed to have soil under my fingernails, I now wear my grubby hands with pride.

Through growing food, I see the threads that weave through and between all things, and I bear witness to how profoundly we are tied to one another. From verdurous out-breath to mammalian in-breath, from petal unfurling to reveal a dusty yellow stamen to the soft nudge of a fuzzy bumblebee. From pollen meeting stigma to the incremental transformation that follows, cells dividing and multiplying into the gentle swell of fruit. From the plants that grow in seemingly implausible places to the fungi that help the trees talk amongst themselves, to the bowls that spill over with steamed rice or sautéed greens or fiercely hot red chillies.

*

Alongside the squash and courgettes, I sow Mauritian cucumber seeds once more. This season I want to grow the food that raised me, the food of my family. Little seeds, placed on their side and kept at a comfortably warm temperature. I check on their progress, the next day and then the next. And soon enough there is a pale-green sprout breaching the surface of the compost. Neck first, this small cucurbit, the young charge I've been awaiting, is appearing. The third year that he asked, the second time that I tried, and the first time that they've dared to grow in my care. I go to call my dad, but think better of it. I'm not certain that this one will survive. Through quiet, silly tears, I take a picture instead. I'll show him when I feel more certain that this time it's going to grow.

CHAPTER 9

The weather has been unsettled lately and it persisted in its strangeness until yesterday, when it reached a crescendo of thunder and lightning and pounding rain. The pressure broke, at last, and with it went the dull ache in my head. The evening sun broke through the storm clouds and cast a glow the colour of Himalayan salt. When I find myself looking for something to love about being here, I watch the sun set over the woods. I look west and see how, after a rain passes, mist settles into trails that run through the uppermost branches of the trees. As the sky turns violet, before the sun drops away to darkness, I feel steadier than I did before. The more attention I pay to the shape of the clouds as they go by, the faces of the wildflowers I'm getting to know, the wizened trunks of ancient trees that I weave a path towards, the more I feel that I might come to love this place.

The tender summer plants are growing more swiftly. They spend their nights in the conservatory, where I indulge them with heat mats and fleece snuggled around their pots and then, from the morning until the evening, I set them out to lounge in the sun and grow accustomed to being jostled by the breeze. I'm readying them for their life in the ground, outdoors and without my protection. I shuffle them around, shunting them towards the sunlight and exposing them incrementally to the reality of a life without coddling, in the hope that the transition won't be more shocking than they can handle. I don't trust them to the night yet and so, instead, I give the rampaging squash plants some fresh compost in larger pots, for them to fill with their roots.

We head off for a walk through the village, which takes us down a narrow passage edged by banks of three-cornered leek in flower and to the brow of a hilly field of cattle. Through stiles and kissing gates, we follow our neighbour's directions along the public footpath that leads to a patch of hushed woodland. Once inside, sunbeams shine through the gaps in the canopy, silhouettes of leaves put on a performance in the dancing light, which shows us the way through the trees. The sound of a hungry woodpecker drums fiercely above us but it is impossible to spot, lost against the glare of the midday sun. We've been heading out to the woods more often lately, wanting to watch spring stepping into the first days of summer. Our walk takes us in a loop, down to a field carpeted with purple-spired bugles, past a tree adorned from bottom to top with a ladder of fungi and through a pet cemetery, which is as unlikely and as serious as it sounds. We walk up and down the rows of miniature graves of red brick, some from decades ago, and read the names on the tombstones out loud.

'Patch. Snowy. Cleopatra. Buster. Lucky.'

'Maybe we'll find some nice names to call our chickens?' I suggest, half-joking.

All the names have a decidedly feline or canine energy. No birds – and certainly no chickens – have been laid to rest here, as far as I can tell. Coming back on ourselves, we retrace our steps to head home. More walkers, most of them out with their dogs, come towards us but keep their distance, as the government has instructed. As each person approaches, I try to predict whether they'll be friendly. I decide whether or not to greet them, or to compliment their dog as a way of parading my RP accent, in the hope that I might pre-empt and disarm any misgivings about my presence. I've long tried to be more amiable than I'm comfortable with, in a bid to fit in, and mostly it does the trick. Everyone we pass is pleasant today. One remarks on the glorious weather, another jokingly complains about wearing the wrong shoes for their walk. We pause by the village allotments to snoop at what's growing, and we chat to a generous allotmenteer who sends me off with a pocketful of perennial kale cuttings and a muddy clump of chives to plant in our garden.

We head down another path, and a man wearing sports gear and leaning on the gatepost in front of his house says hello and waves, and a passing nod turns into a chat, pleasant enough at first. We tell him that we're new to the village and are attempting to get to know the place and the people, despite the national lockdown. I want to avoid talking about the pandemic, as the news is relentless and disheartening and we walk for a little respite from it. But it proves impossible to steer him away, and it takes only one conversational handbrake turn before he's talking about bio-warfare and terrorism, and how this virus is a wake-up call for us to recognise the threat to the Western world posed by China, Russia, North Korea and Islam. I couldn't tell if he was seriously referring to Islam as a country, and I wasn't about to ask. I try to keep my facial expressions under control and squeeze Sam's hand hard, to let him know I'm not okay. I've previously cursed my inclination to smile, be accommodating, laugh along for the sake of peace, and here I am again, wishing I'd made my excuses and left before the conversation went sideways. The problem with trying to fit in is that sometimes it works too well, and someone thinks you're just fine with their bigotry and conspiracy theories.

I don't know what to say, so I don't say anything. I wasn't about to cause a scene in front of this man's enormous house, and risk the whole village hearing how the newest and most conspicuous local resident lost her mind at a beloved member of the community. I let Sam make our excuses and we walk away in silence, hurrying to get out of earshot. Putting his arm around my shoulder, he leans down and whispers, 'What the hell was that?' and I don't let go of him until we're at our front door.

*

LORD FARINGDON: 'My Lords, I beg leave to ask the Question which stands in my name on the Order Paper. [The Question was as follows:] To ask Her Majesty's

Government what is the latest information that they have received of the extent of the devastation in Mauritius and, in particular, how many houses and how many huts have been destroyed, and what percentage of the sugar crop and of the tea crop, and whether the damage to the [Government's] tea factory will render it inoperative during this season and finally what is the estimated value of the losses suffered.'

Hansard, 17 March 1960

When Cyclone Carol hit Mauritius, he was five and she was six, and many people lived in houses made of straw and wood and corrugated iron. Cyclone season comes every year from November, although some years the strong winds and lashing rain stay out at sea and follow a trajectory that misses the island. But not that year.

Everyone prepared in a panic, securing what they could before the cyclone hit. The house he lived in with his family was built not long ago and it was sturdier than most, so they opened their doors to all the people in the village who were scared that their homes couldn't withstand what was coming. After moving his boat to the cove, where he prayed it would be safe, his father took the thickest of his fishing ropes and threw them over the roof of their house, lashing them to the biggest boulders they could find, before securing the doors and windows as best he could. Inside, the floor was covered with people who lay awake all night, listening to the howl of the 160mph winds and the thundering force of the rain. Tree branches and dislodged pieces of corrugated iron flew past, smashing into whatever they met along the way.

Her mother was ill when they heard the cyclone was on its way. Their home in the city wasn't going to be safe enough, so she, her parents and her three sisters left immediately, carrying nothing with them, and headed to Beau Bassin, where they could shelter with her father's sister. But they got word that this cyclone was going to be the worst in years and became fearful that her auntie's wooden house wouldn't protect them, either. So they left, as the wind gathered pace and the rain started to fall, to another relative whose house was made of béton. The force of the gale was so strong that her little legs couldn't keep up, so her father scooped her into his arms and carried her to safety. It was quiet enough once inside the concrete building and she slept all the way through the night.

When the cyclone passed, the sun seemed especially bright against the clear blue sky, as everyone emerged to survey the damage. Many houses had pieces missing, some were left roofless and others had been flattened entirely. Trees were torn from the earth, their roots exposed and all the lowest points along the roads were flooded. They were excited, though, as all the children were, to collect what fruit had fallen to the ground. Mangoes, coconuts and longans – they hoped – if there were still some growing before the wind blew in. While their children made their hands and mouths sticky with fruit, the adults swept up the debris with coco-brooms and made plans to rebuild what had been lost and destroyed.

THE MINISTER OF STATE FOR COLONIAL AFFAIRS
(THE EARL OF PERTH): 'My Lords, cyclone "Carol" which
struck Mauritius on the 27th and 28th February was the
most severe ever recorded in the island's history. There
were over 1,700 casualties; 42 people were killed and 95
seriously injured. Over 100,000 buildings and huts were
destroyed or seriously damaged. Nearly 70,000 of the
island's total population of 600,000 are now in refugee
centres.'

Hansard, 17 March 1960

*

The sound of the side gate smashing into the house startles me
awake. The wind is back and has already set to rearranging the
garden. I had hoped that we'd left the incessant wind behind,
but it's followed us from winter through spring and into summer. The other day I set out the chard and beetroot seedlings,
the first into the ground. They have two sets of true leaves –
glossy and green, yellow and red – and, although a little on the
small side, I was convinced they'd be happier outside. If they
had to, they'd survive a chilly night or two. But now I'm watching as the willow ripples like a windsock, and I wonder if there
will be anything left of the seedlings by the time the weather
has settled. Gusts shudder through the roof tiles, tearing fistfuls
of spring's new leaves away from their branches and swirling
them into tornadoes that deposit them elsewhere. This wind
has been unsettling. Although the house feels secure, I fear the

wind is part of the character of this place. Perhaps our position, halfway up a hill, with nothing to interrupt the weather coming from in front or from behind, has us exposed to these rattling gusts that upend the furniture of my mind.

Once the boisterous weather calms down, it leaves behind a cool, bright day and I venture out into the stillness to survey the damage. Everything looks a little battered and lopsided, but is mostly intact, aside from the newest, tallest fern fronds, which have been snapped, and the remaining leaves, which look scorched. A terracotta pot lies smashed on the gravel, and there are twigs and branches and the purple petals of wisteria blooms lying scattered over the ground. Yet the chard and beetroot are upright and unbothered. Low to the ground, they appear to have escaped the worst of it and, if anything, are probably stronger for surviving.

The temperature has fallen low once or twice in the last week and brought with it the threat of a late frost. It's the moment in the growing year known for its precarity. The days are warm and encouraging, but the possibility remains that, come night-time, the temperature will fall and remind us of how fickle the weather can be here, and how little say we have over it. There's no way to truly know when the last frost will occur. At best, it's an educated guess. You make an estimation based on what you remember of last year, and what you know of the space in which you plant. You count back from when you hope it might be, and sow your seeds undercover accordingly: four or six or eight weeks prior, and some even earlier if you can offer them enough light when they sprout. Then you watch as those tender plants grow on windowsills and under sky-lights, and you protect them from being kissed by the cold. You hold back your runner beans and tomatoes and squash until you're absolutely, positively (fingers crossed) sure they'll make it through the night on their own. I don't know this place or when the last frost occurred a year ago, but the forecast is looking promising. The tomatoes have thick stems and are ready to be planted, while the courgettes and cucumbers have been outgrowing their pots for some time. It's always a gamble, but I am daring to say (with fleece clutched at the ready) that it should be safe in the ground, and overnight, for these plants from now on.

The older of the cucurbits are looking a little gangly. I'm worried they'll be too weak to do well outdoors. The younger plants are faring much better. Later sowings often catch up in the strong light and warm days. Last week we filled old rubble sacks with ten-year-old horse manure from a huge pile near our friend's house. It's been sitting there for so long that nettles almost as tall as I am grow out of it, letting us know that it is nutritious. Into a hole dug through a thick layer of compost and into the dense Sussex clay, we throw a trowel's worth of old manure. Anchoring the stems between my fingers, I tip each tomato, squash, cucumber and courgette plant into my hand, loosen their roots and push them into the ground. Carefully but resolutely, I firm the compost around their stems and surrender their tenderness to the earth.

Back inside the house, I go to check the propagator. I've been checking several times a day. It's the only place unbothered by the unsettled weather and, inside it, I'm trying to grow okra for my mum. While she concedes that she isn't much of a cook, she loves lalo and she cooks it well. It's because of her that even in my childish fussy stage I loved it, and will defend it from anyone who sneers at its texture. I've never known how she does it, but it's not slimy when my mum makes it.

I sowed the first round of seeds at the beginning of April, after soaking them in warm water. Knowing they could take up to twenty-one days, I waited for weeks before running out of patience and tipping the compost out of the pot and into my hand. I carefully searched for a sprouting seed, but there was only warm, sodden compost and the faint smell of decay. I tried again that same day with seeds that I decided not to soak, and they too refused to germinate, choosing instead to remain intact, like stubborn little stones. But for the third attempt, with the last of my seeds, I slowly and precisely ran the blade of my harvest knife against the tough seed coat, being careful to leave the eye, where the shoot will emerge, unharmed. After soaking them for only an hour or so, I planted them as before and muttered something hopeful as I covered them with compost. Okra would prefer to be growing in Mauritius, really. Or where its origins were traced, in present-day Ethiopia. Anywhere tropical or subtropical or with a warm and temperate climate. Anywhere, it seems, but here.

But I urge the seeds to be defiant and to push roots into the earth here anyway. I implore them to try and grow. I will them to seek the sun and take up space, to gather the energy they need to bloom. I feel hopeful that they will find the strength they need to turn their flowers into seedpods and that, one day, there will be enough of them to throw into a pan of frying garlic and ginger being stirred by my mum. Today, at last, there is a short green stalk sporting its first tiny clamshell leaves. The next day I find there are three more seedlings emerging to join the first. It took me three tries to get these four seedlings to grow. Four chances for one dish of toufe lalo.

A flurry of long-tailed tits dance through the branches of a rangy holly bush. From behind a nearby tree, we watch in silence as they dart about playfully and chatter. Snub-beaked, blush-bellied, all fluff. Implausibly long tails and surprisingly loud mouths. We've returned to the same woods as the last time, making sure to hurry past that man's house. My heart has been growing heavy again and I'm seeking the shelter of these towering hornbeams and their dappled sunlight across the fern-covered woodland floor. These last few days I've been trying to avoid a video that's been circulating online. It is nine minutes long and it shows the dying moments of a Black man who shares my father's name. Instead, I watched a video of a woman calling the police on a Black birdwatcher, for pointing out a mistake she was making in Central Park, and I've spent too long wondering how easily it could have ended the same way for him, with a knee on his neck until it was too much to bear. I'm haunted by the moment when the tone of the woman's voice shifts, when she uses what we all know about whose safety the police prioritise to sound as though she's in danger. The sound of her voice ricochets about my mind and won't leave me to walk in peace.

It's quiet here, but my thoughts are not. She must have known that in that place of nature, preserved for wildlife, her presence was a more natural fit than his. That despite her being the rule-breaker and letting her dog run around unleashed, she could weaponise her identity to endanger his. It reminds me that no matter where – even when we seek the tranquillity of the outdoors – we can be denied our peace, and that it is not our decision to make. It reminds me that even in the midst of one of the most diverse cities in the world – a city I lived in for four years, and a park I visited often – the natural world is still the domain of whiteness. After years of fighting my way back into the embrace of the natural world, my presence there is somehow considered incongruous at best, and suspicious at worst. I won't feel peace here in the woods today.

I'd prefer to put that incident down to one person's prejudice. It would be far easier to. But it's more insidious than that, deeper and more toxic than one woman's actions. It connects together the many times I was the only person of colour in green spaces; the horticultural language imbued with disdain for the other; the flippant racism against which I've had to grit my teeth while growing vegetables; how there are rarely experts and teachers in my industry who look like me; how the colonialism and imperialism that are ingrained in horticultural and agricultural history – the 'plant hunting', bio-prospecting, renaming and weaponising of plants in oppressive profit-making enterprises – are so rarely spoken of; how protecting the environment has been adopted as the pet cause of neo-Nazis who seek to protect their green and pleasant land from those they believe don't belong there. People like me. It exposes the many structures and forces, histories and injustices, displacements and destructions that are at the core of the disconnection I felt to the natural world, and why it has been a battle to claw my way back to it.

The video is just over a minute long. Within it I see a whole universe of power and cruelty. A timeline stretching back through decades and centuries of a people being coerced and controlled, excluded and denigrated. A vast and tangled history of exploitation and prejudice that has left too many of us with the wounds of our parents and our grandparents and our ancestors and kept us from our motherland, and from our home in the embrace of the outdoors. When we try, we endanger ourselves. We are not safe. We are the anomaly, the peculiarity, and we have to live with the psychological burden that comes from being an outsider trying to make space for ourselves in hostile terrain.

The long-tailed tits fly away eventually, scattering and disappearing into the trees. We keep on walking, following the path in reverse to make it feel new. The first person we've seen in the woods today, a tall man in a panama hat and twice our age, is coming towards us. The path through the woods is narrow and, in keeping with the new social etiquette, we know one of us needs to give the other room to pass. He doesn't break stride, so I, not wanting to be rude, leap off the path and into a muddy ditch. I offer a greeting and Sam, further away, says hello, too. A nod of acknowledgement for Sam, a sidelong scowl for me. It is a tiny gesture, an indistinct expression, but it was a choice to respond to Sam and not to me. It is close to nothing, but I've seen it before. A furrowed brow and then a turning away. A muted but familiar disdain. And it landed, and felt pointed. Its energy akin to the quiet scrutiny of those regulars as I stepped into the village pub, or the vexed elderly woman who wrenched open the door of her cottage as I admired her pretty garden, her glare following me as I hurried away. I know that look too well. It's been the first sign of trouble, in the past. I look down at my feet in the mud. A passing scowl is gesture enough for my body to remember what it means to feel unsafe, to feel precarious and exposed, and to brace itself for what may follow.

It lives in my bones, this melancholy and trepidation. In my aching bones and broken heart. I carry it around, and it's weighty. Thief of joy and stealer of peace. It is a wound that half-heals, before being torn open again by a look intended to intimidate, a flippant remark, a prying question, hands that reach towards my hair or an outright slur. I'm braced for any and all of them. Even the smallest thing, invisible to the naked eye, is enough to make me flinch, cortisol rising, poised to flee. How my body holds itself, battle-ready, is almost as taxing as when a punch finally lands. Whether it's in the news, in a video online or in person, my body doesn't seem to know the difference. When you say it about them, you say it about me. What differentiates me is a veil of good fortune, which offers little protection for my heart. I am weary from years spent withstanding, from years feeling the abuse of others inside myself, tearing through my muscle tissue and wearing it thin.

*

Trou d'Eau Douce, 1963

He had lighter skin than his brothers, so they called him mulâ-tre and said he must be the milkman's son. He didn't know it at the time, but his parents treated him differently from his brothers and sisters because they had high hopes for who he'd grow up to become. He worked hard at school, because that's what was expected of him, but also because he was smart and determined. Speaking French in the classroom, writing in English for his exams and chatting in Morisyen to his friends in the playground. He was a bookish boy but mischievous, too. Playing tricks on his friends and trying to look fearless in front of his brothers. The relief of tears was never worth the merci-less teasing that would follow him, if he cried when he was the victim of their pranks. After school he would run home through the sugarcane fields, filling his pockets with guavas from the trees that grew wild.

At home there were always jobs to do, but the chore he liked best was cooking dinner for their eight hungry bellies. He would coup so zepiss and cook rougaille ourit, mine frir and cari pwason with rice because his dad always brought fish home for the family. Apart from in the winter, with its treach-erous seas, when his dad would spend his days fixing the holes in his fishing nets and they'd eat salted fish instead.

They had a garden behind the house in Trou d'Eau Douce, but it was a garden without many plants. A few citrus trees grew there, but not much else. If there had been any plants in the ground, their animals would have eaten them, so they never really bothered trying to grow them. He and his brother would be sent to the banks of the river nearby to collect fodder for the family's pigs. Cutting back the foliage, he'd dig up the tuberous roots and carefully gather them into hessian sacks. The caustic sap that would ooze from the freshly cut stems could burn a young boy's skin.

On Sundays he and his two brothers would take the boat out to Île aux Cerfs and cut down a tree for firewood. Once it was sawn into pieces, they carried the wood on their shoulders to where the boat was waiting under the filao trees by the shore. Once they'd rowed back to the other side of the water, they'd haul each log up the hill to their home in time for a slightly late but appreciated lunch of bread and zasar legim. They'd split the wood and use it to light a fire, which boiled the water to cook the roots they'd gathered for the pigs. They'd start early in the morning, to the sound of crowing cockerels, and only finish when the sun had passed its highest point. Some chores took most of the day.

When the family sow was at her most fertile, his mother would always know. He'd tie a rope around her neck and, with his brother's help, convince her to walk up the road to 'spend some time' with their neighbour's waiting hog. Some-how the hog knew, too, and would be there, standing by the fence, waiting for her to arrive. Three months later there'd be a new litter of piglets to care for, until they were sold to whoever in the village wanted one. All these years later, he can still remember the noise the pigs made when they were being slaughtered, and that piercing, sickening sound comes

back to him any time someone offers him pork, and he
politely refuses.

*

The cardboard box on my lap is suspiciously quiet. I hold it
just above my legs to protect them when the car runs into
bumps and potholes in the road. The radio is off and we stay
quiet, hoping to hear their little noises, but they stay silent.
They're not as heavy as I imagined they would be. If I hadn't
watched the man at the farm put them in this box, I'd be
tempted to check if it was empty.

The advice is to put them in their house as soon as possible, and leave them for an hour or two before opening the
door to let them out. In theory, this should teach them where
to go when it's time for bed. Sam's holding the box next to the
propped-up lid of the henhouse, and I open it carefully, half-
expecting them to make a break for it as soon as they see
daylight. But they stay entirely still, all four squished together
in the corner of the box and looking as worried as it's possible
for a chicken to look. Each one is distinct from the others –
black and white, grey speckled and two gingery-red: one that's
dark, and the other light and speckled with white. They are a
feathery mass, and I'm sure they won't appreciate being separ-
ated for even a minute, as nervous as they are to be somewhere
new and unfamiliar. I lift them out of the box quickly but gently, wrapping my hands around their wings and placing them
inside the house. They're smaller than I expected, smaller still

between my hands. They feel like they're made of nearly nothing. They're about fourteen weeks old – somewhere between chicks and adult hens – and over the next months they will grow bigger and fluffier, then start laying. As Sam closes the lid, they run towards each other and snuggle into a corner, pressing their feathery bodies against each other again.

These four birds are my first 'real' pets. My family are not pet people, and the only living creature they allowed me to bring into our house was a goldfish in a plastic bag that I won at the funfair at the end of the road. It was a tiny little thing, about the size of eight-year-old me's little finger, and I named it Amber. Amber didn't last long, and when my dad found her floating lifeless in the bowl, he sent my brother to the pet shop on his bike for a replacement. New Amber was a chubbier, longer fish, with a pretty fantail, and I was gullible enough to buy their story that, well, sometimes fish just grow up and change. I loved that fish. I'd clean out her bowl in the bathroom sink willingly, and offer her my finger and laugh when she'd suck on it to see if it was food. They would have got away with the deception, if not for a squabble that my brother won with the knockout blow of the truth of Original Amber's demise. There was an imposter in my fish bowl and I never forgave her for it, so when Amber No. Two died, I was too angry to replace her.

It's a warm day, so I don't want to leave the chickens locked in for long. Plus I'm excited to meet them properly and watch as they explore their new coop. I want to see them get to know the place, and get used to us, but when I open the door, they won't come out. They stay cowering in the corner together, looking suspicious of us. And then the black-and-white one strides out of the door, skids down the ramp and crashes to the ground. She pecks around, walks around the feeder and starts to explore while the others stay inside. She's the leader, I'm sure, the most confident of the bunch, and we agree that she, with all her assertiveness and beauty, has chosen her own name. From then on, she'll be the hen we call Grace Jones. Over the next few hours the other three follow Grace and venture out of the house, but choose to hide away on the other side of the coop, to escape the two imbeciles who are trying to befriend them by making chicken noises and offering them mealworms. After a while of trying, we leave them be, to get accustomed to the place without an audience.

I harvest a handful of rocket and a bowl full of lettuce leaves, throw a blanket onto the ground near their coop and we settle there to eat our dinner. We watch bats darting about overhead, hunting moths in the evening light until it's nine and the sun is gone. It's been a long day and the chickens settle down in a pile on the ground; they don't remember where they're meant to sleep. We pick up their drowsy little bodies and place them gently in the nesting box, and although they fuss and cheep a little to protest at being disturbed, they're tired, so they let it happen. The following night, as the daylight grows dim, they flap into the henhouse of their own accord and put themselves to bed.

CHAPTER 10

The chickens seem to mind me a little less with every morning that goes by that I'm here to open their door and bring them food. In their first days here they gave me a wide berth, eyeballing me as they edged towards the feeder. I'm sure they can sense how desperate I am that they come to love me as much as I already love them. They've been getting a little more confident and adventurous, flying up to the higher roost and chasing each other around, and today they ignore me and run straight towards breakfast. They remain unconvinced by the clucking noises I make, or how I sit in their coop and tap the ground as a mother hen would, to teach them where to look for food. All in a vain attempt to gain their trust. They don't really cluck and I don't know if they will. They peep quietly and chat to each other, but they don't yet talk to me.

Nonetheless, their characters are becoming more distinct and certain, although I still can't tell who's at the top of the pecking order. Sometimes I think it's Alan, who is bossy and fierce; and sometimes Grace, whose lead everyone follows still. Ti Coule – whom my dad named for the love he has for my mum – is the bolshie middle child, getting on without too much fuss, but poised to elbow another hen out of the way if she thinks she's getting less than her share. While Mimi, sweet thing, is an unhelpful mix of shy, nervous and vacant, and sometimes the other three walk off, leaving her behind to stare into space, lost in her daydreams. When she realises she's alone, she squawks and flaps into flight, desperate to find her sisters. I don't know if they're related by blood, but they grew up together in the same flock and it has made them inseparable. They prefer to be together even when they're finding each other irritating. They spend hours clustered together, heads disappearing under wings, pulling at their feathers with their beaks. Sometimes I spot them gently pecking and preening each other; and every night they go to sleep squeezed together into a nesting box made for one, as they did when they arrived.

I've only found the courage to grow annual plants so far. I've not committed to planting any perennials of my own, but thankfully the front garden overflows with them. Hardy geraniums in magenta and violet, dark-red geums and salvias in bloom. The fluted velvety leaves and frothy lime-green blossoms of lady's mantle cover the ground. Lilac globes of alliums stand tall, while wild strawberries with tiny fruit, and fleabane covered in white-and-pink daisies, clamber out of the bed's edges and romp down the path. Leaves and flowers grow cheek-to-cheek. I'm grateful for the beauty and abundance that lives here in the soil already.

The first purple and pink radishes tasted spicy and enlivening. The first salad of lettuce and baby chard was satisfying and delicious. These initial harvests from the vegetable patch lead me to believe that my murmuring doubts about being here could be displaced. When misgivings rose to the surface, I dropped fresh marjoram from the herb bed into a pan of frying garlic and onions, so that their comforting smell could quieten them. But as much as I try, I can't shake off how much that video has rattled something inside me. And I can't stop thinking about the man in the woods, either.

I need healing practices. I go to sit on my meditation cushion, but my agitation demands something physical, something to restore my faith. I spend the day with the soil. I clear the just-germinated little weeds out of the bed where the tomatoes will go. I plant out dill and sunflowers, pot on the smallest tomato plants, sow four different kinds of bean and the next succession of courgette seeds. Two varieties – one nearly black and the other light green and striped. The first round of courgette and cucumber plants have stems that are thick and sturdy now, calloused but robust and a darker shade of green. I split clusters of purple basil plants and give them more room to grow, and more compost to grow in. I need the garden today, I need its fortification and its blessing. I drink deep of its medicine. These are meaningful movements. I nudge the plants forward and the garden moves on.

The work calms me. My swirling thoughts become less frantic. I feel the urge to say something, but the mess of internet back-and-forths and text messages and social-media posts have left me frazzled. I pause in the sun to wait for my thoughts to settle and try to hear the words I think I want to say. I want to describe how I've always whitewashed myself and code-switched for other people's comfort and approval, and that I cringe at how my learned proximity to whiteness makes me seem more acceptable. I want to explain that I've felt held back from the natural world here, because of how unwelcome I feel in this country and how clearly and deeply I know that I don't belong. I want to say that living in the countryside feels like an act of defiance, a rewriting of the stories I believed about who gets to make a life here and call it home. And I want to explain that the work of growing plants is not frivolous to me; it has changed me from the outside in. I want to say that this world I've entered – the world of plants – is not exempt from society's prejudices, and the fact that its past and present are knotted up with colonialism and imperialism is something that I wrestle with most days. I want to say aloud what I've been holding in my heart for years now: that this work that oppressed my ancestors is the work I reclaim in their name. And that I know they existed and cultivated before they were stolen and exploited, and that I nurture the soil to honour who they were when they were free. I want to speak words that lay bare the trauma that is my inheritance, and the strength that has been bestowed upon me, too. That while I will never know their names or their stories, I carry them with me as I kneel down and touch the earth.

So I write. I add the title 'I Don't Belong Here'. Then I hit 'publish', turn my computer off and walk away.

*

I spend the next hours outside, to keep away from my phone. I'm not sure what I'm more afraid of: people reading what I've shared or people ignoring it. I think I'm most afraid of hearing the words I've heard before, the words that erase me and remind me of how I erase myself: 'I don't see you as different. I don't think of you as Black.' I've heard it from old friends as well as new ones. Spoken by people who've known me for decades and by those who don't know me at all. I understand what they're trying to say, but it's the opposite of what I need to hear. They want to show me that they think we're the same, but I want to assure them that we absolutely are not. They mean it as a compliment but, believe me, it is the opposite. To say that you don't see the part of me that's more visible than anything else is to tell me you don't – you can't, you won't – witness my wholeness. You won't look at all that makes me. That you'd prefer to flatten me, to make me more manageable. But you're doing that for *you*. Don't tell yourself it's good for me. To say that you don't see my race tells me to be quiet. That you don't think it's a thing, so it's not. That if it's invisible to you, then it ought to be invisible to me, too, and so therefore should my struggle. It tells me that I've contorted myself to fit in, broken the bones of one identity to shape myself around another. The completeness of my fitting in here is an awful success and a terrible failure. And I've lost so much because of it. Most of all, it tells me that I'm not as honest as I believe myself to be. That I'm not courageous. That there are people I care for that I hide from. That I have disappeared important parts of myself within the relationships that I have chosen. That I have participated in my own erasure, such that you have received the message that it's okay to say, 'I don't see your race' to me. Well, now the truth is out, and I pray that I never have to hear those words again.

I keep away from the internet long enough to make sure I can't take it back, even if I wanted to. I lie on the grass, looking up at the sky without shielding my eyes, and the colour of the willow branches over me turns from green to silhouette-black. I watch as they sway gently, before closing my eyes to see the colours inside my eyelids, bright yellow-white and ruby-red. There's an ache in my belly that's telling me to pack up everything – my books, my shoes, my seed box – and head back to London. Abandon this experiment and return to the place that knows me best. But to do that, I'd have to abandon the plants that I'm already growing and the chickens who've only just arrived. And I'd have to admit – to myself and everyone else – that I couldn't figure out how to make it work here. But I am making it work. The plants are rooting into this earth, and the chickens grow bigger and bolder with each passing day. I grow plants through my unsteadiness, and soon enough there will be fruit. The currants are turning red.

With each exhale, I sense my body sinking, moving down-wards towards the earth. I'm merging into the darkness, the soil and stone and clay. I'm heavy and I'm light, and disappear-ing down to join the roots and creatures, and the threads of mycelium woven through and connecting it all. I fall apart into it, pulled down and held up. I am the soil, and the soil is me. We are one and the same. The same rock, the same lignin, the same carbon and sun and water and moonlight. In the distance, clouds darken and bring the hope that a storm will soon come. I will the wild and unsettled sky to drift towards me, I will the rain to fall. The ground is thirsty and I am, too.

I listened to an interview with a horticulturalist the other day and, while speaking about their countryside upbringing, they said, 'You just are from where you're from.' It was a passing comment to describe how their early inclination towards plants follows them wherever they go. My heart sank, hearing those words spoken as if they were a universal truth. Such a fatalistic notion presented as though it were indisputable. What if where you're from is a troubled or dull or dismal place? Are you destined to be troubled, dull or dismal? And what if where a person is 'from' is not a straightforward question to answer? For me to be living here in the countryside, I need to believe that it is possible to change and transform. That if we don't identify with the place where we grew up, we can learn ways of being that feel new and true. I need to believe what Buddhist teachers have taught me: that no immutable self exists.

When I was in Gloucestershire, someone I worked alongside would ask, 'Is that an urban thing?' whenever I used a word or described something they hadn't heard of before. The implied message, as I felt it, was that there were things about me that they couldn't comprehend because I was too urban (read: Black) for their countryside mind. While I choose to believe they weren't being malicious, that little question reinforced the belief I held that rural life would always be wrong for someone like me.

Before we committed to this move, I thought about what it would take, often and at length. Making lists in my head of what I'd gain if I did it, and what could go wrong once I'd arrived. I spent hours making hypothetical plans in daydreams of how I could make my way back to the city if, no matter how I tried, it all fell apart. Before taking the leap, we visited as often as we could, explored the little villages and pebble beaches around this area that seemed to be calling to us. We nudged one another gently in the ribs whenever we saw a couple who looked a little like us, hoping that they lived here and weren't just visiting, as we were.

The notion that people of colour are more likely to live in cities is borne out by the statistics. Of the 17 per cent of the population who live in the rural parts of England, only 2.4 per cent of that percentage are not white. That's 0.42 per cent of the total population. It's not a lot of people of colour, once they're spread throughout the countryside of this land. There's little safety to be found in these scant numbers.

There's more safety in community, in not feeling perpetually conspicuous and in seeing faces that look like yours and your family's most days. That's why I lived for most of my adult life in London and New York. Yet the evidence that points towards the ravage of an urbanised existence, a life that is solid with concrete and glass and devoid of sufficiently abundant green spaces, is mounting by the day. City life, while rich in many ways, is associated with higher rates of cardiovascular and respiratory diseases as well as an increased risk of depression, generalised anxiety disorder and psychosis.

Negotiating bouts of depression and immobilising anxiety has been normal to me since I was a teenager. It is still part of the dance that I do now to ensure I remain functional and healthy. With a decade of yoga and meditation practice at my back, a couple of years with a really good therapist, and a relationship with the natural world that I nurture daily, I'm okay more often than I'm not. And I know now that the gap between me and feeling well has been woven together by the plants I grew in that space. Becoming more able to move through green spaces, and becoming more comfortable when present in plant-filled places, is what offered me the healing I was so desperate for. My life now has a meaning that I couldn't find elsewhere. Whether it's due to the exhaustion, the satisfaction or the peace that I find through working with plants, I am finally able to sleep deeply through the night. So I am here in the countryside, trying to take root and connect with the earth, because my mental well-being depends, in part, on this garden.

We need trees and leaves and flowers. We need green to feel steadiness and peace. As the theory of biophilia hypothesises, we feel most whole when in the presence of the natural world that we co-evolved with. And, even more so, when we are in deep kinship with the plants and creatures, landscapes and bodies of water that make up the world beyond our brick walls. Studies demonstrate that spending time in nature can reduce stress and improve our mood, support us to recover from illness and even restore us from our mental fatigue – as put forth by Attention Restoration Theory. One such study conducted by the European Centre for Environment & Human Health at the University of Exeter found that participants who spent at least two hours per week in green spaces were significantly more likely to report good health and mental well-being. Prompted by a project that treated cancer patients with *Mycobacterium vaccae* – a type of bacteria commonly found in soil – which saw them reporting an improved quality of life, researchers from Bristol University and University College London conducted a study giving the same bacteria to mice. The researchers found that *M. vaccae* stimulated their neurons to produce serotonin, the hormone associated with well-being and happiness, prompting the lead author, Dr Chris Lowry, to consider whether 'we shouldn't all be spending more time playing in the dirt'. I sense the emotional truth in this finding whenever I take my hands to the ground and tend the soil.

To have a garden of my own, to own a small piece of land, is an immense privilege. It's a privilege that my parents created for me through their devotion and hard work, from the very little they began with. They pushed me into the safety and advantage of being educated and financially secure – and, from this place of privilege, I sow seeds of my own choosing and grow plants for joy and nourishment. Once I'd learned how to choose a decent waterproof and had saved up enough to afford one, the barriers I encountered between myself and knowing the natural world were (and are) principally emotional and psychological ones.

I know how lucky I am now, because meaningful access to green spaces for city-dwellers (a group that contains 98 per cent of all people of colour in Britain) is not guaranteed – and it certainly is not equal. City neighbourhoods where residents are likely to have gardens or green spaces nearby are more expensive to live in. So when the homes with adjacent green spaces are unaffordable, and the cost of gear for getting outdoors or for travel is more than a budget will allow, and there's no time between work and all of life's other commitments for a person to get out into the natural world, issues connected to income intersect with issues around race, since households of colour are more than twice as likely to be living in poverty as white households. So, given the fact that those who live in cities are more likely to become unwell and experience mental-health challenges, it strikes me as no coincidence that here in Britain a Black person is four times more likely to be detained under the Mental Health Act than a white person. And it bears mentioning that there are many other factors – including, but far from limited to, gender and sexuality, neurodiversity and chronic illness, accessibility and ableism – that routinely converge to withhold access to the natural landscape from certain people more than others.

While the reasons for all these issues are manifold, being deprived of a connection to the natural world certainly played a part in my mental-health struggles; and – as the evidence attests – nature has a role to play in soothing our troubled souls and bodies. So with all of this in mind, it feels imperative to ask ourselves: what can we do to dismantle the barriers that render the natural world inaccessible to those who might need it the most?

*

I let a handful of freshly picked sugar-snap peas tumble onto the kitchen counter and go to pick up my phone. The screen is filled with notifications. My solar plexus tightens, and from it a flush of anxiety starts to rise. I'm not sure I've done the right thing. I could have kept this to myself, but I chose to write. I could have left it at that, but I posted it online instead. It could have been ignored, but then people have been reading it and sharing it, and now I feel more exposed than ever before. I take a deep breath in and force it out. Then I lose the rest of the day to the screen. I watch as my words bounce around social media. Emails ping, messages beep. There are likes and shares and comments. It is breathless, I am breathless, and I'm tiring myself out by reading and responding to the stream of commentary. There's a sugary taste in my mouth. It's the taste of unease and restlessness. It happens when I'm losing my equilibrium.

The messages are a mix of responses. Mostly supportive, surprised and upset. I don't hear from some people I'd hoped to, but I get messages from people I haven't heard from since university, and others from even longer ago than that. They're checking in and wanting to know how I'm doing; it's been too long and we should catch up. I know I should probably be grateful, but I don't feel it. The overfamiliarity is making me uncomfortable. We haven't spoken for years and those years turned into decades, and you thought today was the day to say hi? I get messages from people who want to pick my brains and ask me how to fix the 'lack of diversity' in their projects and workplaces. Clearly baring my soul and sharing my words on the internet wasn't enough. Apparently it's also my responsibility to figure out how we remedy the inequities I've gestured towards. If only I knew how. I drain myself, being polite. I find ways to say no without being rude, because I've trained myself to be agreeable and accommodating, even when people interrupt my day with questions that ask more of me than I'm willing to offer up.

An idea starts rebounding around Instagram, suggesting that this could be a week to 'amplify Black voices'. I don't know where it started, but I see it gaining traction. The idea is a fairly simple one. For a few days people will quieten down and, as a consequence, the voices of those who are under-represented and have less visibility – in all domains – will have a chance to be seen and heard in a way that ordinarily they are not. It's not the most meaningful of gestures. Social media visibility isn't going to challenge the structures of power that perpetuate injustice, but in this strange moment, while I sit watching protesters in Minneapolis chanting in unison to tell the world that they can't breathe, I appreciate watching this modest expression of solidarity replace the images that normally fill my Instagram feed. I watch a flood of black squares being posted and, after that wave of darkness, I wait for the quiet, to make space for the words and images and creations made by Black people to rise up and take up some room.

It appears as though most people have accepted the invitation and are making the effort to hush for a few days. But then I see a picture of pink dahlias in bloom pop up. Then a video of someone pruning the side shoots on their tomato plants, and someone else holding a pot of lavender. I see gardeners posting as though nothing is happening and it enrages me. Institutions and individuals, I watch them as they carry on regardless, posting pictures of flowers and vegetables, continuing as though there isn't an overdue conversation happening now about the right of Black people to exist in peace. Either they're not paying attention or they don't give a damn. Either way, I am furious.

Would it really have been that hard to quieten down for a couple of days? It's as if they don't realise that someone like me exists. It's as though they haven't considered the possibility that there are Black people who are part of the horticultural community who can see that they haven't stopped talking. I accept that there will be people who think this moment is irrelevant to them and, as painful as it is, I know that some don't agree that Black lives matter at all. But I wasn't prepared for this level of disregard amongst the horticultural community, which so often presents itself as compassionate and caring. I know that my anger comes from envy. I'd do anything to not feel this way. To have the option to turn away because racism doesn't affect me, and not mind the images because indifference to racism doesn't wound me. That feeling is starting to simmer in me again – the same thing I felt a few days ago. It's the feeling that prompted me to write and to share my words. But I pause and let it move through me. I'll wait. I don't want to use up what little energy I have left.

*

Today there are more thoughtless posts. Pictures of green-houses, pea pods, seedlings and asparagus pressed against grinning faces with requisite banal captions and hashtags. Primulas, rhododendrons. . . oh and a hastily posted video featuring a Black gardener posted by the same organisation that hastily emailed me yesterday to be interviewed for their podcast. They're trying to inject a dose of emergency diversity. I thank them for getting in touch and ask: 'Would you be open to organising a recorded conversation for your podcast between me and a member of the senior management to explore issues around representation, inclusion and accessibility in horticulture, and to discuss what is being done to address your organisation's shortcomings in this regard? If so, I would be open to participating at a point when I've had sufficient time to rest and heal from what is a very challenging and upsetting time for Black people everywhere.'

A polite response that doesn't use the word 'no', but absolutely is a no, arrives in my inbox in less than an hour. I'm tired. I can feel the frustration gathering in my belly, burning a path up to my chest and, like the first outpouring, I see the words materialising in my mind's eye. The words before came from a place of sadness, but today I'm angry. There's more that I need to say:

This morning I tapped into a little rage and gave the unfollow button a little workout.

I don't think that everyone does (or should) feel equipped to speak up at this time. Not everyone feels able to articulate their distress, or solidarity, or plans to decolonise their mind, heart and actions. That I'm ok with.

It's all the people who thought it was just fine to keep posting their trite grow-your-own bs with no reference to the fact that some of us are trying to reckon with the repercussions of centuries of racism and white supremacy.

So to them I say: Fuck your fucking french beans. If you don't know what to say, the option to pipe down is always available to you.

I send these words into the social media bubble and let them burn there. For the most part, they are surprisingly well received. Of course there are a few people who don't appreciate the feedback, and I watch my follower-count tick downwards as I read the vexed messages that appear, uninvited, to tell me I'm wrong, or rude, or too angry. They tell me that I have no right to tell them what they can and can't do – as though that were even possible. They tell me how I'm supposed to feel, and suggest more acceptable and palatable ways of expressing myself. And some people simply don't like seeing the word 'fuck'. I consider taking a moment to respond, but I don't want to waste my breath now that I've got so little to spare. I go back to scrolling, despite the fatigue that is settling into my brain. Switching from the news to Instagram, then texting and then back again, until I can no longer keep my eyes open. I sleep restlessly and have nightmares that I've seen before and know well. I don't get enough rest to recover for when I wake up the next day, pick up my phone and live the same day all over again.

Every weekend Sam walks to the village shop to pick up a newspaper for an elderly neighbour. He's been doing it since the start of the pandemic, to take the risk on their behalf. It's taken him longer than usual today because he ran into another neighbour on his way and they stopped to talk about the protests. I'm glad I didn't go with him. I am in no mood to talk to someone who says he 'understands their grievance', but keeps describing the protests as riots and the protesters as looters. I'm glad that Sam was the one who had that conversation, so I didn't have to, and that he has the confidence to explain how that narrative is designed to distract from and undermine the very reason people are marching in the first place. I'm not marching, though. I'm too nervous to go to London and I haven't had word of any protests going on nearby. So I just stay sitting in the shade by the ferns, watching online videos of people gathering with signs and banners in cities across the country. I watch as a group of people in Bristol push a statue of the slave trader Edward Colston into Bristol harbour. It feels like something is shifting.

'Are you growing parsley, Claire?' a voice calls from the field at the end of the garden.

The question snaps me out of the trance I'm in. 'I am, Anne, would you like some?'

What Anne actually wants is advice on how to grow parsley because hers isn't doing so well, and she asks me for a blow-by-blow, seed-to-harvest description of how I get my plants to grow. The request is pleasingly mundane, and I enjoy offering her a little guidance. It's a change from talking about the pandemic or race. Most of our conversations are like this one, over the rabbit-proof fence as Anne pauses for a moment while walking her dog. If she's not asking me what bread recipe I use, or how to find something on the internet, she's mostly talking about her plants. Her garden is a wilful chaos, grown for her enjoyment, but mostly for the benefit of wildlife. She lets the trees and shrubs grow high and unwieldy, and it means that bullfinches and goldcrests visit often, but the shade they cast means the sweet peas and tomatoes that she's trying to grow struggle to get the sunlight they need. This is likely the reason her parsley won't grow.

'You don't transplant it, though, do you?' Anne asks, sounding serious.

And I assure her that I do, as I do with all the seeds I sow in spring. I place a small cluster of parsley seeds in a module filled with seed compost, and keep them watered and protected until they sprout and grow a number of true leaves. And then, yes, I do the unthinkable! I transplant them into the ground to stretch their legs into the soil below.

'I don't transplant parsley, I just put seeds where I want them and leave them to grow on their own, because my mother used to say that if you transplant parsley then there'd surely be a death in the family,' Anne goes on.

Well, this is news to me. Especially as this is my fifth year in a row of successfully following the same approach and, lucky for me, it hasn't killed anyone I love yet.

She goes on to tell me some other parsley-based beliefs. Like if a garden has an impressive lot of parsley growing, then the 'woman of the house is to be obeyed'; or how you're giving away your good luck if you share your parsley harvest. Nonetheless, I go and pick her a bunch and hand her the bouquet over the fence with my fully outstretched arm. She thanks me and asks how I'm doing, and I almost tell her, but think better of trying to explain what's been going on. She watches the news and pays attention, but she doesn't live her life on the internet. I don't know if she'll get it, if I describe the last week or so, and I haven't got the energy to explain. Plus she's in her late seventies, so I'm not sure she'll have the energy for an honest answer anyway. So instead I reply with, 'Oh, I'm fine,' and go back to my spot in the shade, feeling envious of anyone with a quiet life, no presence on the internet and perennially protected by their whiteness.

Sam walks into the room with a smile in his eyes. He's made something for me while I've been staring at my phone. It's a painting. Leaves and streaks in all shades of green and in solid black capital letters, in his distinct style, are the words, 'Black Lives Matter' and, beneath that, 'Fuck Your Fucking French Beans'. I burst out laughing. It's beautiful and sincere and hilarious and a gesture that is unmistakably him. A way of showing that he's supportive while dealing with how helpless he feels, watching me thrashing about online for the last week and a half. I want to keep the painting for myself, but I show it to a friend who thinks there will be people who'll like it, and Sam's up for painting ten of the same, so we decide to give each one away for a donation to charity. It means putting my head above the parapet again and the thought of doing so is taxing, but if there's a chance we can turn these last tumultuous days, this anger and sorrow, into something generative, then I think I can manage one more go around the block.

The photo I share is of the painting nestled between the marjoram and a sedum. I put my phone on silent, hit 'share' and then walk away, worrying that this might be a huge mistake. Indirectly but openly criticising the horticultural industry, through the medium of a painting that swears, will not be a message everyone wants to hear. It will live on the internet for ever and may well be the reason I don't get hired for one thing or another. But it's angry because I'm angry, and it's true because I am, at last, being truthful, so I let it have a life of its own and resign myself to taking what comes, as best I can. By the time I pick up my phone again, the image is pinballing around. The likes and comments and messages light up the screen and I can't keep up. The ten paintings that we offered have been claimed, and then some. The requests keep coming. I call to Sam to come and sit with me, so we can watch this thing come alive. It looks like he'll be painting a few more than ten. Like most of what I've shared lately, the reception is a mixed one. Some of the comments are angry and nasty, but I'm not above blocking people to maintain my sanity. I try to focus and figure out how many paintings I can ask Sam to paint before he leaves me. One day later and we've raised £2,234 and

Sam's got fifty paintings to paint, and I'm feeling a little less wretched for the first time in a while.

I make dal using channa, like my dad does, trying to remember the recipe he once described down the phone to me. It was that time, a few years ago, when I was missing him and his cooking and needed dal to ease my agacement. Garlic, ginger, turmeric and chilli. A tomato, I think. I chop slowly, keep the fire low and let the simmer rise gradually. I stir in slow motion, watching it bubble and steam, letting the process take up more space than is necessary. This time has not been my own. This time has been a hijack. Of my thoughts, my emotions, my body and my brain. I can't settle. I'm contracted and hypervigilant. Outside what I've chosen to share and create, and the support and conflict it's garnered, most of this experience is something I did not fully consent to. We're being held in place by a pandemic, living our now-smaller lives through the screens of our smartphones and computers. People watched – or avoided – that damn video, and the howls of collective sorrow have been echoing around the globe ever since. People are marching and demanding change in all the spaces where Black people exist. They are demanding justice and will keep demanding it because, as painful and draining as this has all been, it's felt deeply necessary, too.

Still, it's a fight I'd rather not have. It is confirmation that, as Black people, we can be drafted into battle at any moment. Our lives will never be wholly our own. We can try to tell ourselves that our existence is one defined by self-determination, and then a Black woman is killed in the night by policemen shooting carelessly into her home, and a part of us dies inside, too. Then the next day we have to figure out how to resist the lure of despair and keep going. We endure the fury of those who think we're complaining about nothing and have no reason to protest, no grounds to demand better in the present, or redress for the injustices of history that live on in us. Their disdain, their words, move through me like bolts of electricity. My nervous system is hyperactive, my heart pounding so loud that the noise, the throb fills my skull. Each time a tremor of sadness or horror or rage moves through me, it trembles my insides and a little of me disappears. I'm becoming dull. Worn away, worn thin. I'm disintegrating and turning to dust.

What becomes of us when we are trapped in a cycle of defending our humanity? Will there be anything left in the end? Will we always be defined by our racial identities or measured against the yardstick of whiteness? Will we ever be allowed to exist outside these racial constructions? And should we even want to? I have fought my way back to myself after a childhood, a young adulthood, of rejecting who I am. My racial identity is something that I, at last, hold with pride, so to question it now would feel like an undoing. Nonetheless, I want to know what would be possible in a life lived outside it. What might I want to say? What might I write or create? And what parts of me will never see the sun, will never flourish or bloom? What am I missing because I'm being distracted and drained by the battles for my right to be considered – and to consider myself – a whole human being?

And yet I would never give it up. If you'd asked me as a child, my answer would have been different, but now I hold my Blackness – our Blackness – close to my chest and I will defend it with all that I have. This sense of the collective, vast and varied as it is, feels deep and profound and alive. It is forged between those of us who are thrust towards each other through the marginalisations that we experience. While prejudice seeks to coerce us into a fallacy of homogeneity, we know better than to believe that falsehood. Our Blackness is expansive and beautiful and manifold, and it binds us to each other with a depth that means that to bear witness to Black pain and Black trauma is to feel it in our bodies, too. Knowing this gives me a way of understanding why events across an ocean feel as though they happened on my doorstep. And it gives me a way of understanding why this time has left me feeling ravaged. My body is weary. Not solely from the pain of these last few weeks, but from the trauma it has dragged to the surface. Watching the protests and the debates, reading the news and the opinion pieces and the tweets and posts, it forces me to relive the racism and prejudice that I'd really rather forget.

I'm sitting at the bottom of the stairs, listening to Sam's voice through the wall. He's speaking to his grandad, whose ninety-first birthday is coming up in a couple of weeks. Sam's been video-calling him more often since the pandemic has kept the whole family from visiting. I can't bring myself to talk. I'm too tired. And when Sam tells him how distressed I am, his grandad says, 'I can't believe this is still an issue.' For someone who has lived through the Second World War, witnessed the apparent dismantling of the British Empire and felt the whiplash of seeing Nelson Mandela painted as a terrorist in one moment and as a peacemaker in the next, he's borne witness to how often societies, governments and individuals persist in acting on their prejudices. I hope that if I live to my nineties I'll have something more encouraging to say than 'I can't believe this is still an issue.'

This strange time has taken me away from the garden, away from the big and little changes happening outside. The plants have been growing while I've been lost in the internet, and I'm certain I've missed a lot. Flowers that have bloomed and already faded, new tendrils searching for and finding something sturdy to climb. I let the chickens wander out of their pen and into the garden for the first time, hovering nearby to keep watch. They know the sound of corn kernels rattling in a yoghurt pot, so I know I can persuade them to come back if they wander off a little too far. They seem happy to be free, following each other around to scratch at the grass and peck the ants that run along the low brick wall. I lie by the shadiest bed, at eye level with bright-pink geraniums, petals curling back in the heat, stigmas jutting out. We've let the grass grow long and it's peppered with butter-yellow ranunculus and wrinkly-leafed plantains in flower. The sun is climbing and so is the temperature. I stare at the page of the book I'm trying to read, but the heat makes the words swirl. A tiny seed, jet black and round, drops onto the page I'm not reading and rolls into the spine, propelled from a ripe geranium seedhead. I throw it back towards where it came from, in the hope that it will find a welcoming patch of earth to germinate in. This is all the gardening I have the energy for today. I chase the shade, shuffling to keep my head cool, leaving my feet to catch the sun. The chickens do the same, huddling in a row under the tree that was the last to come into leaf. It is covered in little buds, but nothing has bloomed yet. My mum thinks it is a hibiscus but I'm not so sure. I've not seen a hibiscus growing here, but I remember seeing them in Mauritius. Could a flower that I've only seen growing near the equator be flourishing in East Sussex?

Sam's been getting on with the painting. He's finished twenty-four already, nearly halfway through. Every surface of his studio is covered in paintings of curse-words over brushmarks in green. He needs a break from the paint fumes and the repetition, so we pack up some lunch and head down to the sea. He wants to put his feet in the water. Hopefully it will be cooler down there. We turn in the direction of our favourite spot, snaking through quiet country lanes and hoping it won't be too busy when we arrive. My phone beeps and it's my friend who lives in New York. We've been leaning on each other like we used to when we lived in the same city, because these last weeks have been shit for her, too. She wants to talk, so I call once I've taken off my sandals and pushed my toes through the hot pebbles and found my way to the cooler ones below.

We don't ask each other how it's going, because we already know. She tells me about work and people and friendships, all going sideways – mostly necessarily – because everyone's talking about race. We speculate together about why George Floyd's

death is hitting people so differently from all the other times a
call to the police has ended the same way. Maybe it's the existence of the brutal video that lasts for nine whole minutes, or
how many millions of people around the world have watched it,
or how he used the last of his earthly breaths to call out for his
mother. That's what we've heard. Neither of us has watched it.
Couldn't bear to. Bearing witness, albeit it indirectly, to this one
death would mean reliving all the others, and a reminder of our
vulnerability – and of our relative value – compared to our white
friends. We talk about all the statements being released by companies and brands, and whether any of it really means anything.
We talk about whether change is even possible, and whether
those with power will even allow it. And we talk about how battered and hurt we both feel, and whether her mental health or
mine can withstand what lies ahead. This time presented an
unexpected opportunity for me to speak truthfully about race in
a way that I hadn't felt able to before. And for better or worse, I
spoke up, and it has caused a deep unravelling of the wounds
I've long tried to keep hidden from view.

Beads of sweat gather along my hairline. I pull my shirt over
my head and lie back on the stones. She sounds far away, but her
words and her anguish feel close. They're familiar, and she sounds
exhausted. I ask her if she's sleeping enough, but I know she
hasn't been. We're similar in that way. By the time I put the phone
down, I've been out in the heat too long. My head is swimming
from the noontime sun, and from the thought of all the conversations that are happening between Black friends and in Black
families right now and over this last fortnight, full of distress and

trauma – new and old – wasting our time and our precious energy. I track my eyes along the shoreline, looking for the outline of Sam. He's dragging his feet through the surf at the water's edge. I watch him slopping around until he's wearing socks made of khaki-coloured sand, while the sun glimmers off the sea.

The first suggestion of yellow courgettes appears on the day my nephew is born. I sowed and planted them for his mother because she once told me how she liked them more than the green ones. I sowed a few extra seeds, with the plan to give her a strong seedling to watch grow as she waited for her child to arrive, but we haven't seen her or my brother since the start of the year, so I made space for those plants to grow here. We missed the pregnancy entirely, only waving to her growing belly on video calls. And now he's here – quite suddenly, it seems – changing the nexus of our family's little world.

It must take a great leap of faith to become a parent. Especially at a time when the signs that the climate and ecological crisis is reshaping the planet are undeniable. I am already gripped by terror at what the future might hold when I consider which parts of Mauritius, or of the nearby beaches I've come to love, or the areas of London I once lived in, will disappear under water as the sea levels rise. I wonder if, when my nephew is old enough to pick garden peas by my side, there will still be tortoiseshell butterflies flying past and willow tits singing overhead. I wonder if he'll be angry at us all for not doing more to address our role in the changing climate while we still could have. And I wonder, too, if he'll feel Mauritian and will want that sense of identity to be part of who he is, or whether he'll lean more into his Englishness and let our heritage slip away.

I know it disappoints my parents that motherhood is not a journey I feel called to embark on. While they're too kind to pressure me into something I don't want, it aches not to feel capable of giving them that particular gift. Even if my heart yearned for a child of my own, I doubt my anxiety about the planet would allow me enough peace to become a parent. Still, having children is not the only way to create life. I grow it out of the earth. I show those I love what they mean to me by placing food that I've grown from seed on their plates.

Days later I pick a fully grown yellow courgette to take as a gift for our first visit. Outside my brother's house I touch my nose to the window as they stand on the other side, holding up my nephew's tiny, clenched body for us to see. I wave and coo at his crumpled little face and tightly held fists. He looks just like my dad. His namesake. I try to catch a glimpse of his jet-black eyes as he pries them open for a moment against the warm summer light. He's beautiful and I am overcome with new love. He's divine and worth trying to make the world a more hopeful place for. He's not mine, but he feels like a part of me, and in these first moments I know I'll do anything I can so that he has a good life. I watch him gently squirm in my brother's proud embrace until it's time for his next feed. I wonder when I'll get to see him again and if, next time, there will have to be glass between us still. I wonder if by then I'll be able to hold him for the first time. And I wonder if, when he's old enough, I'll tell him about the summer he was born.

CHAPTER 11

I harvest daily. Pulling dark-red and golden beetroot from the ground, brushing off the soil that clings to them. Snapping thick, wrinkly cavolo nero leaves and twisting free the courgettes that grow fatter by the hour. I pinch the tips off the sweet basil and pull up a handful or two of pungent spring onions. The kohlrabi swell to a dusky purple, rotund and teetering on a thin, woody stalk. Trusses of tomatoes wearing tiger-stripes ripen from bright green to deep red and warm yellow. The air smells deeply and sweetly of jasmine, and the marjoram and sedum flowering side-by-side call the furrow bees and marmalade hoverflies to forage. Every couple of days we venture out to buy sweet cherries and fat strawberries grown in Kent from a stall in a lay-by close to the house, and eat so many that our fingers and lips turn red.

A week ago Sam and my dad put up a greenhouse in the place where the rotten shed had been, before we smashed it to pieces. The weather was breathtaking. The closeness and humidity reminded me of Baie du Tombeau, where my mum's side of the family lives. The microclimate there makes the unmoving air feel heavy and sultry on the hottest days.

At a distance, they worked together while wearing sweaty masks that rubbed marks across their noses. I chose the cheapest greenhouse option and the wooden pieces arrived unlabelled and so, through the heat, the task became exasperating. I spent the day keeping their cups filled with iced water, when I wasn't weeding the docks and creeping buttercup in the sun. My mum, keeping her distance too, did the same in the shade of the cherry tree, finding some coolness in what little breeze there was. Ordinarily we're deeply and, sometimes, unthinkingly honest with each other, but we didn't talk much about what had happened through June. I couldn't find the words to describe how all these conversations about race have been unfolding for me, and I think she knew that I didn't want to be asked.

Sam built planters for the greenhouse out of scraps of wood and, on a cloudy day, we wheelbarrowed the last of the compost up through the garden and filled them. I plant the remaining tomatoes – three varieties, two cordon and one bush – and cucumber plants into them, in the hope that they'll keep the summer going a little longer when the nights start to cool. I tuck the one bitter melon that germinated and grew into the corner by the door. I suspect there won't be enough of the summer left for it. As I'm planting out a second round of climbing beans while munching on some pickings from the first, I let the chickens plop down the step and into the vegetable patch with me. I keep one eye on the task and the other eye on them, and whether they're pecking at the worms that appear where I've disturbed the soil or are stripping the chard leaves down to their midribs. My third eye I keep, as I've done since they arrived, on the lookout for passing predators. The early springtime memory of a rusty-red fox and her two cubs frolicking in the frosted back field is never far from my mind.

During these difficult weeks the chickens have been a balm. They arrived in my life at a time when it was deeply helpful to have something to take care of and get to know. They gave my heart something to do other than ache. In this short time their feathers have become a shade darker and more vibrant, their bodies rounder and more substantial. And I'm getting better at recognising their different voices. Each one makes her own distinct noise and so, more often than not, I know who is calling out for attention or demanding that I feed them the redcurrants they can't reach. I watch them bask in the sun, splaying their speckled wings out to get the best of it, relaxing their chubby little bodies that spread out like tyres deflating; and I watch as they chase flies and snatch them out of the air with their beaks, and I plead with them not to do the same to the butterflies because, for some reason, it feels more tragic.

Alan is acting strangely today. Stomping around, stretching her neck to yell at the others and then coming through the back door to yell at us, too. She's been knocking things over, climbing into boxes and squeezing herself into any small space she can find. Once she's got our attention, she suddenly runs towards the henhouse, flapping off in a panic. While the other hens peck the bugs off the decking, Alan continues with her irate and relentless protest. I think she's trying to find something, but I just can't figure out what. By the late afternoon the sun drops behind the house and the garden starts to cool off. Alan has quietened down and is next to the greenhouse, fervently scratching at the pot of camomile that I was trying to grow there. And by the back door she's left us a surprise. Her first little egg – half the size of a regular one – laying on the ground for me to find. It's a very odd thing, living with birds.

When asked what they know of Mauritius, people usually speak of sandy beaches and the clear blue sea, expensive flights or honeymoon plans. If you get your holiday advice from the *Daily Telegraph*'s travel section you might be tempted to seek out the 'reassuring remnants of the British Colonial era' that, it believes, you can find on a trip to the island. If not, then almost invariably people will name the only other thing commonly associated with the country – the dodo. The story is so well known that it almost doesn't bear repeating. This flightless bird, native only to Mauritius, was extinct within a matter of decades of the arrival of the island's first colonisers, the Dutch. The way the dodo's story is told paints the bird as a halfwit, so accustomed to a life without the threat of predators that it failed to flee from those who sought to devour it. Almost turkey-like in shape, but larger at around a metre tall and twenty kilos in weight when fully grown, the dodo had little wings and short legs, and a large beak that sloped towards a bulbous end. Some historical records show that certain

Dutchmen ate dodo meat reluctantly and rarely, finding the taste and the texture quite disgusting and calling them 'Walgh-voghel', which loosely translates as 'tasteless' or 'insipid bird'. Other records contradict this story of their unpalatability and describe how Dutchmen hunted and ate them daily. The creatures that came along on those Dutch ships – the rats, and then the cats and dogs brought to control the rats, and the pigs that soon escaped and became feral – also hunted the dodo, its eggs and its chicks, while other introduced species competed with them for food. Alongside the arrival of predators and competitors, it was the decimation of the rich habitat upon which the dodo relied that caused its eventual extinction.

The story that is told about the dodo is one of a humiliating demise, the inevitable upshot of their innate stupidity rather than a tragic tale of a bird that might still exist, had it not encountered colonisers at all. Whether through naivety or physical incapability, a gentle nature or not swift enough instincts, these birds were not destined to survive the colonisation of their home. The peaceful life they led until the arrival of Europeans left them ill equipped to defend themselves against those whose actions would lead to their total obliteration. A sad story, whatever way you look at it, and a cautionary tale, if humanity had only learned from it.

Colonialism was (and is) an ecological disaster. The vast sugarcane fields, historically grown as a monocrop, that still dominate the agricultural landscape of Mauritius are a testament to that. Yet, the dodo – the island's most famous victim – has become one of the most recognisable symbols of Mauritius. Depictions of the dodo are quite literally everywhere: on beach towels and key-rings, on shop signs and postcards, as fridge magnets and souvenirs, and painted onto the hulls of fishing boats. Its outline can be found on the rainbow of the national flag, the country's coat of arms, and is stamped in your passport as you pass through immigration. I find it baffling that the image of this now-extinct bird, with its embarrassing reputation and calamitous story, has become synonymous with, and ubiquitous in, the land of my family. I can't fathom celebrating it, let alone centralising it in the imagery that identifies the island. Turning the dodo into a brightly coloured character removes it from the historical context that led to its annihilation, and reframes its extinction as a funny mishap, erasing the truth that it was an extermination. It's a story that, to me, foretells the decimation the island would go on to endure over the centuries that followed. It is a story that exemplifies the degradation of the natural world and the unbalancing of ecosystems that was (and is) one of the many side-effects of colonialism. It is a story that has made a cartoonish mascot out of a tragic tale of the price paid by one (of the many) species that suffered due to the boundless self-interest of colonialists and their relentless hunger for the accumulation of wealth. It papers over one of the most visible examples of how ecological devastation was (and still is) both a tool and consequence of colonial rampage, as were (and are) the eroded soils, denuded forests, extinct species, decimated habitats, disfigured landscapes and altered weather systems.

There are only a few remains of the dodo still in existence. Oxford University Museum of Natural History has a dodo head and foot in its collection, and the British Museum in London was once in possession of a dodo foot, but it went missing around 1900, while an almost-complete skeleton was sold by an auction house in West Sussex for £280,000 in 2016. I search for what is left of the dodo and who possesses it, because it feels wrong to me that any remains are kept outside Mauritius today. In fact the Mauritian government has made the export of dodo remains illegal. I find the story of a naturalist whose fascination with the extinct bird inspired him to collect paintings, souvenirs, knick-knacks and carvings of the dodo and fill his home with them. It all started when his father, an ornithologist, left two dodo bones to him when he died and, from then on, this man became obsessed with the bird. When I stand on my front-door step and look towards the horizon, where I've been watching the sun set for the last ten months, I face the direction of his house. The Dodo House – as he named it – is on the other side of the woods, about four miles away. I want to ask him whether he still has the bones or whether he's had the good sense to send them back to Mauritius. I find his email address and send him a message to introduce myself, but it bounces back, unsent.

*

Suikerriet. Canne à sucre. Sugarcane. Karo kann.

It was brought to the island from Java by the Dutch in 1639, but it was the French governor, Mahé de La Bourdonnais, who would encourage the commercial development of the crop almost a century later. Yet it did not become the principal driving force behind the plantation economy in Mauritius until the early nineteenth century when the British took possession of the island from the French. Well suited to the subtropical climate of the island, its thick canes bend under the force of the wind during cyclone season but, unlike other crops, they recover when the sun and calm return. The work of cutting and cleaning the cane, and the spine-contorting toil of carrying full baskets to the ox-carts that pulled the harvest to the mills, was the labour of 90 per cent of the island's population – almost all of whom were enslaved. The hugely productive plantations led to a rapid economic expansion, which in turn caused many slave owners to rename their captives, attempting to organise them by giving them new, simplistic (and sometimes offensive) names and surnames, further removing them from a connection to their past.

Under the British, sugar was mostly grown and produced on plantations that were still owned by French colonists, located in the north of the island where the land was more productive. The plantation owners would then export the lion's share of the crop to London. Anticipating the abolition of slavery, Mauritius was the first of Britain's colonies to experiment in indentureship – the 'Great Experiment', as it came to be known – with thirty-six Indians of the Dhangar caste who arrived on the island in 1834 as indentured labourers. They were sent to a plantation in the north-east of the island to work alongside the 200 enslaved still toiling there.

Slavery was abolished on 1 February 1835, at which point

Mauritius was one of the largest slave colonies in the British Empire and was notorious for its extraordinary cruelty. Nonetheless, the slave owners were richly compensated for their 'loss', and the now-emancipated were forced to continue to work for a period of 'apprenticeship' while indentured labourers were imported to replace them. Also called 'girmitiyas' or 'coolies' (now considered an offensive term), indentured labourers were brought to Mauritius as free men and women who signed contracts for five or six years and received a wage, huts in which to live en masse, and medical care if there was a hospital close enough by. Unlike the enslaved, groups were often recruited from certain villages simultaneously, enabling them to maintain a sense of identity and community when they landed.

They withstood a ten-week journey from their homeland across the Indian Ocean and, despite the terrible living and working conditions that met them when they arrived, found ways to build lives of their own. They practised the religions they'd brought with them, praying to their gods, celebrating festivals and laying offerings on altars made of stone. They cooked the food that raised them, the farata and lentils and rice, and spoke the languages of their homeland – Hindi, Urdu, Tamil or Telegu – while learning Kreol Morisyen from their new countrymen. With time, they gained their freedom from indentureship, and those who chose to stay in Mauritius rather than return to India took what money they had saved and established themselves as landowners and planters – and became the largest ethnic denomination on the island.

By 1920 half a million indentured immigrants had arrived in Mauritius, most of them working in the sugarcane fields, which by then covered almost 80 per cent of cultivatable land. Under the British, as with the other colonisers before them, the area of land that was deforested and exploited for the establishment of plantations rose, and kept on rising. Each plantation was established on soil that had once been dense and verdant forest. Unique and robust ecosystems were cleared and transformed into an economy based on a monoculture. The plantation system devastated the habitats of the animal and plant life, while steadily eroding and depleting the island's once-fertile, volcanic soil.

*

I have a list on my phone of all the places we planned to visit and all the things we hoped to see when we moved towards the south coast, but in the last five months of lockdown we haven't ventured much beyond the five miles between us and the sea. Today we're heading out, with a rucksack full of food and a bottle of sun-cream, to visit the gardens at West Dean. It's a good day for an adventure, sunny and pleasing, but the journey takes two muggy, sweaty hours. We cross from East Sussex into West Sussex with the car windows down, feeling absurdly excited and somewhat unnerved to be stepping out of the shrunken life we've been living within.

Today the gardens aren't as they 'ought' to be. The lockdown caused operations to shut down for a number of crucial weeks over spring, and hard decisions were made about what to grow and what plans to abandon. It can't have been easy, and yet the gardens still look wonderful. A purple-blue display of salvias and eryngium framed by clematis clambering across a trellis. Soft blushes of astrantia; an arch of trained pear trees; the pergola dripping with climbing roses, jasmine and grape-vines. If I didn't know any different, I would assume that the bindweed flowers cascading over the bear's breeches are meant to be there. It isn't perfect, and I'm grateful for that. It shouldn't be. The disarray is honest and reassuring. What use is the pre-tence of normality in the midst of turbulent times?

Formal gardens like this one interest me. Despite what I know about plants, I find the presentation and execution of this level of botanical performance intriguing. It is an art form, a tableau painted in blooming flower and foliage, a kind of choreography. It's a dance akin to growing food. You come to know the plants, their wants and needs, watch the weather and, as best you can, curate the conditions for their thriving. But the desired outcome is principally beauty, which is where I find myself losing interest. The performance and grandiosity speak of a time gone by, but do not speak to me. It feels to me a manifestation of an idealised Englishness that embodies restraint but also dominion, of seeking to control – especially over the unruliness of the natural world. I find the formality, the exactitude, the perfectionism, the opulence quite beauti-ful, but somehow it fails to enchant me.

Traditional gardens don't affect me in the way that market gardens do. My heart belongs to edible plants. The purpose of growing food is more obvious, of course, and the harvesting and eating feel like the completion of a cycle. For me, the natural crescendo of journeying lovingly with plants is finally getting to put them in your mouth. I also happen to believe that edible plants are just as beautiful as ornamental ones. The fuchsia midrib of rhubarb chard is as glorious as the most perfect pink camellia, in my eyes. And then you get to eat it, which is the most captivating thing I can think of.

I was a teenager, maybe thirteen or fourteen, when my parents first took me to Pamplemousses Botanical Garden in Mauritius. It was named after the village nearby, where the grapefruit trees – imported from Java by the Dutch – still grow. Now it also bears the name of Sir Seewoosagur Ramgoolam, the first Prime Minister of Mauritius after the country gained independence from Britain in 1968. I remember the famous pond of giant water lilies, *Victoria amazonica*, 'discovered' by Robert Schomburgk in Guyana (then British Guiana) and (re) named by botanist John Lindley in honour of Queen Victoria. Enormous round, reptilian lily pads turned up at the edges like serving trays, looking sturdy enough to take the weight of a person. The sacred banyan trees with vines dropping from their branches and touching the ground, before rooting down and weaving around to become part of an expansive trunk. The day was characteristically hot and humid, and we got caught in a rain shower so heavy that we had to take shelter under umbrella-sized leaves – from a type of monstera, possibly – clasping them over our heads and screaming with laughter. Fat plops of tropical rain splashed on the ground and filled my sandals with warm water. And later that day, to cool off, we drank the sweet, fresh water straight out of coconuts cracked open by the side of the road.

If you only read the tourist literature, you'd be forgiven for thinking that Pamplemousses started as a humble garden created by Mahé de La Bourdonnais to grow fruit and vegetables for his household. Rarely are the workers – whose labour built the place, who sowed the seeds and who ensured there was a harvest to gather – mentioned. Left out are the details about how the garden was a colonial tool, used as a nursery in which plants that could be utilised for profit were grown and acclimatised. Like the manioc – native to South America and able to grow abundantly in parched earth – which was introduced by La Bourdonnais to be grown as a cheap and nutritious foodstuff to keep the enslaved population (and livestock) from starvation while they built the country's infrastructure and laboured on its land. Blessed with the island's generous climate, La Bourdonnais would have been provided with bushels of produce grown using the skill and knowledge of those he considered insufficiently human to share it with.

A few decades later the garden was transformed into a more formal botanical garden by a French botanist named Pierre Poivre – the Peter Piper who picked a peck of pickled peppers in the nursery rhyme. After a number of years engaging in spice espionage, in an attempt to undermine Dutch dominion of the trade, Poivre became General Intendant of Mauritius. He oversaw the collection and propagation of the plants that grew at Pamplemousses, including a great number of stolen specimens of commercial interest, such as nutmeg, cinnamon, pepper and cloves, which he wanted to introduce into the economy of the island. Poivre has been hailed as one of the first conservationists, as he put forward a theory that deforestation was connected to changes in rainfall, and attempted to institute regulation and legislation to protect the environment and prevent soil erosion. And yet he was also responsible for the introduction of more than 600 plants to Mauritius, which has undoubtedly led to environmental repercussions that persist to this day.

Plants were 'hunted for' and 'discovered', and then moved around the world, from coast to colony, and weaponised for their most profitable qualities. The crops that were found to prosper as commodities – cotton, sugar and tobacco – were shipped from one colonised territory to another and used as instruments of subjugation, extraction and capitalisation. As serviceable as the whip or the brand, these plants became the tools of colonialism and enslavement. On decimated land, crops were grown as monocultures and turned into exportable products to line the pockets of the British, Dutch, French, German, Portuguese, Spanish and (new) Americans with outlandish riches. That money built those countries into what they are today. No part of what they have accomplished since would have been possible without this bloody institution.

Like most botanical gardens, Pamplemousses is presented as a tourist attraction, and I thought it was that and not much more. Beautiful, ornamental and benign. When it came to visiting Kew Gardens for the first time – only a few years ago – my understanding of these spaces hadn't deepened much. The beauty of botanical gardens, the diversity of plant life and even the scholarship that developed from those places do little to convey the environmental pillage and destruction that are integral to their story. And all the way through to their positioning as places of rational science and into their reimagining as spaces of leisure, they did little to depict the blood and the toil that nurtured and stained the soil in order for them to exist. These grand places filled with exquisite flowers and lush foliage, framed by ancient trees and housing rare plants from all over the world, were the tools of empire and, despite the historical obfuscation of this truth, they stand now as living monuments to both the environmental and human exploitation that was foundational to colonialism. There is no part of the history (and, thus, of the present) of botanical gardens that arose independent of their role in enabling the rampage of colonial endeavour.

Even now, looking out at my garden, I see colonialism's heirlooms growing in every corner. These plants from all over the world were once incubated and acclimatised in the nursery beds and greenhouses of the empire's gardens. Those considered beautiful and capable of thriving in the less welcoming British weather were ushered into horticulture and, depending on the prevailing fashions, have persisted to populate British gardens to this day: the gangly cotoneaster and abundant, sweet thorny olive from China. Fragrant jasmine from the Himalayas. Seducer of bees, the hebe, from South America or New Zealand or Australia.

The narratives of these plants exist. Specimens of their

predecessors are pressed between paper and annotated in scratchy ink scrawls to tell us the wheres and whens of their first encounters with European eyes. We have some understanding of who they were when they grew in their homeland, and where that homeland happened to be. The names that their indigenous stewards called them before they were uprooted and displaced may have been erased, but enough information was documented to trace some of the lines between what grows now in English soil and who they were before their identities were rewritten. We can find our way to some of their origin stories and, if we choose, stop believing that roses and geraniums and periwinkles were 'discovered' by plant hunters and botanists from Europe.

Enslaved people were treated with less grace than the plants in our gardens. For so many of them, no records of names and homelands were kept. While I can ask the internet to show me digitised copies of plant specimens collected in the eighteenth century, there is no database I have found that enables me to follow the connections from who I am today back through bloodlines or family trees to tell me where my ancestors came from. East Africa maybe, Madagascar probably, or even as far away as Senegal. Provinces in India certainly, too, from Tamil Nadu and maybe Malabar. More recent migrations and unions persist in the echoes of names and stories held loosely in the fading memories of my illiterate grandparents. Yet all those who came before them remain lost to me. Where I look and hope to find them, there is only silence.

*

I'm up for the chickens, as is my duty, and I go to drag the hose to the end of the garden, as is my habit. This morning still holds some of the moisture from last night's rain, and the cucurbit bed looks especially resplendent with its glistening lily-pad-like leaves turning towards the early sun. Beneath these fleshy leaves, sitting proudly above the ground, are the fruit that have begun to fatten up. The squash – 'Hokkaido' and 'Fictor' – are growing happily, their vines crawling away from the stem, adorned with lantern-shaped gourds. The fruit closest to the stem are the largest, and the skin has started to darken from lemon-yellow towards pumpkin-orange. Tracing the voyage of the vine where it has crawled along the ground, I follow it along the bed, across the path and away. The further I get, the smaller the fruit become, and I tuck a handful of hay under each one to protect their undersides from rotting. Bumblebees buzz loudly nearby and while I'm certain they'll find the right flowers, in the right order, and do the good work of being reproductive conduits, I can't help but intervene to make sure. I look for an open flower on a slender stalk – the one that contains the dusty pollen – and gently scoop a little onto my fingertip. Then I find my way back to the youngest, smallest fruit with a blousy flower still attached and, less gently this time, rub the pollen on the stigma and hope that nature will take care of the rest.

The brassicas that I forgot to net against the cabbage whites are being steadily munched by their well-camouflaged caterpillar offspring, while the rocket and kale that the butterflies have ignored are peppered with holes made by flea beetles.

I chase the butterflies and they flutter away, leaving clusters of tiny yellow eggs on the underside of the purple-sprouting broccoli leaves for me to find. I pick off the caterpillars and, one by one, feed them, squirming, to the chickens. The chard, the lettuce and even the lowest beans are covered with holes and trails of slime where the slugs have feasted at night. They've slunk away into the long grass to rest up for now and will almost certainly reappear for more destruction, come nightfall. Dotted around the patch there are small hills of soft clay from burrowing moles who occasionally surface to unearth a crop or two. I'm grateful that there are worms and soil life enough to tempt them here, but am less charmed by the decimated plants and their disregard for my no-dig approach to growing.

The field beyond the patch has been left unmown and the grass has grown tall and full of wildflowers. It sends flutters of meadow brown, painted lady and brimstone butterflies over this way and I watch as they fly amongst the dandelion seeds that swirl on the breeze. A red damselfly lands on the fence, a grasshopper clings to the ridged edge of a cucumber leaf, a mining bee bombs towards the grass and disappears underground into its nest. Honeybees, solitary bees and marmalade hoverflies fly from tomato flower to orchid-like French bean flower to open-mouthed nasturtium. Overhead, two coal tits and a wren dart about, and a robin drops down from the willow to forage on the ground. I pause for a few moments to listen to the rumble of buzzing and humming and chirping. It is raucous and divine. I grow, in the hope that these creatures will join me here. The garden is their home as much as it is mine. Even those that I wish away (and occasionally relocate or feed to the chickens) have as much right to be here as I do. They are necessary and they tell me there is balance. And when there are losses, as there inevitably will be, I try to remember that losses for me often mean gains for the ecosystem. Less of an individual failure and more a contribution to the universal good. It means that my vegetable patch and my garden are far from pristine but it's my kind of perfect.

There are two courgettes ready to pick. Most days there are. Courgettes with every other meal at summer's peak is a grower's joy and their family's and neighbours' burden. Sam cobbled together a trellis from scraps of wood and old chicken wire, and the cucumbers have been clambering up it readily, with a little coaxing and gentle encouragement. I take the vines that are trailing along the ground and show them where to go, picking up each one carefully and weaving it through the wire, placing their tendrils to suggest where to grab on. Underneath the leaves now lifted away from the soil, I see that the first of the cucumbers I promised my dad has been pollinated and is starting to grow.

With a little lump in my throat, I do the other jobs on my mental list. Prune the side shoots on the tomatoes, then feed them from the smelly bucket of comfrey tea. Trim the grass edges around the squash beds with a large pair of scissors, where the strimmer can't reach. With a pocketful of little orange tomatoes, I place the courgettes in the cradle of my elbow and head back into the house, but the raucous buzz of a bumblebee catches my attention as I pass. It is thrashing about drunkenly, covered all over in pollen, face-down in the blood-red centre of a hibiscus flower. The first bloom to open on the tree that I'd been waiting to reveal itself since we arrived. Although I thought it impossible, my mum was right. This tropical flower can grow and blossom here.

The term most often used to describe a plant that comes from another country is 'non-native'. When it comes to the hibiscus, its exact origin is unknown, but it grows throughout the tropical and subtropical regions of the world, so although it is categorised as non-native, it's rarely described this way because it happens to behave as gardeners wish it to. Where the term 'non-native' is most often heard – whether in horticulture, agriculture or conservation – is when paired with the term 'invasive'. A term that describes a plant or creature that reproduces prolifically, is inclined to spread and proves hard to control. The two terms have become intertwined and the phrase is intended to cause alarm. Often enough there's a legitimate cause for concern, such as how Japanese knotweed can grow up through concrete or how giant hogweed can blister your skin. Both plants will grow rampantly if they're given half a chance.

To hear the words 'non-native' even when it is uncoupled from 'invasive' makes my stomach turn, but it is the unquestioned connection between these two terms that I've come to find troubling. If the concern is a plant's growth habit and the consequences of it spreading unbridled, why is it necessary to note that it is 'foreign'? What wisdom does that impart? What useful understanding does it confer? Is there something inher-ent to its 'foreignness' that causes it to behave differently? Why name their 'non-nativeness' at all, unless it is pertinent to the behaviour that you're trying to describe? Is it true that all non-native species present in this country are invasive? No, as evidenced by the hydrangeas, fuchsias, camellias, hyacinths, hellebores, gerberas and thousands of other species that all behave acceptably and are grown in the gardens of many. Not even English roses are English, as their ancestors would likely have been from Asia, and most probably would have been Chinese. And is it true that all invasive species are non-native? Also no. The bracken that romps through the English country-side is a problem all over the land, threatening to poison cattle and horses if they make the mistake of eating it. If you want a phrase to have utility, then surely it needs to have specificity, clarity and accuracy? To be careless with these words risks cre-ating a fallacious concept that feeds into a narrative of generalised disdain towards those believed to be 'other'. Many 'non-native' plants are of benefit to shifting ecosystems and in the context of the climate crisis, we may find that their pres-ence is necessary and welcome.

While a conservationist's concern is likely legitimate, the way these terms are used divorces the issue from its historical context. Most of the plants that refuse to behave as we want didn't come here of their own accord. They were not invaders or interlopers or parasites. They were hostages, stolen out of the earth by those who hunted for plants to bring back for profit, status or study. They were taken by those who viewed the world as a place of endless riches to be explored and exploited, and who took all they could when they arrived somewhere that, to them, was new. It's possible that some plants arrived here by chance – maybe a seed on the sole of a shoe or in the soil of another specimen – but it's more likely that they were brought here wilfully by someone with the kind of power and influence that can alter the course of history. I think it is worth bearing in mind that when you're cursing the Himalayan balsam's exploding seedpods, for example, you should probably be swearing at Dr John Forbes Royle, who brought the first specimen to the Royal Botanic Gardens at Kew in the late 1830s.

I know that there is virtue in making attempts to remediate the effect that certain species have had on the landscape, but I can't help but find that mindset troubling, too. It's impossible to know what unexpected repercussions our actions may have in our bid to undo the changes that have taken place. Or what possibilities we are laying to waste in our bids to turn back time. It seems that humans cannot help but believe that the remedy for historical human interfering is even more interfering. And to what point in the past are we trying to return, in these efforts to restore and 'rewild'? Surely we don't believe that there was a moment when 'nature' was pure and perfect and entirely untouched by humankind? And who gets to determine what type of landscape we should be trying to re-create and what gets to stay or who has to go? How long do plants have to be growing on this land to be considered native enough that they can remain? I have many questions about this endeavour that fetishises the native and seeks to reclaim the soil for their roots alone. Because I can't help but hear the arguments of the ecofascists who believe that 'foreigners' are a danger to their land. I can't help but shudder at the thought of the nationalist group that, just the other day, hiked up to the top of a hill in Derbyshire and unfurled a 'White Lives Matter' banner, and that recruits members with messages that equate nationalism with environmentalism, and believes that the decline of countryside is the fault of those who aren't white and English, describing us all as 'invasive'.

Plants and seeds, creatures and spores, they know nothing about the boundaries that humans create to carve up the world. They hop over borders every day and if they have travelled great distances and wrought havoc where they landed, it's likely because of the actions of certain humans, not because of their non-nativeness. The story of the non-native is incomplete if you only hear the term used when describing a problem. In the English landscape I am a non-native. Yet I happen to believe that my presence is of benefit to this place, no matter where my origins can be traced. (Not that I believe that only those of us deemed 'worthy' or 'beneficial' should be made to feel welcome either.) If we must use this term, let's use it every time we describe the many plants that are welcome and of benefit here, but happen to be from somewhere else. And if not, then let's dispense with the term altogether, because it doesn't serve its purpose well.

Whether you believe it or not, words are powerful. They shape the way in which we understand the world. They allow us to create stories so that we can skip to the end, and to simplify narratives so that we might circumvent the complex. Yet words don't stay contained in one corner of meaning, even when it's what we want them to do. They creep out and misbehave and transform, taking root in conceptual spaces they weren't intended for.

If you don't think there's an issue with connecting 'non-native' and 'invasive', then you haven't lived a day as an 'other'. If you think that the terms are for the use of horticulture, agriculture and conservation alone, then you haven't been paying attention. The dehumanising language of invasion, of pests, of vermin, has been used for centuries to demonise those arriving from elsewhere. Whether they are immigrants, refugees or asylum-seekers, that language has been use to strip people of their humanity for many years. If you believe that this language will behave because you use it in the right way, then I'd hazard a guess that you've never had your belonging questioned or your nationality challenged. If you use these words, I'd ask you to consider: what are you really trying to describe?

The Mauritian cucumber looks ready to harvest. I look through photos on my phone and find the picture I took in the market in Flacq. The same market where my dad and my uncle would go to buy vegetables for their family. The same uncle who took Sam and me to the market that day to step out of the sun, and under the shaded canopy were long tables piled high with squat pineapples, chubby bananas, thick chunks of manioc, thin aubergines and bundles of thyme and coriander and, by our feet, khus-grass baskets filled with okra and margoz and long green beans. We watched a Tamil man take a machete to a fresh coconut and, once it was beheaded, present its water to us to drink.

Yes, these cucumbers look the same as the ones I saw that day and they are beautiful. I imagine asking my dad if they're ready. I imagine asking my grand-père, who would tell you the size of a thing by holding out his forearm and tapping his finger to show you the length and asking, 'Sa longer la?' And if you were happy with it, you'd reply, 'Oui ta!' I snip the hefty fruit from the vine, the cut stem oozing with glistening sap. It's smooth and weighty, and I am proud. I hand it to Sam, who wraps it in thin paper and bubble-wrap like a precious artwork, then places it inside an old shoebox, ready to go to the post office in the morning. I'll taste one, of course – maybe the next one, but not the first one. The first one's for my dad.

CHAPTER 12

There's a point at the height of the season when the plants become abundant and unwieldy. The heat kicks into a higher gear, and the garden and vegetable patch take on a wildness, growing up and over, stems bending under the weight of themselves and their fruit. It's generous, too. There are congregations of short light-skinned cucumbers, clusters of climbing beans and the last of the purple-podded peas. Tomatoes, split open from the other day's sudden rain, have fallen to the ground, and where I have left the dill to grow tall and spindly, sunshine-yellow umbrellas have burst into flower and are buzzing with the hunger of hoverflies. I 'stop' the cordon tomato plants and the squash vines by snipping off the main shoot, the leader, which will now direct the plant's energy into the fruit that has already set.

I watch as a tractor rumbles past the rabbit-proof fence, chopping and flattening the tall, swaying grass, and I'm sad to see it go. A murder of crows scours through the newly mown grass in search of palatable casualties. Sam leans out of the bedroom window to cut back the wisteria vines that have been growing in a tangle across the glass. I felt as though they were slowly engulfing the front of house, weaving a protective basket around where we sleep, and I'm sad to see them go, too. All else, though, I leave to amble onwards as the hot days get steadily and noticeably shorter. I resist the urge to tidy, unless it really seems necessary. I feel more at ease when flanked by thick foliage and tangled vines. I feel more at home when I'm amongst the plants that I have grown.

The chickens are feeling more at home too. I've even managed to convince all but Mimi to fly onto my lap in return for a few kernels of corn. I keep stock-still when they do, in the hope that they'll linger for a moment and even concede to a stroke, once the treats have run out. Ti Coule stayed for a while, even preened herself while sitting perched on my thigh, and it made me deliriously happy. Sometimes she walks through the open door and flies onto the back of my desk chair to look over my shoulder while I type. Grace has taken to singing loudly when she's lain an egg, and if she spots me stepping outside to listen to her tuneless song, she flies towards me in celebration, all flapping wings and triumphant squawking. All the while shy little Mimi keeps her distance from us, no matter how we try and tempt her over. And she hasn't lain her first egg yet.

I'd been warned that Pekin Bantams have a tendency towards broodiness, but I was entirely unprepared for how it would make a chicken behave. Alan, who is full to the brim with hormones, is as moody as a teenager. She spends her days fighting her way to the nesting box to sit down, head low and backside up, whether there's an egg underneath her or not. And she'll stay there all day in the vain hope that – if she can get hold of one – the unfertilised egg that she is keeping warm under her chest will hatch and give her a chick. She persists in sitting, in something of a trance, on eggs that will never hatch, and it's quite sad to watch her do it, knowing that her efforts will ultimately prove futile. We do our best to intervene, even though she'd rather be left alone. From her vicious pecks and low rhythmic growl, it's clear that she doesn't know that we're doing it for her own good. But if we leave her to it, she'll get hungry and dehydrated, won't preen or bathe in dust, and will forsake her own needs in the vain pursuit of motherhood. So I lift her out of the henhouse as she clucks, angry but quiet, with indignant feathers raised, and set her on the ground. The trance persists for a few moments before she realises I'm waving a mealworm in front of her face and she snaps out of it. She snatches it greedily from my fingertips, but however much I try to keep her distracted with more treats – some corn or kale or something red – she'll invariably run off, ten or fifteen minutes later, in the direction of the henhouse, where she'll meet the door that I've now closed.

When she can't sit, Alan gets annoyed with the others, pecking at and chasing them around. Today is especially warm and, on warm days, she is especially broody, so I pick her up and hold a cold paper towel against the space on her chest where she's pulled out her feathers and left her plucked hot skin exposed. This isn't as odd as it sounds. It's quite normal for a broody hen, who hopes that pressing her exposed skin against an egg will coax it to hatch. Cooling it is supposed to soothe her and, after a few annoyed fits of flapping, she concedes to allowing me to cool her off and settles in my arms, claw holding my finger gently, her body resting against my chest. I feel her breathing rise and fall alongside mine, her pupils dilate and, after a few minutes, her eyes close and she drifts off for a little nap. I put her down eventually and reward her with a treat, and for a little while Alan forgets her obsession. I know she'll go back and try to sit again, but for now she's pecking around with her sisters.

It's barely the morning, and thunder rolls from one side of the sky to the other. It wakes me first and, a little later, Sam too. I keep my eyes pressed shut against the start of the day, trying to convince myself I'm still asleep. But the sun pushes itself in, orange and pink, through the murky grey clouds and pouring rain, nudging at the gap in the curtains. The colours move with the stirring sunlight, before disappearing into the storm clouds. Sam pulls the curtains open as a flash of lightning smashes white, purple and blue across the sky and bathes the garden, the air, the bedroom in the pink of blushed roses. I lie for a time and listen to the rain falling, fat drops on the roof, against the window, on the thirsty parched earth. The heat starts to break and I breathe it in deeply. Another flash of light, three 'Mississippis' and a deep, low rumble. I start to drift back to sleep and dream of goldfinches landing on the washing line.

More than 6,000 miles away, oil is pouring by the tonne into the ocean off the south-east coast of Mauritius. Ink-black spilling into the clear turquoise lagoon. A Japanese-owned tanker got too close to the island and ran aground two weeks ago and is breaking up in the rough subtropical winter sea. The images are devastating. The thought of what it has done – what it will do to the precious ecosystem, to the coral and fish and birds and mammals, as each undulation pushes the poison further and deeper into the water – is unbearable. There are no images of what's happening beneath the surface, but it's not hard to imagine. How the oil drifts downwards and coats the centuries-old bright, white coral. How it fills the cracks of a hawksbill turtle's shell and pours down the throat of a melon-headed whale. Waves splash oil against the shoreline of Île aux Aigrettes, which is home to some of the most unique and rare species on the planet. There are many Mauritians there. Volunteers stuff straw and sugarcane leaves into fabric sacks to soak up what they can of the spill. They wear white boiler suits that display how the thick, shiny oil clings tightly to their arms and legs, as well as masks to protect themselves from Covid and the stench of petrol fumes.

I watch on Twitter as picture after picture appears of this unwelcome shadow leaching outwards, into and through the water. I feel the destruction of it as though it's moving through me, its toxicity seeping into my blood vessels and engulfing me. I imagine how heartbroken my fisherman grand-père would have been to have witnessed this.

If I'd grown up there, I might have lived near the sea. Maybe I'd have learned how to swim properly. Maybe I'd have been less afraid of the water. If I'd grown up there, I could have been there today and done something – anything – to help clear up the mess. Seeing it is breaking me, but I can't look away. It is an ecological catastrophe. The government has declared a national emergency, one that it has neither the resources nor the funding to cope with. It is appealing to the French, its former colonisers, for support. I sign a petition. I donate to the clean-up fund. I share it online. It's all I know how to do. I look at the hills and woodland out of my window and see an ecological catastrophe there, too. A landscape whose biodiversity is in disastrous decline. One of the most 'nature-depleted countries in the world', according to the *State of Nature* report of 2016. I sign another petition and watch as the crops I've left to flower for the pollinating insects to gather nectar from bend in the late-summer breeze. It's a small thing that I can do.

It is unclear why a ship of that size would stray 100 kilometres off-course from the shipping lane it should have been following. It is unfathomable that a bulk carrier would veer so dangerously close to the island, let alone in proximity to Blue Bay Marine Park, which is home to a 1,000-year-old brain coral and an ecosystem that is so fragile it is listed under the Ramsar Convention as a Wetland of International Importance. Having said that, I'm never certain that such designations, made in the name of environmental protection, mean what they purport to mean, especially in the face of capitalism and imperialism.

*

Bassas de Chagas. The Oil Islands. The Chagos Archipelago. British Indian Ocean Territory.

The Chagos Islands are a coral archipelago in the middle of the Indian Ocean, made up of sixty-four tropical islands, the largest of which is Diego Garcia, at sixteen square kilometres. The history of the population of the island runs almost adjacent to that of Mauritius from 1770 onwards, when France allowed companies to establish coconut oil plantations on the land and transport enslaved Africans from Mozambique and Madagascar to labour on them.

In the mid-1960s, when the government of Mauritius was in the process of negotiating the terms of its independence from Britain, it was forced to cede control over the islands – which were considered part of the territory of Mauritius, despite being more than 1,000 miles away – to Britain, in return for its freedom. The then-governor of the Seychelles, Bruce Greatbatch, was tasked with 'cleansing' and 'sanitising' the islands, and he described the Chagossians as 'unsophisticated and untrainable' and determined that 'these people have little aptitude for anything other than growing coconuts'. So in a handful of years after Mauritius gained its independence, the nearly 2,000 Chagossians who were living on Diego Garcia were forcibly removed to make way for the British government – now calling the archipelago the British Indian Ocean Territory (BIOT) – to rent the island to the US, who would go on to build a military base there.

The British government orchestrated a campaign designed to erase the existence of the people of Chagos and to mislead the international community by maintaining 'the pretence there were no permanent inhabitants' on the islands. The

Permanent Under-Secretary of State in the Foreign Office, Paul Gore-Booth, wrote, 'We must surely be very tough about this. The object of the exercise was to get some rocks which will remain ours; there will be no indigenous population except seagulls.' The Chagossians were forced to leave behind their homes, their possessions, their land and their waters and, carrying just one suitcase each, were dumped elsewhere without resettlement assistance. And they have been fighting to return ever since.

Before their expulsion they led simple lives on their island. They had jobs, grew vegetables and fruit, raised livestock and caught fish to feed themselves and share with their community. They grew sweet potatoes, gourds, peppers and chillies, breadfruit and yams. They would grow custard apples, mangoes, citrus fruit and pineapples, papayas, bananas and guavas. In the countries where they ended up – Mauritius, where the majority were left, as well as the Seychelles and Britain – without the capacity to sustain themselves as they once had, they faced lives of poverty. To this day the exiled population sustains a connection with their homeland through the food they share, the plants they grow and the cultural practices that ensure the memories never fade. Crushing leaves, brewing tisanes and preparing herbal remedies, they soothe their ailments and the sorrow of their uprooting, while fighting and hoping that one day they will be allowed to go home.

In April 2010 the Commissioner of the BIOT declared the archipelago to be a 'no-take' Marine Protected Area, banning all commercial fishing and extractive activities in order to protect the largest living coral atoll in the world, as well as the species that live in and around it. This designation was made unilaterally by the British government under the Labour Party, and understandably met with approval from a number of environmental groups. Then-Foreign Secretary David Miliband declared the move a 'demonstration of how the UK takes its international environmental responsibilities seriously'. Yet later that year WikiLeaks disclosed a US diplomatic cable revealing that Colin Roberts – an official from the British Foreign Office – had told a US State Department official that establishing the MPA 'would have no impact on how Diego Garcia is administered as a [military] base', while 'effectively end[ing] the islanders' resettlement claims'. The US official replied in agreement, stating that 'establishing a marine reserve might, indeed, as the FCO's Roberts stated, be the most effective long-term way to prevent any of the Chagos Islands' former inhabitants or their descendants from resettling in the BIOT'. The Americans and their military operations were welcome there, but the Chagossians were not. Marking out an area of 544,000 square kilometres of rich marine environment for safeguarding is unarguably a good and necessary thing, but doing so in order to consolidate a neo-colonial grip on a strategically positioned island is less so. This part of the Chagos story has been described as 'conservation colonialism' and it's not hard to see why. Even if the Chagossians won the right to return, limiting their capacity to fish for subsistence would make living there untenable.

The dispute over the islands goes on. The Chagossians' right to return has been repeatedly refused by the British government, despite their expulsion being deemed unlawful by the High Court in 2000. In 2019 the International Court of Justice in The Hague ruled the British occupation of the islands illegal, and the UN passed a resolution demanding that Britain return control of the Chagos Islands to Mauritius – not that handing over control to Mauritius would guarantee repatriation for the Chagossians.

Nonetheless, Diego Garcia remains a US military base, the archipelago remains colonised and the Chagossians remain displaced.

*

In what has always been the warmest month of the year – the month of plentiful light and heavy yields – the wind is blowing again. The wind has returned and the temperature has dropped, and the plants are looking troubled for it. The supports that steady the tomatoes are coming out of the ground, and the arch that the French beans have climbed is wobbling and looks liable to fly off into the field. This storm, it feels, is trying to force summer to give up the last of its days and blow autumn in sooner than expected. Tumultuous weather unsettles me. It makes focusing a struggle. I check the news and see images of dead dolphins washing up on the shore near the site of the oil spill, and videos of volunteers dragging shovel-loads of dark sludge off the base of the mangroves. I read how the schools nearby have been forced to close to protect the children from the overwhelming stench, and see pictures of protesters dressed in black marching through the streets of

Port Louis. They are chanting their frustration at the government's inadequate response, as well as at the corruption and
negligence that allowed the spill to happen in the first place.
The poison of it all reaches far and deep and the clean-up will
take a long time.

In one video, three young Mauritians speak of their sadness at what they are witnessing. They feel deeply connected
to, and protective of, the ecology of their nation. They so clearly
comprehend that to disrespect the environment is to jeopardise their future, and part of me envies their sense of kinship
with the natural world. I ache with envy at how profoundly the
ecology of the island is intertwined with their sense of who
they are, but even more of me aches for their despair and feels
despairing, too. How agonising it must be, as a child or a teenager now, to be living with the consequences of the extraction
and degradation of the natural world. To be young in the face
of systems of power and wealth accumulation that refuse to
consider what the future will hold, and who will be left to deal
with the fallout. To witness the lacklustre promises on pollution and missed climate goals, then try to convince themselves
that we adults care about what will be left of the earth to
inherit. It must be unbearable.

It's not the first oil spill I've watched on the news. It's far
from the only environmental disaster that's happened this
year. There were oil spills in Russia and Venezuela, too. And
deadly floods in Indonesia, Brazil and Rwanda. There were
landslides in Myanmar, Nepal and Nigeria. And wildfires in
Australia and the USA. I see them and ache for them, and then

they drift from my mind. I'm not strong enough to hold the heartbreak of each catastrophe for long. But this one, I imagine, will endure. I'm certain I'll worry if the migrating birds – the curlew sandpiper, whimbrel and sanderling – will find somewhere to land and something to eat in Mauritius, so that they might return to the shores of the south coast when we're walking at low tide. I'll worry about what of the coral reef will not survive this, and what fish will disappear when it's gone. I'll worry whether there will be any dolphins still swimming in that part of the ocean by the time I'm able to return. And I'll worry about the lives and the livelihoods that have been, and will be, lost because of this destructive act of negligence.

I feel powerless, so I take this feeling of powerlessness out into the garden. I crush the dried lavender flowers between my fingers and take in their calming sweetness. I pull at the nettles that have snaked under the wire fence and grown amongst the strawberry plants, until the tingle in my fingertips becomes unbearable. I snap the desiccated seedheads off the calendula, then tumble the gnarled reptilian seeds into my pocket and resolve to sow them a little earlier next year. In the greenhouse I fill trays with seed compost and press it down until it is firm, then tip some brassica seeds into my cupped hand, one variety at a time: 'Mizuna', 'Green Wave', 'Purple Frills', 'Dragon's Tongue'. All mustard greens, all seeds that look similar but will grow up to be different kinds of fiery leaf. I place a few seeds in each module, then crumble compost through my fingers to cover them. All I know to do when I feel helpless is to sow seeds. As I go to water them gently, the sky above me darkens and soon rain thumps down onto the greenhouse roof. I watch the heavy drops bouncing off the baked ground, before the earth finally relents and lets the moisture in. I stand and listen to the noise of the rain thundering down and it sounds like the centre of a waterfall. It's as overwhelming as it is soothing and I'm comforted by the rhythm. Some minutes later the rain stops and the air turns a faint honey colour, and what is left feels like a palpable exhale. The fresh moisture hangs in the air and my next inhale is so cool and sweet and lush that it works its way into the depths of my lungs.

By the next day the heat has returned. There are no clouds in the sky and the air is still. It's as uncomfortable outside as it is in, so we take ourselves to the sea. We head to the same place that we visited when we moved, on the cusp of winter when the wind blew so fiercely it whipped our words into the waves as they crashed towards us on the incoming tide. It's the opposite today. It is calm and quiet and searing. While I settle in, tucking our things and myself into a sliver of shade by the breakwater, Sam throws himself towards the sea. I envy his confidence as he runs, barefoot, at and then into the water. I hang back for a time to gather together some courage; it always takes me a while to gear myself up to get in. But the mind-bending sun is persuasive. I'm starting to feel unwell, and my head is already swimming.

I go to walk across the hot pebbles, but the soles of my feet can't take it, so I tiptoe back to get my flip-flops. I try again and by the time I get to the water's edge, the impossibly cold saltwater laps around my toes and causes my breath to catch in my chest. It's a wonderful and terrible feeling. It's the cure for this bristling heat, but to get to it, I have to shake off the shock that's pounding through me and hit it with everything I've got. I take off my flip-flops, hold them over my head and throw myself into the water, backside first and screaming. It feels incredible and relieving, splashing around in this shallow, cool sea water. The waves are easy-going and it's barely deeper than a bath. I don't know why I was quite so afraid.

These waters are a balm for me today, but I'm one of the lucky ones. For other people, these waters are contentious. The beaches of the south coast are where migrants, most of whom are fleeing war, famine, persecution or encroaching climate change, have been taking what they hope will be the last leg of a perilous journey towards safety and refuge. If you only listen to the outrage of right-wing commentators, the angriest users of social media and a particular contingent of Conservative MPs (who you'd think would be busy dealing with the pandemic), then you'd believe that the small number of migrants who have made it across the Channel in overcrowded dinghies are more of a threat than the highly contagious respiratory disease that continues to barrel through the country.

The rhetoric is the same every time. The main actors are often the same, too. And the incendiary language is age-old – not that different from when I was a child. They call the migrants an invasion. They insist on describing them as illegal, even though they are yet to be offered due process. They say that they're criminals, intruders and probably terrorists. They say, 'Send them back' because 'this country is full'. They say we don't owe them safe refuge, while refusing to see the many ways this country has led them to these shores. The language is familiar and painful. The inhumanity of their words overwhelms me. I fall apart at the thought of what vast suffering someone must have been endured to face such danger to get to a country that declares itself fair and believes itself humane, only to be met with such hostility. Some will think me naive. Too soft in the face of each tragic story and too gullible to know the truth from a lie. But for now, and for the rest of my days, I will choose this way over hard-heartedness. I won't let my heart become empty of compassion.

I wade in a little further as the waves grow stronger. They push me about as I attempt to stay upright. I try to keep my feet touching the sea bed while the sand and pebbles shift beneath me. But the next moment I reach down and find nothing. I kick and splash, panicking, my stomach dropping as I frantically search for something to steady me. Salt water catches in a gurgle at the back of my throat. When my toes finally find stone and sand and solidity, the terror subsides and I can breathe again. I paddle closer to the beach, my heart beating loudly in my ears, remembering all the times I've been afraid of the water. What a thing it must be to trust yourself to the sea.

There were only four or so months between our move and the start of the pandemic. We've been living here in some version of a lockdown, in a cloud of Covid-anxiety, for more time than we haven't. When people ask me how it's going and if I'm set-tling in, I'm not sure how to respond honestly. It's hard to tell if this move is working out or not, while we remain stuck in this strange time. We haven't seen our friends for months, and after a few heady weeks of pleasant chats with our occasionally tipsy neighbour in the spring, she's gone back to avoiding cas-ual conversation. I think of that cold Saturday last November when Linda burst into the house to wrap me in a welcome hug and I wonder whether I'll see her again. All the people we were hoping to meet are working from home and keeping socially distant. It's been harder than I imagined to be far from those I love and not yet know if there are true friends to be made here. I have moments of longing when I wish I could still skip across the road we lived on in Hackney, and spend an hour or two laughing with my friend.

Although I have more space, my world – like almost every-one's – has contracted around me. We go for early-morning walks in the woods but don't wander too far. We eat our dinner in the garden by the chicken coop until the sun drops behind the house and takes the warmth with it. Our only real-life social interactions are with Rachel and Graeme, who stand in the field at the bottom of the garden and ask us how we're doing while Winnie, their dog, ignores the Covid rules and wanders into our house for a sniff around. Despite the feelings of distance from other people, I know that I am so fortunate. The garden is abundant, the vegetable patch provides and the chickens lay little eggs with outsized yolks most days. I have the space that I was craving when we left the city, and I don't think it's my imagination when I say that, out here, it's easier to breathe.

I go to step through the greenhouse door, but the low thud of warm, thick air chases me out. I leave the door ajar and go to fill up the watering cans while I wait for the fug to clear. I check the okra plants daily to look for new buds as their flowers are pretty, hibiscus-like and fleeting. I don't want to miss them, as they bloom and drop in less than a day. I've only picked a few pods, but they were especially delicious because of their rarity. I let the purple basil in pots run to flower by mistake, but their sweet smell sees them busy with buzzing creatures foraging. I gently cup my hand around the butterflies that find their way into the greenhouse and frustrate themselves bouncing against the clear roof. Their wings flutter against the insides of my fingers before I release them to fly away.

The bitter melon has been advancing at an astonishing speed, putting on inches of growth every day. Each section of its exquisitely lobed leaves is a fluctuation of smooth curves and jagged points, each new tendril reaching out in search of something to hold on to. When its gently curling tips find the wire, they spiral around it tightly to steady themselves as they grow on. When I was nine or ten years old, my hair was long, weighty and wavy. I asked my mum to cut it short, holding the unspoken belief that it would fall into a sleek bob. With each snip through my wet hair, huge chunks fell to the floor, and what remained attached to my head began to curl. I watched, horrified, as my hair was doing the opposite of what I wanted and showed the true nature of my follicles. My entire head of hair sprung into a chaos of corkscrew curls, and I was completely and utterly crushed. These cucurbit tendrils remind me of that fateful day when I believed that, if I dared to try, I could look more like my straight-haired school friends. Watching how these vines reach out defiantly and then curl themselves tightly, so they can keep pulling themselves towards the sun, makes me smile. I didn't know it at the time and it took many years to accept, but my curls are a fierce part of who I am. They're my inheritance and, now, I wear them with pride. I wouldn't know who I am without them.

From where I'm standing I can see the mildew creeping across the courgettes and cucumbers, despite the way I keep spraying them with a milky solution to hamper its spread. They will succumb to it eventually, but I hope not yet – there's more fruit to come, I'm certain. Another bout of unexpected wind has scorched and curled the tomato leaves on a few plants and has snapped one of the towering dill plants at the middle. There are holes where the slugs have munched through the chard, and gaping holes where hairy caterpillars have chewed through the leaves of the romping nasturtiums. The other day I thought I saw signs of mosaic virus on the squash and, worried about it spreading to the other plants in the bed, I harvested the most mature fruits with bright-orange toughened skin and got rid of the plants earlier than I'd planned.

I can see three new molehills and am wondering where the next one might appear. Maybe there's a pattern or some logic to how the moles move that means I can guess what bed or plant they'll destroy next. While I want the garden to feel replenishing, it can be arduous, unruly and disheartening.

Sometimes it feels like too much, and the more overwhelming it feels, the more unmanageable it becomes. It is at this point – and at this time of year especially – that relinquishing the urge to control is most necessary. I pause to take note of what hasn't gone to plan and hope to learn from it, come the next season.

And I remind myself that while there have been disappointments, and while this year has been anxiety-inducing and distressing, I am standing in the midst of one of my dreams coming true. I am standing by my greenhouse, in a garden where I am growing the plants of the food that raised me. This is the closest to home that it's possible for me to feel, living in the English countryside, through a global pandemic, during a conversation about race like nothing I've experienced before. Watching the Mauritian cucumbers zigzag towards the sky, and waiting to see the chubby pod that remains after the okra's flower withers and falls, and noticing how the bitter melon has its first buds – although it's too late for there to be one to hand to my mum before the season ends – is a grounding and delicious triumph.

CHAPTER 13

My body always knows when autumn is coming. I sense the little slips as one season loosens its grip and invites the next one to find its feet. The dawns are misty and tiny beads of dew sit atop each blade of grass as the low early sun shifts to shimmer through each drop. After the late-summer months of mostly cawing jackdaws and laughing seagulls, I can hear the sound of sweet birdsong again. The starlings have returned and chat through the bedroom window in the early morning. The chickens are moulting and their feathers and the first of the fallen leaves blow in through the back door, along with the occasional daddy-long-legs, who then bumbles, frustrated, around the house. As growth begins to slow and the light starts to lower, the irresistible nature of change makes itself known. My gut, my spirit recognises the first of autumn's gestures long before my brain can discern what is changing. There's a gentle ache in the pit of my belly that speaks of possibility, a feeling weighty with potential and buoyant with hope. A new pencil-case, cracking the spine of a fresh notebook and imagining the journey ahead in the year to come.

We've been in the countryside for almost a year now and making it through a cycle of the seasons is an accomplishment that I want to repeat. I want to stay here and keep watching the evening light dance through the wisteria leaves, and try to grow bitter melon in the greenhouse again next year. While I wonder whether winter will be hard in the shorter days and colder nights, because winter has been hard before, I welcome the deepening light and the slowing of energy, and the guidance that this seasonal change is imbued with – the call to quieten, withdraw and rest. I'll relinquish my grip on all that I didn't get round to, that didn't work and didn't grow and, in doing so, accept whatever comes next.

At this time my favourite fruit of the year arrives: the first apples and greengages. And for one glorious year I worked on a site where the late raspberries ripened into September. After spending another year of being terrorised by rogue brambles sneaking under fences and clambering out, thorns poised, from beneath bushes, and after the many times I have tripped in the woods and almost face-planted after catching my foot as a branch scrambled unscrupulously across the path, it is finally time for me to remember why we put up with it all, because, at last, the blackberries have arrived. Every few days, in the mid-afternoon, we gather together a collection of old yoghurt pots and walk up the back field to prickle and stain our fingertips purple collecting their ripe berries. I push my body into the chaos of spiky stems, getting as close as I can stand, sweatshirt snagging, to pick as many as possible. The best ones are always just out of reach, but I sneak up on them nonetheless, trying to avoid the thorns that scratch white lines into my summer-darkened skin. Even when I press a berry still warm from the sun against the roof of my mouth and it is cruelly tart, instead of sweet as I'd hoped, I'm grateful to this plant that I curse in winter and spring, when it redeems itself with its voracity and generosity.

It's also the time when damsons arrive – a fruit I've known only for a few years but adore over all other plums. Rachel and Graeme have been sharing their garden's bounty with us since late summer, filling our pockets with tomatoes and Victoria plums. But since springtime, it's their damson tree that I've kept half an eye on and now, finally, it is dripping with ripe fruit. Sam pulls the branches down gently towards me and I pick as many as we can carry home in our canvas bag. The damson is a strange little thing, but I think it is delectable and has come to symbolise the beginning of the end of my busiest growing months. So dark an indigo that it is almost black, with rich yellow flesh that clings tightly to its stone, it's a fruit that asks you to work for the privilege of its flavour, as they are bitter and unkind to eat raw. You have to cook them before they give themselves up to you, and it might be that this effort is part of why I cherish them as I do. I bake some to stir into porridge, turn another handful or so into a clafoutis, and the rest I cook into jam. To cut the flesh from the stone is impossible, so I cook half a panful with some water until the fruit falls apart and the mixture turns a deep, bloody red. After the sugar is added and while the mixture is steadily rolling, I peer into the pot and, through steamed-up glasses, fish out the stones, one by one, with a wooden spoon. I could leave them in, but I can't fathom doing that. I prefer to put in the time to make sure my jam is flawless.

I pay more attention to the time and tone of the sun rising and setting here. On bright days the skyline at daybreak and dusk is a riot of beauty. Brushstrokes of warm peach, soft cerise and parma violet fading into a cool, regal blue that quickly turns to or from darkness. I'd always thought magnificent beginnings and endings of the day were rarities, as I couldn't see them in the city where the horizon is obscured by buildings. But they are not rare; they are just hidden from view and fleeting. It is a grace to have the space to witness a day as it shifts into night, or the blackness of the early morning give way to an emerging sun. Majestic for only a handful of minutes on a clear enough day, and visible only to those fortunate enough to see the full-ness of the sky. With an unobscured view of the treeline, I watch the moon crest, large and low, glowing silky orange in the evening sky and so luminous that you could draw a map of the crags and ridges that mark her surface. To witness the alchemy of this space and time where change is at its most divine, where the impermanence of existence is at its most vivid, is a gift. So I watch the place where the sky meets the earth for as many of those moments as I can. Holding my gaze on the horizon line steadies me. So unlike the cityscape, which can be so dizzying.

Some of the most remarkable and intimate moments that I've experienced with the natural world had taken place in the city, and yet it was because of those moments that I came to crave the space and quiet that I believed I could find in the countryside. I thought that here is where all that is nature – including me – would have more room to take deep lungfuls of fresh air. There is plenty of life to be found in the city, but there isn't much welcoming space for it. Trees are planted along roadsides with their roots encased in concrete, branches torn from their trunks by passing buses. Bushes and shrubs placed as street furniture become the receptacle for empty drinks bottles and crisp packets. Pigeons with deformed claws, deterred from roosting by spikes mounted on walls, and dandelions sprayed with toxic weedkillers. The foxes that root through the bins run off into the night to escape our frustration and fury. Most of the plants and creatures making a life for themselves in the city are seen as pests and weeds and vermin. I myself would curse at the squirrels who dug up my freshly mulched beds, and I'd pull plants from the earth, calling them weeds when they competed with those I grew for a living. I was not always welcoming there, and I won't always be welcoming now that I'm in the countryside, either. When the currants start to ripen next year, I'll net them in good time to keep those bloody blackbirds from eating them all.

Although there's space and quiet in this place where I live now, there's no wildness to be found. With city eyes and ears, it seemed as though the countryside was more 'natural'. It was what I thought I wanted – to be somewhere the mark of man was less apparent, where living things had more space to thrive. Yet now I'm here, I see it is quite different from the wilderness I imagined. This, too, is a man-made place. These rolling fields of gold and green are private, denuded land and have been wilfully carved up by hedgerows of holly and bramble and barbed-wire fences. There's no true freedom to explore. The paths and desire lines, stiles and yellow arrows tell you where to go and remind you that trespassing is forbidden. There is woodland, yes, filled with hawthorn and oak, woodpeckers and bullfinches, deer and badgers, but these spaces are not as 'natural' as they seem, and it might be that there's nowhere in this part of the countryside that is the kind of 'wild' that I had imagined.

I've come to realise that what I really crave is the intensity and vibrancy and aliveness of market gardens and farms, where humans have encouraged thriving ecosystems to arise. Not somewhere absent of people, but filled with gardeners and growers who nurture plants and soil with wildness and beauty in their hearts. I crave spaces where people are deeply intertwined with the natural world, not just skirting around the edge of someone else's private land. I want to dwell in places where there is a relinquishment of the urge to partition and control, where the sides of the beds can spill over onto the path. I want to seek out places where plants are grown by human hands as an invitation to other creatures to arrive, so that we all might dance through the seasons together. I want to be in places where the soil is revered as a divine entity and where the beautiful and the delicious grow side-by-side, filled with intentional earthlings, not devoid of them. I want to be in the small-scale farms, community growing spaces and market gardens that are cultivated with intention, overflowing and haphazard and welcoming to all beings, and I want to be in them with other people who grow.

The courgettes and cucumbers in the vegetable patch have succumbed entirely to mildew after putting out their last misshapen fruits. The tomatoes, which have been growing sideways since Storm Francis almost blew them over, are being overwhelmed by blight, one plant at a time. The lettuces are getting tough and bitter as they ready themselves to flower and set seed, so I twist each one out of the soil and put them in the compost. Where the rocket was growing, I plant young mustard greens and imagine the frilled or curling purple leaves that will unfold over the next weeks, then hibernate through the winter, poised to grow again next spring. In the greenhouse the bitter melon plant has formed its first fierce green fruit. Smaller than my little finger and unlikely to grow much bigger, it's not enough to harvest and cook, sadly. I'll try again next year.

The chickens talk to me now. Heads cocked to one side, they look me in the eye and let me know that it's time for their evening's handful of corn. I convinced myself that, being small, they'd be less likely to fly away, but their small size and light weight make them better at flying than full-sized chickens, and Grace, it turns out, has a taste for heights. She's taken to flying onto the highest fence post at the end of the garden, where only a few vegetables separate her from the big, wide world beyond. And I just have to watch her and the iridescent green on her black feathers glinting in the low autumn sun, with breath held, hoping that she flies back down towards me instead of flying off. Mimi is still shy, except when I'm clearing the mess out of their henhouse when she keeps a close eye on whether I'm doing a thorough job. At first we would shoo the chickens out of our house if they wandered in, but it only took one instance of slack boundary-setting for them to get the confidence to march into the kitchen when we leave the back door open. Most mornings they come in and sidle up to the table, hoping for some crumbs from breakfast or a scrap of sweet fruit. If there's nothing forthcoming, they slowly pad around, searching the kitchen floor meticulously for edible detritus. I move around the garden differently now that I share it with the chickens. They follow me back and forth, getting under my feet and nosily interfering with whatever I'm doing, forgetting that I'm there only when there are woodlice to scratch at or beetroot tops to pull chunks off.

We take walks in search of fungi and, every so often, I spot something and crouch down to inspect the offerings of the woodland floor. Fat saucers of polypore bloom out of the fallen trunks of birch. Frills of velvety cobalt crust fungus cling to dead bark. Clusters of custard-yellow golden pholiota sit, proud and slimy, on an upturned piece of old trunk. Cartoonish fly agaric push their way up through the dead leaves, phallic at first, before opening out to form red umbrellas with white spots, telling tales of fairies, hallucinations and flying reindeer at Christmas. I once took a workshop that explained the process of how mushrooms grow and was immediately struck by how curious and profoundly different they are from plants. Having no need of sunlight to grow, the majority of a fungus – the mycelium – lives threaded through the ground, permeating a piece of wood or occupying whatever substrate it has taken possession of. What it lives in, it consumes, and so it is a decomposer par excellence. What we think of as a mushroom is merely the fruiting body of a fungus when it is ready to reproduce, bursting out into the light to spread its spores and start the cycle again. What fungi are capable of is virtually unfathomable. Cleaning up pollutants, detoxifying radioactive waste and enabling trees to care for one another. How they labour steadily in the cool, dark and quiet, remaining unseen until an opportune moment for their emergence arrives, is a model for a humane existence worth aspiring to.

Today we follow a path that drops us downwards to a reservoir that the summer has emptied out. The earth is cracked as though arid, but still holds enough water to squelch disconcertingly underfoot. I step out onto it, sinking a little, but eager to explore a space that is rarely seen by human eyes. Trickles of water burble streaks of orange and red over the rich brown sodden ground. The point that would be deepest is bare, but towards the edge of where the water once was grows pygmy-weed and smartweed. I follow the footprints of a deer and a fox, pushed into the mud, and stop where the deer turned around but the fox continued on to the other bank, because I don't want to sink any more, either. Sam wants to follow the river back up to the path, but as we walk the water starts to reappear, deepening with each footstep until we find ourselves climbing up a steep and ungenerous bank, looking for a way back into the woods through the dense trees. This is Sam's way. Follow your nose and if it leads you astray, scramble through the bushes until you find your way to the path.

On the hike back up, I see a familiar fungus. One that, at last, I don't need an app to identify. Thick fuzzy bracts, fluted like a tutu with concentric circles of lemon-yellow, then coral. It is chicken of the woods – and this one is a handsome specimen. I ate it for the first and only time in Gloucestershire, when one of the other farm workers showed me what it looked like and cooked it for our Monday night dinner. I check the internet to make sure I'm not going to poison myself and, feeling certain, snap it gently at the base before tucking it carefully into my coat pocket. I'll cook it when I get home, with garlic and some parsley from the garden.

The temperature is starting to tilt. Letting the chickens out in the morning is becoming an ever-chillier task, and I'm watering less and less. As I generally do when the autumnal equinox arrives, I've started to panic because I 'haven't enjoyed the good weather enough' and I want to squeeze in more walks and adventures before the season turns. As I make breakfast and Sam tries to find somewhere for us to spend the morning exploring, the voices coming out of the radio are discussing the National Trust and a report that it is soon to release. It's going to state the obvious: that the existence of some of the manor houses and other properties in its care was made possible by the slave trade and colonialism. You'd have thought the work of historical inquiry would be welcomed by those who find this country's history interesting, yet there is resistance, and the radio presenter – in a bid to provide 'balance'– feels compelled to mention it. My heart sinks.

This reluctance to acknowledge how the dominant accounts of history are incomplete feels as illogical as it does dispiriting. Excoriating 'settled' history is more than a search for what has been erased. Deepening the excavations of these ugly and complex periods of our collective history can offer us a lens through which to view the many ways in which the exploitative dynamics of imperialism and colonialism are still alive and well today. While I reflect on the colonialism in my past and the way it arises in my present, international investment companies and global agribusiness have bought up millions of hectares of farmland throughout the continent of Africa; private companies hold patents on products developed using the plant knowledge they gleaned from indigenous communities; and the destruction of ecologies and the displacement of people from their lands, to make way for the interests of those who seek to profit from it, carry on. All I hear are the fading cries of a dwindling set of the Empire's apologists and I'm determined not to give their dissent more attention that it deserves.

Although the early morning was cool, the sun has started to climb. I've never trusted the English weather as it steps from one season into the next, so I put on an extra layer, just in case, while Sam tells me about a walk in a nearby village around a set of structures with a strange origin story. An eccentric squire, a known drunkard and an MP at twenty-three years old in 1780, built a series of functionless monuments – follies, they call them – in and around the village of Brightling. Intriguing and odd, and close enough for us to fill our flasks with tea and head out for the next couple of hours.

The drive takes us steadily upwards, noodling through single-file country lanes, until we're high enough to see the landscape open outwards in all directions. From here, it is just about possible to look south and see the blue line of the sea at the horizon. The air is hazy warm and entirely absent of moisture. The sky is a soft light blue and a red kite hangs, hovering, in the middle of it. The trail doesn't appear to have a start or an end point, so we park up and head in the direction of the nearest structure. We follow the directions along a hedgerow of bramble and gorse and, on the other side, newborn calves, their mothers and a bull with a face framed by curls watch us as we pass them by. The first folly we come to is a tower – a turret really – mostly hidden from view by a circular woodland of trees surrounding it. It's an imposing structure made of stone, with barred windows, and where it stands, disembodied, it has no obvious purpose. There might have been a time when you could have climbed the circular staircase inside it, but to what end is unclear. The vantage from the ground is impressive enough; a tower here is quite pointless.

Following the dropped pins on Sam's phone, we head back over the field and into the village, past a pretty little stone cottage with a tree full of apples that are just out of reach. The next folly that we find is in the churchyard. It's a pyramid and it is this man's mausoleum. It's an odd thing, maybe twenty feet or so high, taking up far more room than the weathered headstones of its neighbours. The story goes that he organised its construction before his death and was entombed inside it, seated upright at a table with a bottle of wine. We laugh at its absurdity and ostentatiousness, and how strange it is to see a pyramid in a little village churchyard. I circumnavigate it and peer into where the door would have been, as Sam reads out more about John 'Mad Jack' Fuller.

'Mad Jack was a patron of the arts and sciences, bought Eastbourne its first lifeboat, bought Bodiam Castle to save it from destruction and was an outspoken supporter of slavery. This article describes him as a vociferous anti-abolitionist.'

I should have guessed, and I certainly could have. It's no great surprise that a man with such excessive wealth, who built these idiotic temples to nothing at all, would likely have amassed his fortune through exploitation. I feel nauseous. I've come to hate how a place, a structure or a building can appear intriguing or beautiful one moment and yet, when standing in the fullness of its history – its origin story – can become sour and grotesque. How can I not bristle at the fact that he is celebrated as a philanthropist while also being described as an enthusiastic supporter of slavery?

I walk back to the road to sit on a bench and wait for Sam. He's on a video call to his grandad and I don't want Pops to see me, yet again, feeling blue. There's no one else around, so I quietly watch the dwindling hollyhocks growing out of the pavement. There's an almost-empty noticeboard attached to the wall behind me. Just a copy of the latest parish-meeting agenda, with two items to be discussed and a laminated notice explaining how to spot the 'non-native' Asian yellow-legged hornet. Underneath these notices there is one more piece of paper, pinned to the board, and it reads:

St Thomas a Becket Church and the Black Lives Matter Movement

We are united in our dedication to standing up to racism and oppression, and standing in solidarity with the black community. Black lives matter to Brightling Parish Church, and they should matter to every individual.

The PCC of Brightling acknowledge Jack Fuller's involvement and support of the slave trade during his lifetime. St Thomas a Becket Church operates an open and inclusive policy, and welcomes visitors and worshipers from all ethnic backgrounds.

Brightling PCC, August 2020

These words are far less visible and imposing than the structures they gesture towards. These words that were written by someone on the Parish Council and approved by the other members, then typed out on a computer in someone's home and printed out and cut to size. These words that are pinned on the noticeboard for whoever walks by to read. These words that refer to these nearly 200-year-old structures, which would have been unquestionably celebrated until this summer prompted reflection on what being selective about the stories we tell might do to someone like me.

I wonder who else has seen this notice? It's possible that I'm the first Black person to have read it. This unexpected expression of solidarity tells me that the people in this little village considered the possibility that someone like me would come along one day to see this peculiar pyramid in the middle of a churchyard. And they tell me that those same people want everyone to know that, much as they are committed to preserving the structures Mad Jack commissioned, because they are part of the village's history, they are able to acknowledge the abhorrence of his views, too. They are a handful of words. A small gesture in the grand scheme of things, but, in this moment, they suggest to me that change is possible and offer me a little welcome relief.

There are people who wish for history to be tidy. They don't want to think about the ninety-three National Trust properties with links to colonialism and slavery, or how Kew Gardens is reckoning with the exploitation that is part of its legacy. They wish for the past to stay in the past, because what's done is done, and they would prefer us to believe that while there was domination, there was benevolence and benefit, too. And they want us to concede that, despite the extraction and destruction, no negative consequences persist to this day. They want us to accept that other histories – our histories – are unsubstantiated, irrelevant and non-existent, while refusing to acknowledge what was deliberately left out. It strikes me as

CLAIRE RATINON

strange to want our collective story to be this way. To be incomplete, erased and untold. And for as long as I, and those like me, exist and refuse to accept this erasure, the search for our stories will go on.

After all, what fabrications would we have to accept in order to believe that these powerful people and institutions, with their cataclysmic actions, have left no trace at all? There must be acknowledgement of these truths and restitution for what was taken, and for what continues to be taken to this day. The Chagossians must be allowed to return to their homeland and must be compensated for all they have endured. So where erasure has caused silence to fall, our voices must rise to demand a just world.

The idea of reparations is a contentious one – not that I think it ought to be. But then for me to believe in its potential for justice doesn't compel me to consider what I stand to lose. It is those who know, or at least suspect, that the material comfort of their lives – the wealth, the privilege, the great swathes of land – is disproportionate who dismiss the call for reparations outright. It would need to be a multilateral, international, cross-generational undertaking to create a system that could move incrementally towards equity. The scope is unfathomable and it would cost the privileged more than they could bear to relinquish, and that's why, I believe, the conversation never truly reaches those with the power to deliver it. And yet I also believe that one day – probably not in my lifetime – the notion of addressing historical injustices won't be shrugged off any more. Tiny gestures have been made (like those from Kew

297

Gardens and the National Trust), of truth and reconciliation, that cause me to hope the tide will turn one day.

The word 'reparations', at its root, means to repair, and there's much repair to be done, alongside and beyond tangible restitutions. Reparations in the form of land return, debt cancellation and wealth restoration are justice. Repairing our relationship with the land is the spiritual work of our lifetimes. Because there were other thefts, alongside the stealing of bodies and lands, of plants and soils, of agency and control, of governance and rule. A robbery of spirit took place, and still does. A robbery of history and hope, of culture and tradition, of imagination and dreaming up futures on our own terms. I can barely stand to think of the brutality of those forced migrations and the volume of suffering that was borne. It was a pain so enduring that it persists to this day, in the bodies of its many descendants. All this space taken up by suffering where there might otherwise have been ingenuity and insight, visions and faith, and the chance to wonder and wander. It was a devastating realisation that even my most earnest aspirations took shape within a system that did not have my thriving in mind. The limitations on our imaginings of what is possible persist, as do the oppressive systems that create and enforce their parameters. I will never know who I might have been, outside its burdensome vision. And while I know there is plenty for me to be thankful for – an abundance of privilege and comfort, for starters – I am caught in grief over the possibilities lost because my understandings, my hopes and my thoughts are refracted through the prisms of whiteness, of the English language, of being on this land but not of this land.

And so I seek repair. A tending to the wounds inflicted as a result of realisations like these. Having the room and the grace to seek whatever truths and stories remain, to stitch my heart together with the shreds of ancestry that I can find, and to be allowed to mourn for what will always be lost. Repair looks like being able to trace the threads of the trauma that is woven through my bloodline and allowing it to lead me to the resilience, the marronage, that is also my inheritance. It is naming what was taken, disappeared and erased and daring to reclaim what remains. That is what repair looks like to me, today, as I sit at the base of the copper beech, its silvery bark against my back, and listen to a buzzard call out into the sky above me. As I claim stewardship over a parcel of soil and devote myself to its well-being and choose to see it, not as a piece of this country that troubles me, but as land where the soil is the connective tissue between my body, my labour, my tenderness and the earth.

Repair is reclamation. And to me that has been reclaiming an unbounded relationship with the natural world through growing food. Something that felt unavailable to me for most of my life, and that continues to be a site of discomfort and disconnection to so many who haven't found their way back to it yet. Because we are descended from those who were torn from or left the land of their people, the land that they knew was part of who they were. We are descended from those who were taken to where their bodies were used, dehumanised and broken into pieces, forced into a labour that worked the land from sunrise and into the night, when the moonlight was bright enough. We are descended from people for whom this labour was once a ritual of sustenance and providing – a labour that was honourable and revered, before it was used as a tool of their oppression. We are descended from those who fled that wretched place, running as fast as they could, discarding their chains and undue debt, to escape into the sanctuary of the trees.

I am descended from people who came to see this labour that positioned the work of sowing seeds and harvesting as lowly and undignified and filthy. As work to rise above, and not root into. We must reclaim the stories we tell about the task of growing food and about those who do it on our behalf. We must regard them, once again, with gratitude and reverence, as they are the upholders of life. And we must seek repair not only for ourselves, but on behalf of our ancestors – those whose bones turned into our bones. We must pursue repair for our descendants, so that they might one day know freedom from ancestral trauma while holding fast to the power of ancestral resilience. Repair is not a solo pursuit, even though our journeys are individual ones and the path can be lonely to travel. We must heal in community, at the feet of ancestral wisdom and alongside those who seek the same peace as we do.

Growing food is as sacred as it is elemental. It is one of the few actions we can point towards as the reason we humans continue to exist. With every bite, we consume the offering of an unfathomable number of beings, both human and more-than-human. We consume sunshine and water, the miracle of photosynthesis and the generosity of decomposition. All these entities and elements and processes make our being alive possible. Our aliveness is a community endeavour.

Growing food is how I repair my broken heart and weave myself back into the tapestry of a rich and defiant ancestry. An ancestry that I feel in my pulse, because I have no family records. It is how I have grounded myself into this present – my own particular present – and have grasped the possibility of wading, barefoot, into the long grass and feeling a rootedness manifest as the weight of me pushes down into the earth. It is plants that brought me here. They extended their root systems and leafy branches towards me and showed me where to go. It is with them as my guides that I see now that, although I thought I had nowhere to call home, it's to the earth that I – we – truly belong.

The trees breathe for you, the bees buzz for you, the mycelium burrows deep into the soil for you. Our ancestors knew how to live in accordance with the truth of our interdependence and we must learn to do the same. We must sink down into the structures of our cells to find what was embedded by generations of those who stood in the dignity of their rightful place as stewards of the earth. When the hush of a woodland's silence raises the hairs on our necks, or we shudder exquisitely when our hot skin hits agonisingly cool water, or we feel an expansiveness arise in our heart-space when standing on the precipice of a cliff or canyon or mountainside and breathe deep, we can touch that remembering. The salt that gathers on our skin, the tears that we shed, the breath that flows across our lips are all manifestations of how profoundly we are connected. The earth dwells in the water that steadies our cells and in the marrow that runs through our bones. Our interconnection was known to our ancestors, and it is our duty to remember this now. We must seek to become intimate with what is indiscrete and divine, for the sake of this planet, our only home.

So I am growing the food that raised me – the cucumbers, okra and tiny bitter melons – and I am doing so right here, where I am. Dancing with the seasons and waking up to birdsong, and pausing to breathe in the cool air after the rain. This is how I have pieced myself back together. This is how I have found, at long last, belonging. A sense of belonging that cannot be undermined by that which is man-made. No borders or delineations, no identifiers or manufactured belief in our separateness from one another can convince me that I do not belong. A sense of belonging that is an action. A noun that's more of a verb. A belonging that needs to be nurtured as the soil does and so, when I feel it slipping away, or being wrestled from my grasp, I sow another seed and trust what germinates and grows to this ground where I now live. I'll care for it as it cares for me, and I'll look to it when I need reminding of what it is to know home.

My dad gave me cucumber seeds and he believed they could grow here, when I thought this place to be too grey and cold and cruel. I sowed a few more seeds in June – a little too late, by most growers' advice – to nurture in our new greenhouse. Then, in July, I took them out of their pots and into planters filled with compost and the fine-textured soil provided by the neighbourhood moles. While my attempt to grow okra came to little, the cucumber plants grew in a frenzy through August and started to flower as the month came to an end, and I've been watching them closely every day, urging them to keep limping along into September. At dusk, I close the door and the window against the night, fleece at my side to drape over them if the temperatures drop too low. And today, as autumn's presence becomes undeniable, my parents arrive to spend the day.

As always, dad's distracted by all the things in the house that need fixing, so I get my mum to nudge him into the garden and towards the greenhouse. I pull back the big leaves obscuring the cucumbers that are hanging there, clinging on to the last of the season's energy, so that he can, for the first time, witness his cucumbers growing here for himself. His furrowed brow turns into a look of disbelief, then gives way to a wide and happy smile. It's a smile I've been lucky to see so many times. The smile that is his, and that he gave to me. I hand him the secateurs and he snips one cucumber from the vine, then another. He places them in the crux of his elbow and cradles them in his arms tenderly. Then he turns to my mum, holding them up in the air and says: 'Pran enn foto! Mo bizin montre mo ser!'

Mum, aged eighteen, the day she left Mauritius for England

Afterword

This book came from a feeling as opposed to an idea. After a few years of making my way into the world of growing food, I had a burgeoning sense that there was more to the practice than I was hearing or reading. The work, while arduous, felt profound and transformative, and that sense of profundity was asking to be expressed.

On the one-year anniversary of George Floyd's murder, I planted out the tomatoes and cucumbers, handed in the first draft of the manuscript and then spiralled into something of a breakdown. From what I could see, the landscape of racial justice had – despite the volume of posturing and well-meaning chatter that followed the posting of black squares on Instagram – barely shifted. Against the backdrop of the ongoing global pandemic, the hoarding of vaccines by wealthy nations and the ceaseless unfolding of the climate catastrophe, I emerged from this eight-month period of writing through a winter lockdown feeling self-indulgent and impotent. What use is there in one person writing their very particular story when the world remains ablaze?

Nonetheless, I kept going. And by the time I handed in my third draft, autumn was calling the leaves to change and I, with no words left in my brain or energy left in my body, was heading to the West Country on my way to a training course – six days in the outdoors to learn how to encourage people to better connect with the natural world.

I'm not much of a camper. But I've long wished to find the same enjoyment in camping that so many other outdoorsy people seem to have. I'd hesitated before booking my place but, given that it was the only option for accommodation available, I signed up to the course in the hope that I'd be able to have some fun doing it. Sam showed me how to put up the tent the day before I left, so when I arrived, with rainclouds darkening the sky, I managed to raise my tent before the storm began – and I felt triumphant. Until I tried to go to sleep that night. As the rain fell relentlessly and the temperature dropped to 5°C, the cold shuddered me awake throughout the night, my teeth chattering so much they ached. Unbeknownst to me, the groundsheet of the tent was letting in water from below, so by the morning I was wet, exhausted and chilled through. After that I dropped the back seats in my car (thankfully I'd driven instead of taking the train, because of Covid) and slept there, curled up like a croissant, for the rest of the week.

Every morning I woke to the sound of sycamore seeds falling onto the roof of my car, the morning light pushing through the misted windows. Although I was filled with gratitude for being dry – if somewhat achy – I was stuck feeling anger and shame. I was angry at the tent that failed me, and ashamed that I had failed at what I'd come to believe was an essential activity of the nature-centric, despite the fact that it hadn't been made clear to me that I'd be sleeping in a tent for five nights without access to washing facilities beyond a cold outdoor tap, a toilet without an adjacent sink (I feared the possible arrival of my period) and nowhere to cook hot food for myself. All this, even though the campsite was in close proximity to a building with dormitory accommodation. It seemed that putting up with physical discomfort was an unspoken gauge of who deserved to be there and who didn't. The higher your tolerance, the more nature-loving you must be.

The five days that followed were a very mixed experience. The offering on the part of the trainers was generous. They were experienced in group facilitation and were forthcoming in their sharing and modelling of what they had found were effective approaches to hosting groups of people outdoors. The other participants were friendly and well-meaning but, unsurprisingly, I was – as I have so often been – the only visible minority in this outdoor space. While my handful of years spent growing food in all weathers has equipped me with the necessary uniform – the sturdy walking boots, the thermal layers, the waterproofs – the conspicuousness is always somewhat abrasive.

Even so, there were moments that I found profoundly moving, as I saw how passionate the participants were about the landscapes they loved, and how they felt called to share that enthusiasm with others. Yet there were other moments that felt, for me, fraught and distressing. There appeared to be an underlying belief that permeated the language, the songs, the conversations that implied that all of our relationships to the land must be the same – adoring, worshipful, untroubled, largely Eurocentric – and there was no room to interrogate that assumption. The participants' efforts to connect were characterised by a wholehearted if clumsy lurching towards the trees and the wildlife around us, alongside a simultaneous reluctance to consider the privilege that we held in having access to it. In one group conversation I introduced the possibility that one of our responsibilities – as fledgling nature facilitators – would be to examine the ways in which the expectations we set in place, the stories we believe and retell, the truths we assume to be universal and the constructs that we reinforce can, and do, create barriers for the many people whose existence and experience we haven't considered. But the point was met with a discomfited quiet, and I was left feeling like an antagonist, a disruptor of the peace.

The weather that week was changeable. When the autumn sun came out, it was pleasing and warm, but when the rain reappeared – as it did most days – it took with it the possibility of being comfortable. I was constantly a little damp, always cold and craving a warm place, indoors, to sit for a little while. There was one main route that led up to the outdoor classroom where we gathered every morning, and it was growing muddier by the day. As I trudged up and down this short but steep walk, with each footstep turning the path into a sludgy mess, I was mired in thoughts about all the people who could not access this place. While I may have felt at odds in this group, at least I was physically able to move through that space. Surely we must ask ourselves who is being summarily and systemically left off the invite list when these outdoor experiences are conceived and created?

The feeling that I'd arrived with – that the last year of my life spent writing this book was entitled and worthless – was making room for something else. It was making room for the possibility that, in daring to tell my own story, I would rightfully be taking up space in a landscape that is often considered the preserve of whiteness, of Englishness, of identities that I do not identify with, in places where my presence is an anomaly – and, in doing so, it might encourage other people like me to do the same. And for those who gatekeep (whether intentionally or not) these outdoor spaces for those who are just like them or, at best, those who are expected to conform to their expectations, I hope my words will prompt them to consider who they exclude – whose presence is missing, whose stories they haven't heard, whose voices they aren't listening to – and how we might remedy that. And given that we are facing a climate crisis that threatens to devastate us all eventually, no matter how boundless our privilege, surely our encouragement to connect with the natural world ought to extend urgently to everyone, and so begin with dismantling the obstacles that hold people back from that possibility?

By the time the course was over, I was desperate to leave. The smell of wood-smoke had settled into my clothes and hair, and my body was fatigued from six days and nights of never being fully warm and never being physically or psychologically comfortable. I drove away with that same mixture of shame and relief that I'd felt three years earlier as I travelled from the south-west of this country to the south-east, singing along to that same Beyoncé album in a bid to feel like myself again.

I can hear the sound of starlings crashing against the bedroom window as they swing from the gutter above. I have a renewed sense of gratitude for having woken up in my bed. Sam brings me a cup of green tea and opens the curtains, and I watch as the blush-pink jays pull the acorns off the oak tree that I can see from the window, then fly off to bury them for the coming winter. Lying here, I can see how the trees in the distance have been busily changing colour. I stare out for a time, still consumed by thoughts of how much work there is to do so that every last one of us feels as though we have a place in this landscape.

The next morning the sound of chainsaws wakes us. The couple two doors down want more light in their bedroom, so the precious oak tree that I love to watch is in the process of being dismembered. I listen as its great branches, once sawn through, fall with a depressing thud onto the grass below. There are no birds to watch while the chainsaws buzz. No great tits or blue tits, no collared doves or jackdaws. The starlings are elsewhere and the jays have flown away. They didn't stay to bear witness, so I do, until I can't bear the violent sound thrumming through my body any longer.

I pull on some old clothes and head out to the vegetable patch. The storms that blew through while I was away have made a mess of the place. The bean poles have fallen over, their roots dragged above ground, and there are piles of leaves and branches smothering what little of the crops remains. It's been a strange year in the garden. Our second season here. Wetter and cooler than expected, such that all the tomato plants got blight before even one fruit had a chance to ripen. The Mauritian cucumbers did well, though, and I blame the failure of the winter squash on their success. And I managed to grow my mum's favourite leafy green, bred malbar, and we harvested, cooked and ate it here, together.

Inside the greenhouse is fairly chaotic as well. The red-podded okra spent the summer being bothered by a munching pest and never fully arrived. The long, thin aubergines – the brinzel – that I grew for my dad to make into vindaye have stopped producing fruit and are collapsing into one another. Yet climbing up the desiccated vines of the now-deceased Mauritian cucumber plant, the elegant leaves and dainty flowers of the bitter melon – the margoz – are still growing, and under a cluster of dusty-brown dead leaves I find two bright-green, reptilian fruit hanging there. I've never understood my parents' love affair with these bitter things, but I'm sure that another unexpected harvest will make them happy. I snip them away from the vine as my phone beeps in my pocket. A text from my dad. My grandmère – my mother's mother – died this morning. The last of my grandparents, my newest ancestor.

I look down at the two fruit now sitting in the palm of my hand. She loved margoz. She would have loved that I'd managed to grow them here. And it's probably about time that I learned – like a proper Mauritian, un vrai Creole – to love eating them too.

Acknowledgements

Mum and Dad. You are the reason I do anything at all. You came to England in pursuit of a good life and of better opportunities for your children, and this book is how I've attempted to honour your resilience, your sacrifice and your deep and boundless love for me. I wrote this book about you, for you, because of you, and I'm so glad you think it's good. I hope that your parents, your grandparents, our ancestors would have agreed.

Sam, my love. To say I couldn't have written this book without you would be an understatement. You held me together when writing these words caused me to fall apart. You nourished, supported and loved me when I could think of nothing else – not even you – but the book. I am honoured that I get to cultivate this certain yet wild love with you. Thank you for being my person.

Alice, I know you hate taking credit for anything that I've done but I owe so much of the life I now have to you and to our friendship. The love and encouragement that you have shown me these last few years has been the most precious gift and it was you that urged this book into existence – and then gave me the most generous words to use on the cover. Thank you.

Becky, our friendship was forged in the fire of working the earth in a heatwave and now, I couldn't live without your brain and your heart in my life. You were the only good thing to come out of that awful time and this book wouldn't have come to be without the intensity of our conversations.

Henrietta, you are the sister I wish I'd grown up alongside. I couldn't have gotten through the heartbreaking parts of this writing process without your love and fierce strength. I love and admire you so damn much.

Hannah, dear heart, I can't believe my luck that you live nearby. Your sweet presence, your reassuring energy, and your faith in me were the balm I needed to keep me going through the lockdowns.

To my incredible agent and ray of sunlight, Rachel. You made me take myself – and my words and ideas – seriously, then, tornado-like, you magicked them into the opportunity to write this book. I'm so grateful to you for making *Unearthed* happen.

To my brilliant editor, Poppy. Thank you for choosing to go on this journey with me. There were moments, especially during that mid-winter lockdown, when everything felt impossible yet you were able to gently but firmly steer me back on course. You pushed me to go further and deeper down, and I know the book is better for it. I owe that to you. And to the whole team at Chatto & Windus – thank you for your support.

ACKNOWLEDGEMENTS

To Shiraz. So quickly you have come to feel like family. Meeting you, a fellow Mauritian captivated by the story of our island, made me realise that what I felt called to interrogate was more than a matter of self-obsession. It is an honour that this book bears the beauty of your artwork. Thank you brother.

To all the beloved people who have encouraged me to grow, to think intensely, and be courageous enough to speak up. To those who urged me to write. To Sara, Sophie, Sui, Chelsea, Dee, Josina, Andrew, Jack, Nikesh, Alexis and Tamer. Thank you.

To the countless beings – the human and the more-than-human – upon whom my thriving depends. You have my ceaseless and bone-deep gratitude.